Learning
PageMaker 7

Ramesh Bangia
B.Sc., Dip. Comp. Sc.
Formerly Managing Editor, Software Today
Formerly Incharge Computer Centre, Hindustan Copper Ltd., New Delhi

KHANNA BOOK PUBLISHING CO. (P) LTD.

::: Publisher of Engineering and Computer Books :::

Head Ofice : 4C/4344, Ansari Road, Darya Ganj, New Delhi-110002
Phone : 011-23244447/48 **Fax :** 011-23244447
Regd. Ofice : 1694-95, Nai Sarak, Delhi-110006
Phone : 011-23283211 **Fax :** 011-23256658
E-Mail : contact@khannabooks.com
Website : www.khannabooks.com, www.khannapublishers.com

ISBN: 978-81-87522-95-9

Revised Edition: 2015

Published by:

Khanna Book Publishing Co. (P) Ltd.

4C/4344, Ansari Road, Darya Ganj, New Delhi-110 002

Phone: 011-23244448 Telefax: 011-23244447

E-mail: contact@khannabooks.com

Website: www.khannabooks.com

Regd. Of: 1694-95, 1st Floor, Nai Sarak, Delhi-110006 (India)

Phone: 011-23283211 Telefax: 011-23256658

Printed in India

PREFACE

Learning of a software is both easy and difficult. It depends upto what level you are planning to learn. If you are learning only for the working use, then it is very easy. But, when you try to go deep into it, then you realise how difficult it is to master it.

PageMaker 7.0 is such a vast subject that it will take a lot of time to understand it fully. This book has been written in mind to make you aware of the options available in the software and how they can be used. It is like telling the child about the steps and stairs. You are the one who is to climb the stair. This book will just guide you how to use the stairs.

I am indeed debited to my publishers Khanna Book Publishing Co. Pvt. Ltd., specially Vivek and Puneet for their suggestions and encouragement given in producing this book.

I would like to thank my family specially my wife Sadhna, kids Mayank and Samarth, for without their criticism this book would not have seen the day.

Suggestions for improvement of the book are indeed welcome.

Ramesh Bangia

Contents

1

PageMaker Basics

Introduction

Starting with the year 1987, PageMaker has seen many changes over the years. It was during this year or a little earlier that the first version of PageMaker was introduced. It was then available with just few commands and could be stored in just one floppy. It was introduced by the company called Aldus Corporation. It was so till the version 5.0. This company very happily introduced various changes in the software and went upon making it easier and easier to help the users with lots of new commands over the years.

It was then the company was taken over by Adobe Corporation and they introduced version 6.0 and then version 6.5 and now version 7.0. Each version, as expected has been easier to use and has had many new commands. Let us see what this new version has to offer to us.

What's new in PageMaker

There are lots of new features in this latest version of the software. Some of them which are new or improved are listed here.

Adobe Illustrator Import

Now quickly place Adobe Illustrator files in their original format directly into PageMaker.

Align Objects

Now you can exactly align objects on a page using this feature.

Colour Libraries

Enjoy the support of 17 colour libraries.

Creating Hyperlinks

You can now just drag and drop hyperlinks from Web browsers into PageMaker.

Drag-and-drop

Now easily share elements among various open PageMaker files and with other applications.

Frames

New to PageMaker. It allows you to set up page layout independent of contents.

HTML Export Plug-in

You can now export the PageMaker pages or stories into HTML, keeping intact the hyperlinks.

Image conversion

PageMaker now automatically converts graphics into Web compatible JPEG and GIF formats.

Kodak Photo CD support

Now quickly import and auto-sharpen photographic images using this.

Layers

First time in PageMaker. You can set up a single file for multiple versions of a publication, add annotations, and more.

Layout adjustment, online

Change page size or orientation and quickly reformat publications for online viewing.

Layout adjustment

It automatically repositions and resizes text blocks, frames, and graphics when you change columns, orientation and master pages.

Link management

Now you can reliably track changes to imported text and graphics files.

Masking of objects

It allows you to crop text, graphics, and images easily into polygons, ovals and rectangles using frames.

Multiple Master pages

You can now specify and apply different page designs within a single publication.

Navigation aids

Now automatically create Bookmarks and HyperText links for table of contents and index entries in PDF files.

Object handling

Now automatically align and distribute objects. Combine multiple elements into one unit with a single keystroke.

Opening earlier version files

Now directly open files of versions 4.x, 5.x, and 6.x files.

Page movements

Now quickly move between pages with new Go Back and Go Forward commands.

Photoshop links

Now you can directly open Photoshop and Illustrator from PageMaker.

Polygon tool

Now an enhanced tool gives you the freedom to draw polygons and lines.

QuarkXPress converter

Now enjoy the easy converter of QuarkXPress files to PageMaker.

Right mouse button

Now gain quick access to context-related commands in the Windows 95/98 and Windows NT 4.0 Workstations versions.

Support for Adobe acrobat 3.0

Now you can export files to Portable Document Format (PDF) retaining all the layout and designing.

Table 3.0

A much improved Adobe Table 3.0 allows you to layout text and data in rows and columns and fill them up with colours too.

Templates

A lot of new templates are given in the beginning of the software to make your working much easier.

Typographical controls

Now you can set typographical controls to professional levels using the new tracking and kerning facilities.

Word processing

Now speed up your text processing with a built-in word processing, spelling checker, and find-and-replace feature.

What does PageMaker do?

Let us now try to understand why PageMaker software is very popular. Afterall what it does that attracts so many users all over. Well, it layouts a complete page for you with both text and graphics. It acts as a via media between the user and the printing press. It gives you the output in the form of a page, which looks exactly like the one you would like to read as part of the book or a brochure, etc.

But, starting with an idea and converting it to a printed page, there are lots of steps involved, which we will discuss in the later chapter. At this stage we will just concentrate at the basics of the software.

It is very useful for longer document type of jobs like books, magazines, brochure, annual reports, etc. I will not recommend it for creating a single page with lots of graphics and designs. For that I suggest you use other software, which can be termed as graphics software. PageMaker is essentially a text oriented software with graphics thrown in here and there. It is not that it is not capable of handling graphics but it does not do it with ease as other software do.

PAPER SIZES

In PageMaker you work on pages. This page can be of any size depending upon the type of printer you are using since ultimately it is this printer where your page is going to be printed. Most common among the type of paper which is used in India as well as abroad is A4. It has a length of 11.693 inches and width of 8.268 inches. Since the printer needs about .5 inches on all sides for gripping of the paper, the effective paper size thus becomes 10.693 by 7.268 inches. This is the length and breadth of the paper which can be effectively used for putting the text.

Paper can be used in two ways, which is called the **Orientation** in PageMaker. Portrait is the one when the paper is used with its longer size is in vertical direction and shorter side on horizontal direction. If we interchange the directions, we get the Landscape orientation.

Both of these orientations are shown here.

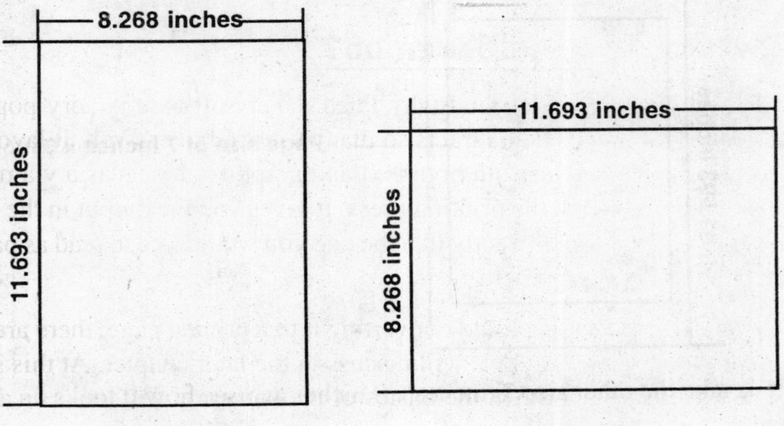

Portrait

Landscape

Most of the time the size of the page will be decided depending upon the type of paper being used. Naturally, everyone would like the paper wastage to be minimum and would like to take out maximum number of pages from a sheet. So depending upon the size of paper available in the market, you would choose the size of the page. The following sizes are the popular ones:

4 inches x 7 inches	Mostly used in the case of novels
5 inches x 8 inches	One of the popular sizes for the text books
6 inches x 8 inches	Another popular size for the text books
7 inches x 9 inches	Most of the magazines are of this size

There are however other sizes too but they are not very popular. For printing of the text, you have to adjust the text on the paper in such a way that it is almost in the centre of the page. This serves two purposes: one it helps in leaving almost equal space on all sides of the paper and secondly it makes the optimum use of the available paper.

Naturally in all these cases you would use the paper in Portrait orientation. However, in the case of 4" x 7", you can use the landscape orientation too. We will see how that can be done later, but lets see how the page size of 7 inches x 9 inches looks in a paper size of 8.268 x 11.693 inches (A4).

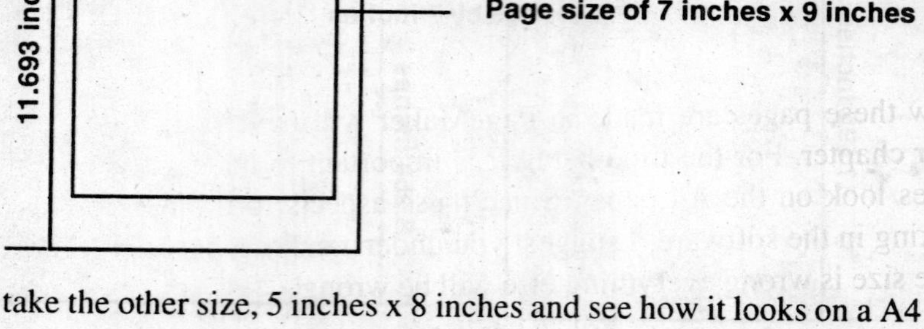

Let us take the other size, 5 inches x 8 inches and see how it looks on a A4 page.

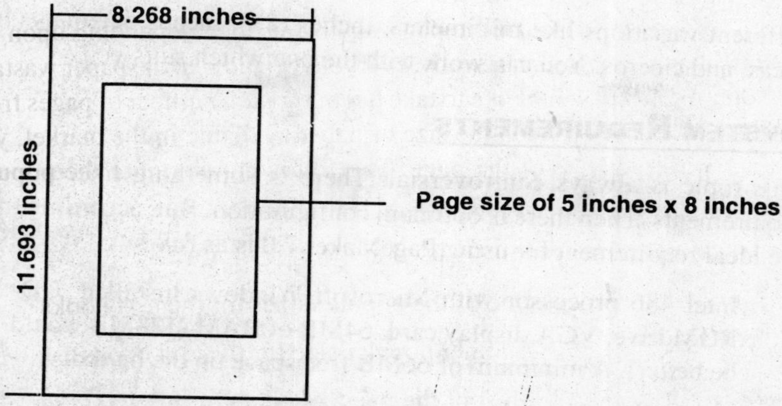

Now let us see how two 7 inch x 4 inch pages can be adjusted into one A4 paper. This is very useful, since it makes the optimum use of the paper space. You would be using less number of pages, less of printer, less of printer toner, etc.

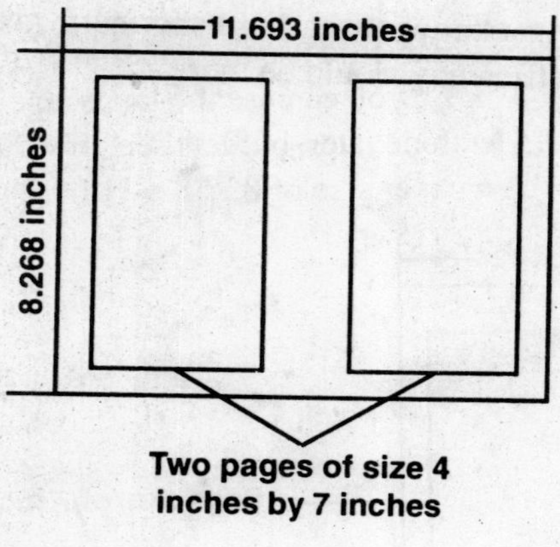

How these pages are made in PageMaker will be described to you in a later chapter. For the time being it is important to understand how these pages look on the A4 paper. Since these aspects form the basis of page making in the software, I suggest you understand this properly, else if the page size is wrong everything else will be wrong.

If you are not familiar with inches, PageMaker allows you to work with different variations like millimeters, inches (8's), inches decimals (10's), picas, and ciceros. You can work with the one which suits you.

System Requirements

This topic is always controversial. There is something like minimum requirements. Then there is optimum configuration. But, according to me, the ideal requirement for using PageMaker 7.0 is as follows:

> Intel 486 processor with Microsoft Windows installed. CD-ROMdrive, VGA display card, 64MB of RAM (128MB would be better). A minimum of 66MB free space on the hard disk.

Best way of working in PageMaker

You can in fact work in PageMaker according to your own settings. Some users I have seen are very comfortable working from the keyboard, using the various keyboard shortcuts. They would use the mouse only in emergency. This is why a list of keyboard shortcuts are given a full chapter in this book. More you know about these shortcuts, faster you can work. Naturally, then the efficiency would be more.

2

UNDERSTANDING PAGEMAKER

INTRODUCTION

Before we go into understanding the various commands of the software, it is essential to learn the basics of the software. First thing first, let us start the software.

PAGEMAKER 7.0

You can start PageMaker by using **Start** button, and going to Programs, Adobe folder, PageMaker 7.0 folder and then clicking at Adobe PageMaker 7.0. There are other methods too, which will be told to you later.

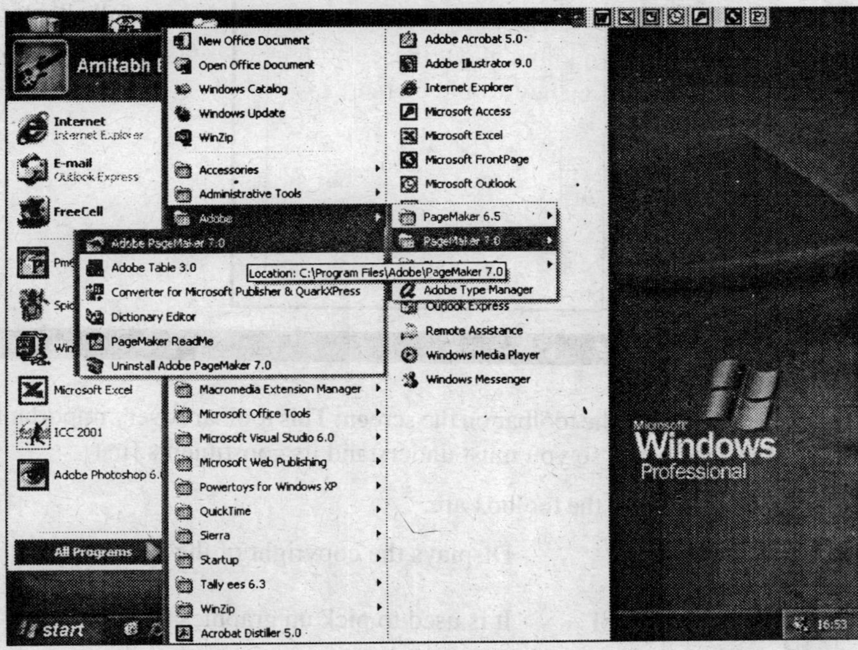

Once started you will see the Adobe PageMaker 7.0's display screen and other copyright conditions. After you have done away with templates dialog box, you will get the blank page as shown here. This blank desktop is your work area and you would be working on it later on. It is a blank page with rulers on the top and left. Scroll bars on the bottom and right side. Buttons for making the window minimum and maximum at the right hand corner. It even has the button for closing of the window. As long as you work on this desktop, the bottom of the screen will show the software name.

Moreover you have the toolbar on the screen. This toolbar is very important part of the software, so you must understand its constituents first.

The various tools on the toolbox are:

 Copyright — Displays the copyright of the software.

 Pointer tool — It is used to pick up graphics and text.

 Text tool — It is used to edit and select text.

	Rotate tool	It helps you in rotating the text.
	Crop tool	It helps in cropping the graphics.
	Oblique line	This tool is used to draw an oblique line.
	Straight line	This is used to draw a straight line.
	Box	This tool is used to draw a box.
	Rectangle frame	This is used to type text inside a box.
	Circle	- It is used to draw a circle or elliptical picture.
	Oval frame	It is used to type text inside a circle.
	Rectangular tool	This tool is used to draw a shape with more than 4 sides
	Polygon frame	This tool puts the text inside the polygon.
	Hand	It is used to move the screen from left to right, top to bottom.
	Zoom	It allow you to zoom to see large or small.

Please note that this toolbar is moveable and you can place it any place on the screen.

Now we come to the very basic of the PageMaker and understand what is there on the PageMaker screen.

A PageMaker screen looks like the one shown on the next page.

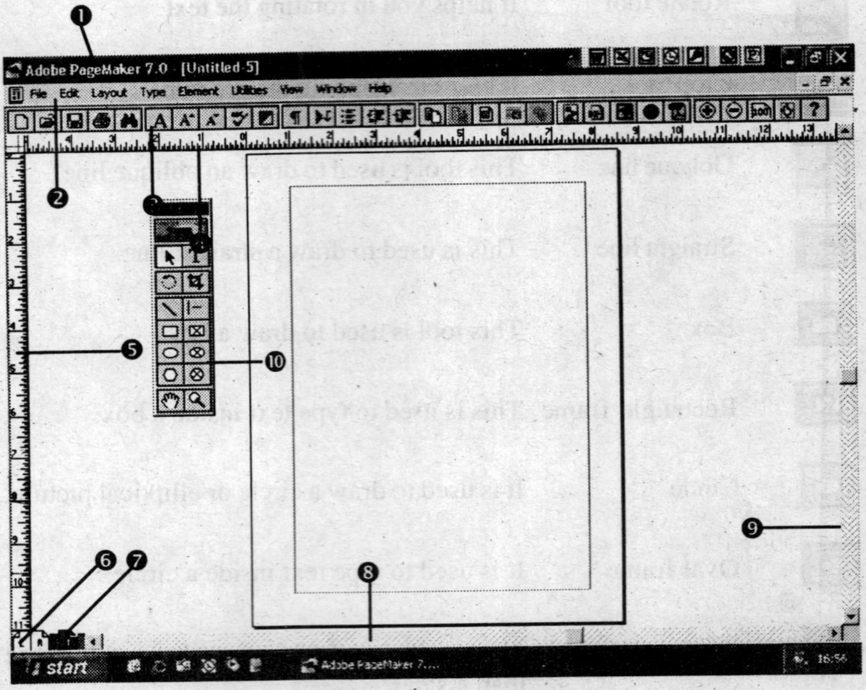

In the above picture, the following items of the PageMaker screen are shown:

❶	Standard toolbar	This contains the name of the opened file
❷	Menu toolbar	This toolbar contains all the menus
❸	Formatting bar	This toolbar has the various tools for formatting
❹	Top Ruler	It shows the ruler on the top of the screen
❺	Vertical Ruler	It show ruler on the side of the screen
❻	Master Page	It shows the position of the master pages
❼	Current Page	It shows the current page number
❽	Bottom Scroll bar	For scrolling the pages left to right and back
❾	Vertical Scroll bar	For scrolling the pages from top to bottom and back
❿	Toolbox	As described on the earlier page

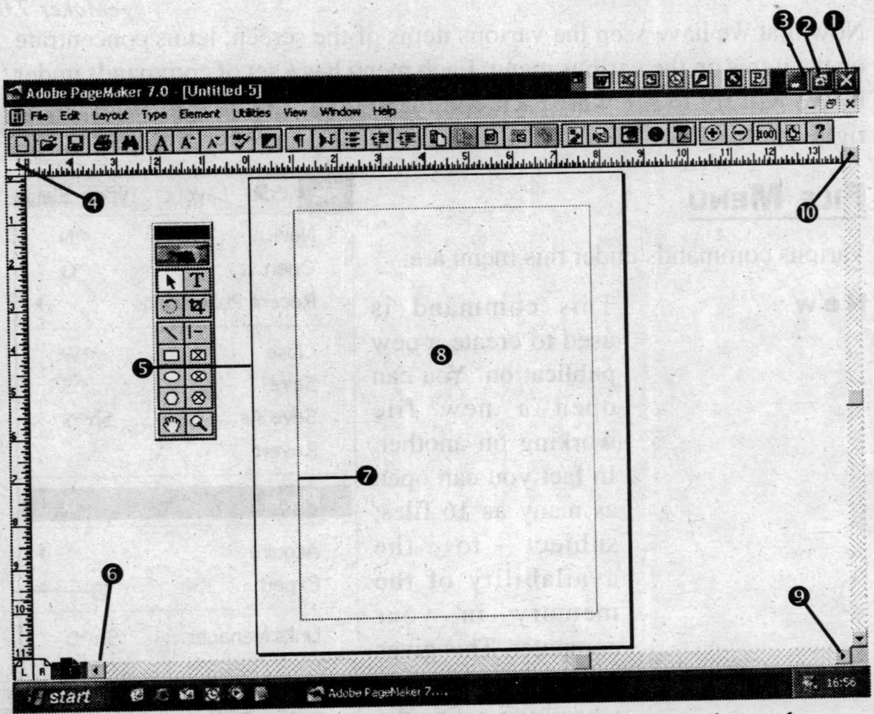

Another set of screen items of the page maker screen are shown here:

❶	Close button	This button closes the PageMaker
❷	Toggle button	This button allows you to toggle between maximum and minimum of screen
❸	Minimum button	This button makes PM into an icon (minimum)
❹	Zero position	It allows you to place zero position on the screen
❺	Paper Size	Outer boundary of the paper
❻	Horizontal button	Button for moving the screen horizontally
❼	Page boundary	Boundary of the created page
❽	Text area	Area where the text will be placed
❾	Horizontal button	For moving the screen horizontally
❿	Vertical button	For moving the screen vertically

Now that we have seen the various items of the screen, let us concentrate on the items on the various menu. Each menu has a set of commands under it. We will try to see what each command does. Let us start from left to right and the first menu if **File** menu.

FILE MENU

Various commands under this menu are:

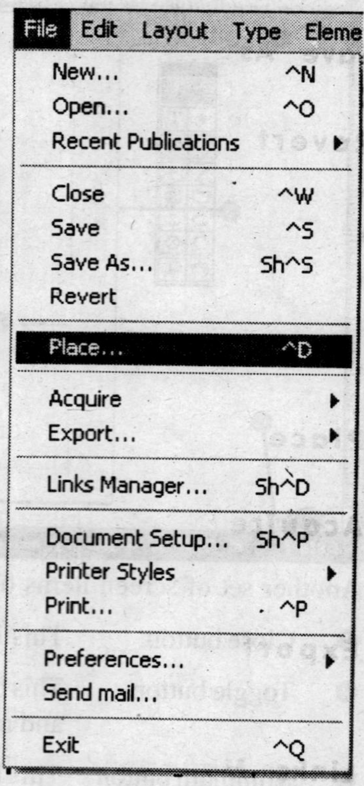

New This command is used to create a new publication. You can open a new file working on another. In fact you can open as many as 16 files, subject to the availability of the memory in your computer. This gives rise to a dialog box, where you define the various options before opening a new page of the publication.

Open It allows you to open an existing file from either the hard disk or other media attached to the computer, floppy drive, CD drive, etc. This also gives rise to a dialog box, from where you can select the file, which you want to open.

Recent Publications It shows you a list of recently opened publications for you to choose one of them for opening or you can choose the **Open** option from above and select the file, you want to open.

Close It allows you to close the current publication file.

Save It saves the current publication file. If you have more than one publication open, save them all by choosing the option of pressing **Shift** key while choosing the **Save** option. The command will change to **Save all** and all the open files will be saved.

Save As It allows you to save the current file under a new name or overwrite the current file.

Revert This command is used to restore the most recently saved version of your publication or template deleting all changes made since the last time you saved the publication. Reverting to the last saved version of your publication is the same as closing the publication without saving your changes and then reopening the publication (assuming that you have not saved the file during the current session).

Place This command is used to place the text into the publication.

Acquire This command is active only if you have the scanner attached to your computer. This will help you in getting the scanned picture into the publication.

Export Using this command you can export the selected text of the publication into a document file in the format selected by you.

Links Manager It shows you the various link files in the publication

Document Setup It is this dialog box which is given when you cli k at New. Here you set the various options of th publication.

Printer Styles You can define here various styles for printing.

Print This gives rise to a dialog box, where you can set the options for printing the publication.

Preferences This command is used to customize your publication according to your preferences. If a publication is open the options you select in the preferences dialog box apply to that publication only. If you have no publication open, the option you choose applies to any new publication you create after that.

Send Mail Using this option you can send e-mail.

Exit Closes your session with PageMaker 7.0.

EDIT MENU

Various options under this menu are:

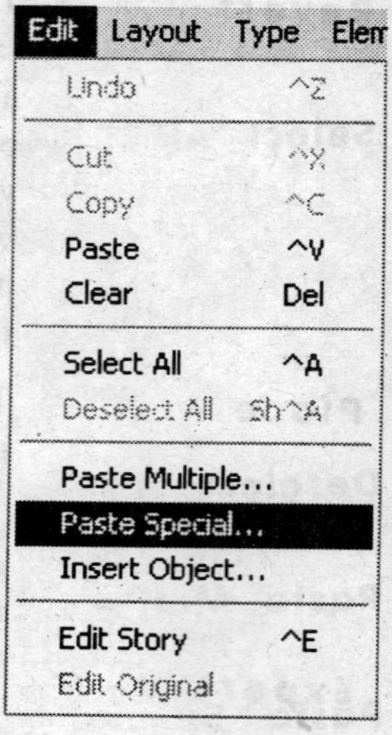

Undo/Redo This command is used to reverse the last action taken by you. However, you can't undo all the actions. If the action can be reversed, the command read Undo on the Edit menu and names the action such as Undo Pasting. If the action cannot be reversed the command is off and thus can be read as cannot Undo. After you have do undo, you can Redo too if it is allowed.

Cut This command is used to cut the selected text or graphics from your file and keep it available for pasting it later to any other place in the same file or any other file or even any other software which supports the clipboard text.

Copy This command is also used to copy the selected text or graphics from your file and keep it available for pasting it later. Only difference it has from Cut command is that it leaves the original text as it is whereas in the case of Cut the original text is lost. When you have more than one publication open, you can copy objects between publications without using the Clipboard. Select an object in one publication, drag it to position in the other publication window and release the mouse button to create a copy.

Paste This command is used to place the selected text or graphics from clipboard, where the text using the above Cut or Copy command has been kept.

Clear This command is used to delete the current selection from your publication without storing it in the Clipboard. This has the same effect as pressing Delete or Backspace.

Select All This command is used as the name suggests to select all. What you select depends on which view you are in and which tool you are using. In story view, the entire current story will be selected. In layout view with the text tool active, the entire current story is selected. In layout tool with any tool but the text tool active, the contents of the publication window are selected.

Deselect All Reverse of the above command, where you deselect all the selected text.

Paste Multiple This command is used to paste more than one copy of the text or graphic.

Paste Special This command is used to specify the format to use when you paste an object from the clipboard into your publication. When you copy an object to the clipboard, the source program often programs the information in more than one format. If there are more than one format on the clipboard when you paste an object, PageMaker picks up the format best preserves the appearance of a format that allows you to edit the text in PageMaker while preserving formatting.

Insert Object This command is used to create an object in another program and insert is an OLE embedded object with a PageMaker publication.

Edit Story Choosing this option you can select word processing mode of the PageMaker without closing the file in which you are working.

Edit Original This command is OLE based command which is used to start the original program in which this selected imported element was created. Once opened you can edit it and return back to PageMaker.

LAYOUT MENU

Various options under this menu are:

Go to Page This command is used when you want to go to a different page then the one which you see on the screen. This is useful—when you to jump ahead or back many pages at a time; or the page icons and scroll bars are hidden.

Insert Pages This command is used to insert new pages into the publication. PageMaker 7.0 allows you to have a maximum of 999 pages in a publication.

Remove Pages This command is used for removing pages from the publication file. Remember the text or graphic on the removed pages will be lost by removing them. If the page you remove has text which is carried from and carried over and is part of the story, then PageMaker automatically joins the last word of the previous page with the first word of the next page to keep the story intact.

Sort Pages When you select this command, a dialog box will appear with all the pages of the publication appearing as boxes. You can then pick up any page and place at it any other place. This way you can change all the pages and once don, click Ok, the new numbers will be allotted according to the new placings.

Go Back Pressing this command you will be able to go the previous page of the publication.

Go Forward Similar to above, you can go to the next page using this command.

Column Guides You can divide the page of the publication into different columns of equal size. You can create columns of unequal length by pulling guides to the required place. However, the text flow from previous page, using Autoflow, does not recognize this option and does not flow the text in unequal columns. The maximum number of columns that you can create on a page are 20.

Copy MasterGuides - This command is used to reflect the master page columns and ruler guides on screen. In case you want to set a different set of guides on the current page, use the toggle option to hide it

Autoflow This command is used to flow the text onto the pages of the publication on its own from a loaded text icon. When autoflow is on, it flows the text into pages from columns to column, if there are multiple columns. It also text around the graphics as per the setting of the text wrap. It adds pages on its own in the publication depending on the availability of the text.

TYPE MENU

Various options under this menu are:

Font This command is used to define the type design used to print selected text or the next text you type. When you choose Font, PageMaker displays a list of fonts installed on your computer, as well as any additional font that may have been used in your publication.

Size This command is used to specify printed point size of selected text or of the next text you type.

Leading Leading is the blank space between the two lines of the text. If the leading is normal the text is more readable, if it is less the text is congested and less readable but obviously the number of lines of the text in a page increases, thus resulting in less number of pages in the book.

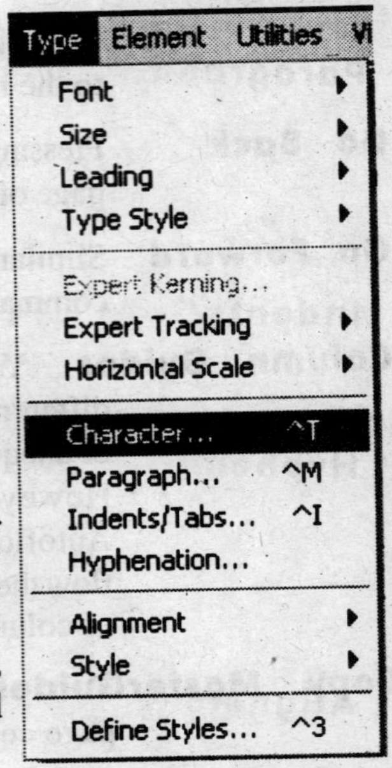

Type Style There are 6 main type of styles to be used in PageMaker. They are: Normal, **Bold**, *Italics*, Underline, ~~Strikethru~~, and Reverse

Expert Kerning It is a method used for keeping the space between the two characters to a minimum. It examines a pair of letters in the selected text and tunes them for optimum spacing.

Expert Tracking It adjusts the spacing of large blocks of text and does it with no regard to individual pairs of letters, as done in case of kerning.

Horizontal Scale This command is used to change the width of the character of the text. It is common to condense or expand the text in typesetting. Setting the width of a particular text to 90% means a condensation of 10% and setting it to 110% means an expansion of 10%.

Character This command is used to set most of the items of this menu at one glance. It has additional commands for setting the text in different position like Subscript, Superscript, etc. You can even change the colour of the text too from here.

Paragraph This command is used to set the various attributes of the paragraph. PageMaker for all practical purposes assumes a paragraph as a set of lines written in continuation till the carriage return (or Enter) is used to end it.

Indents/Tabs These are mainly used in case of tabular matter. This command is used to set the tabs at places where once pressing the text may move to that point.

Hyphenation This command permits two separate operations. Its main purpose is to determine how words should be hyphenated in a selected paragraph or paragraphs of a particular style. You can also use it to add words and hyphenation instruction to your user dictionary.

Alignment This command is used to set the alignment of the selected paragraph. Various options available here are Left, Right, Centre, Justify and Force Justify.

Style You can call the style sheet on the screen by using this command. By clicking at one of the styles present, you can change the attributes of the paragraph.

Define Styles This command is used to create, edit, remove and copy various paragraph attributes which have been selected under its dialog box.

Element Menu

Various commands under this menu are:

Fill This command is used to fill the box or circle drawn by you in the text, with the options available under this command. Most of them are the various type of lines in the box besides options for filling up with paper and solid.

Stroke This command is to select the size of the line drawn by you. It has various size of lines besides some of them being designed ones. You can even have the option of having the line in reverse.

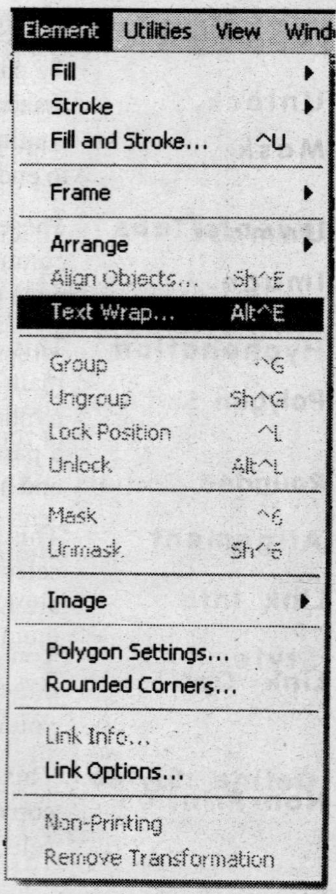

Fill and Stroke It is a combination of the above two commands. Instead of selecting them one by one, you can select them together with this command.

Frame It has the various options of Frame, which you will read in a later chapter.

Arrange This command allows you to bring the graphics to the front or back, depending upon your needs.

Align Objects It is another interesting command which was not there in earlier versions. With this command you can align text, graphics to various positions, like, top of page, centre of page, etc.

TextWrap It has the various text wrap options for you to decide which one to choose for your text.

Group This command was there in most of the graphics software. Using this command you can form a group of the items available on the page. It is like binding them together to form a block.

Ungroup Once grouped using the above command, this command is used to ungroup them.

Lock Position When you use this command with respect to some graphics, the graphic gets locked at that position on the page and cannot be moved anywhere else.

Unlock To unlock the above graphic, this command is used.

Mask This command creates a window sort of effect to see the text through the graphic which you are using.

Unmask To undo the above command, this command is used.

Image This command is used for Image brightness, image contrast, change image screen angle and image's screen patterns.

Polygon Settings Set the number of sides which you want to have in your polygon.

Rounded Corners While drawing a box in Page Maker, you can bend the corners of the box in various options. This command lets you do that.

Link Info This command is used to view additional information about a linked objected selected in the publication.

Link Options This command is used to define whether the linked text or graphic is to be updated alongwith the publication in use and also its frequency.

Non-Printing Using this command you can designate an object to be non-printing so that it does not get printed while printing the other contents of the page.

Remove Transformation Using this command you can remove the transformation used on the selected text or graphic.

UTILITIES MENU

Various commands under this menu are:

Plug-ins This command has sub-command which list the various plug-ins which have been included in the software as additions.

These are:

Add con'td line... Most of the time while using text

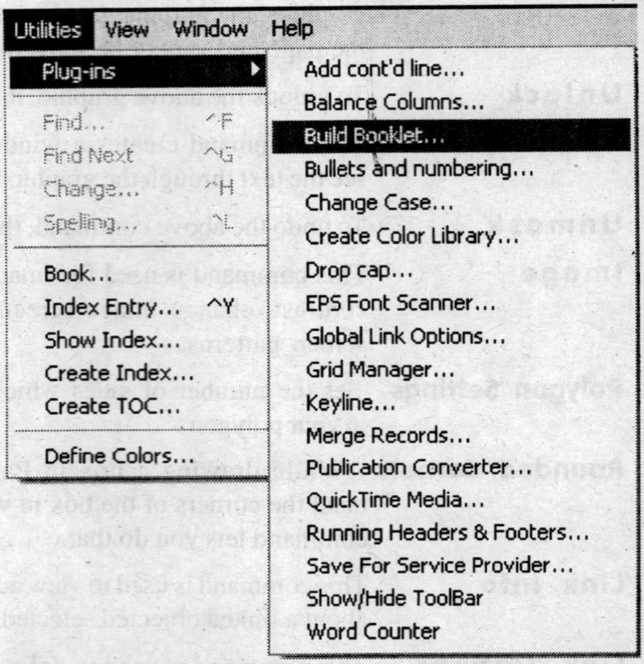

for creation of a book, leaflet, brochure, etc., it becomes necessary to carry the text from one page to another page which is not necessarily the next page. This leads to putting a line at the end of the first page as "Continued on Page no." and putting on the top of text "Continued from Page no." where the remaining text is carried over.

Balance Columns... Sometimes in the text format you are required to balance the two columns of the page. This is mostly required in the case of brochures, magazines, etc.

Build Booklet.. This allows you to create a copy of your publication in which pages are arranged for printing multi-page spreads or signatures, i.e., multiple pages printed on a single sheet when folded assumes the correct page order.

Bullets and numbering... Now it is easy to put bullets in the text. These can be of your choice and can be replaced by special characters too. It is also possible to number the paragraphs. The number style can again be changed according to your choice.

Change Case... Using this command you can change the case of the text from normal to all upper case, all lower case, etc.

Create Color Library.. This feature allows you to save a set of colours as a group and can be used by you in different publications so as to keep the continuity and uniqueness of the colours.

Drop Cap.. It is a concept used to highlight the first character of the text in bold and bigger size. You have a choice to make it of any number of lines, depending upon your text.

EPS Font Scanner... This option allows you to include the fonts in your EPS files.

Global Link Options... It allows you to change the options of links in the publication.

Grid Manager.. This command allows you to set up evenly spaced sets of ruler guide grids, custom ruler guides, and column guides.

Keyline... This command allows you to set up keyline for a graphic.

Publication Converter... It converts the publication to earlier versions.

QuickTime Media.. This command is used for working with Quick Time software.

Running Headers & Footers... It is sometimes required to include on the top or bottom of the page, better known as Header or Footer, to have the first word of the page or the last word of the page as the case may be. This is very useful in case of documents like dictionary, directory, etc.

Save For Service Provider... This command is used by the service provider.

Show/Hide Toolbar.. It is used to hide or show the floating toolbar in the publication.

Word Counter.. Run this command to find out the number of character, lines, paragraphs, etc. in your publication.

Find Available only in Story editor. This command is used to find a particular word.

Find Next Available only in Story editor. This command is used to find the next occurrence of the same word.

Change Available only in Story editor. This command is used as Find and Replace command of the word processing.

Spelling Available only in Story editor. This command is used to spell check the text of the publication.

Book This command is used to create a book of publications of the same book. This is very useful when you are going to create a Table of Contents or Index of the complete book.

Index entry This command is used to mark an index entry in the text.

Show Index This command is used to show the index before printing.

Create Index This command is used to create index on the basis of the entries marked for index.

Create TOC Creates a Table of Contents from the entries marked to appear in the same.

Define Colors This allows you to see the various colours which can be used in the text. It allows to create new colours of your own.

View Menu

This menu has the following options:

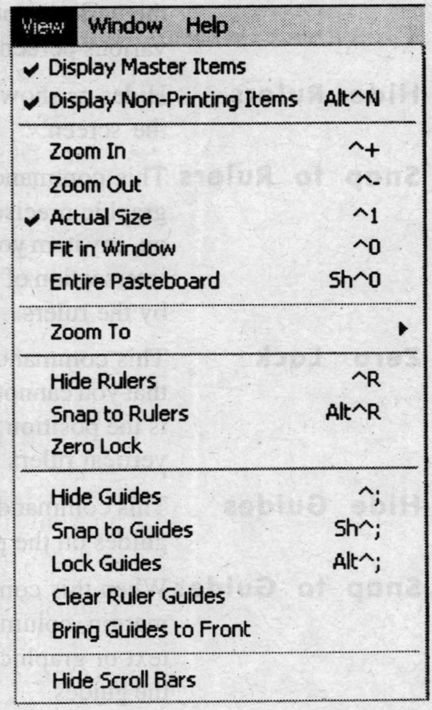

Display Master Items This command allows the matter from the master page to be reflected onto the current page of the publication.

Display Non-Printing Items This command allow you to see even the non-printing items, like paragraph mark, tab character, etc., on the screen.

Zoom In With each zoom in the publication on the screen keeps zooming in for you to see the text in the bigger size.

Zoom Out Reverse of the above. With each zoom out, you will be able to diminish the size of the publication on the screen.

Actual Size This command allows you to see the actual size of the publication on the screen.

Fit in Window It is another view of the publication where the whole page fits into the window of the screen.

Entire Pasteboard This command allows you to see the entire pasteboard on the screen.

Zoom To As you can see from the screen on the previous page, the various options are to see the publication in the various percentages of the publication.

Hide Rulers Hides or shows the rulers on the left and the top of the screen.

Snap to Rulers This command is used to position text block and graphic precisely on a page. When snap to rulers is on, any item you place or move is pulled to the nearest intersection of tick mark on the invisible grid defined by the rulers.

Zero Lock This command is used to lock the zero position so that you cannot change it accidentally. The zero point is the position at which the 0 of both horizontal and vertical rulers meet.

Hide Guides This command is used to hide the column ruler and guides on the page.

Snap to Guides When this command is selected all guides whether margin, column or ruler exert pressure on any tool, text or graphic when they are within short range of the guides.

Lock Guides This command locks all the column and ruler guides so that you cannot move them accidentally.

Clear Ruler Guides It clears all the ruler guides off the screen.

Send Guides to Back All the guides are sent back and not visible.

Hide Scroll Bars You can hide scroll bars through this command.

WINDOW MENU

This menu has the following options:

Arrange Icons This command is used to organize into rows the icons of minimized publications and stories in the Page Maker program.

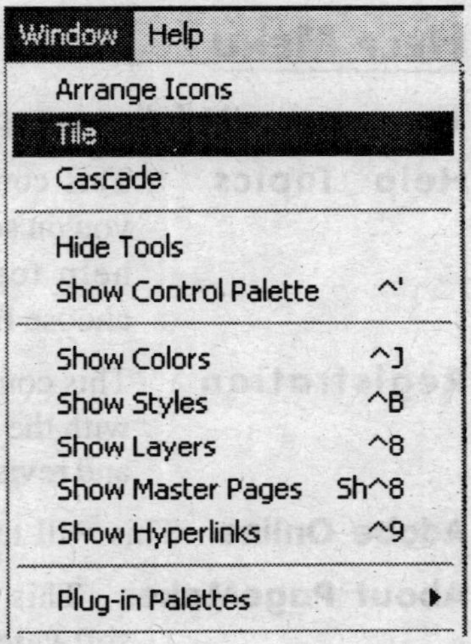

Tile This command arranges two or more windows so that they appear side by side like tiles on a floor.

Cascade This command is used to break the grip of the publication file, so that you can reduce its size and fit it into any place in the window to make available space for more files to be accommodated. It is mainly used when you have to open more than one file.

Hide Tools This command allows you to hide/show the toolbar off/on the screen.

Show Control Palette This command shows/hides the colour palette on/off the screen.

Show Colors This command is used to show/hide colours on the screen or off the screen.

Show Styles Similar to above this command shows/hides the styles of the publication.

Show Layers This command shows the layer palette.

Show Master Pages It shows the information of various master pages.

Show Hyperlinks It shows the various hyperlinks of the publication.

Plug-in Palettes It gives you the information about the various plug-ins.

Open files It gives the information of any open file, including the current one.

Help Menu

This menu has the following options:

Help Topics This command will give you on screen the various help topics for you to choose from.

Registration This command allows you to register your software with the company, so that you can get later versions and revisions.

Adobe Online This will take you to the website of the company.

About PageMaker This gives rise to the copyright page of the software.

Toolbar Options

PageMaker 7.0 has collected a set of commands which are often used in the form of a toolbar, where with just a click, you can access these commands. These commands are available under the various menu commands too, but this is a faster way of accessing them. This toolbar can be accessed from the Utilities Menu, plug-ins, Show/Hide Toolbar.

Various options on the toolbar are:

New Open a new publication.

Open Open an existing publication.

Save Save the current publication.

Print Prints the current publication.

Find Finds the publication file for you.

Character specs Opens the character dialog box.

Increase font size Increases the font size.

Decrease font size Decreases the font size.

Spelling check	Starts the spelling check.
Fill and stroke	Opens the Fill and Stroke dialog box.
Paragraph specs	Opens the paragraph dialog box.
Indents/Tabs	Opens the Indent/Tab dialog box.
Bullets & Numbering	Opens bullets/numbering dialog box.
Outdent	Set the text to outer indent.
Indent	Sets the text to the indent.
Insert Pages	Insert dialog box is opened.
Remove Pages	Select the pages for removal.
Frame Options	Selects the various frame options.
Text Wrap	Opens the Text wrap dialog box.
Blank	Left blank for future use.
Picture pallette	Opens the picture pallette.
Place	Allows you to place files.
Photoshop	Opens Photoshop software for you.
HTML-Export	Allows you to export data in HTML format.

Another very important command here is Preference, which allows you to customize the PageMaker according to your needs.

PREFERENCES

This command is available under the File menu. If a publication is open the options you select in the preferences dialog box apply to that publication only. If you have no publication open, the option you choose apply to any new publication you create after that.

Various options in the Preference dialog box are:

Measurements in You can measure your publication in inches, inches decimal, millimeters, pica & points and ciceros. The unit measure you select becomes the standard for all your publication measurements expect the vertical ruler. You can change the measurements system at any time without affecting anything already on the page.

Vertical ruler You can select to have the unit of measure for the vertical ruler different from the publication overall measurement system. If you select custom, you can set the vertical ruler to match your leading in points by typing that measurements in the edit box on the right, used in conjunction with snap to rulers (from the guides and rulers submenu on the layout menu) and align to grid (in the paragraph rule open dialog box). This feature is also useful in aligning the baseline of the text.

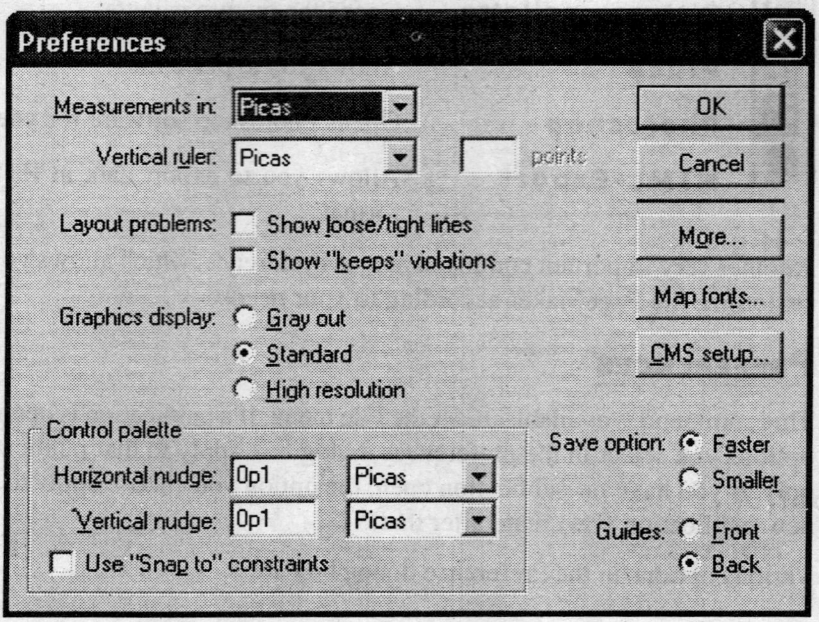

Layout problems

Show loose/tight lines When this option is on PageMaker highlights the lines which have either too much, loose letter/word spacing or too tight. Based on the spacing limits set in the spacing attributes dialog box, you can then adjust these lines to correct the problem.

Show keeps violations If this option is on, PageMaker checks for the violation of widow, orphan or keep with next control that you set in the paragraph specification dialog box. Violation can occur when PageMaker must make composition choice that prevent it from honouring your settings.

Graphics display

Gray Out While using graphics, use this option to allow PageMaker to display gray boxes in places of the graphics.

Normal Again use this with graphics to display non PageMaker graphic as low resolution screen images.

High resolution This command allows the PageMaker to display images including colour image at their full resolution. For PageMaker to display a graphic at high resolution, the graphic link must be up to date or the graphic must be stored as part of the publication, otherwise it will be displayed at low resolution regardless of the graphic setting.

Control palette

Horizontal nudge Type a number and select a unit of measurement to specify the nudge amount for control palette option that measures the horizontal distance. By default the unit of measurement for this option match the unit you choose for measurement system described earlier.

Vertical nudge Same as above to define the vertical nudge instead of horizontal nudge.

Use snap to constraints This allows for the value adjustment to the nearest ruler tick mark or nonprinting guide when you use the nudge button on the Control Palette. This option is used only when snap to constrain are set using command on the guide and rulers submenu in the layout menu and the element is within three pixel of either a guide or a ruler tick mark.

Save options

Faster At the time of saving if this is clicked the PageMaker quickly appends the changes on to the file.

Smaller This option allows you to save the file as if it has been saved in the Save As format, i.e., in compresses the file. Though this command does take a little longer time when you save but on the other hand it reduces the size of the publication since it does not append the changes.

Guides

Front Clicking this allows the margin columns and ruler guides to be shown in front of text and graphics.

Back Reverse of the above command with text and graphics coming in front of margin columns and ruler guides.

Click at **More** to get the **More Preferences** dialog box, which has:

Text

Greek text below Specifies the size below which PageMaker will display text as gray bars in layout view. The default setting is 9 pixels. To increase the speed with which PageMaker displays text, you can set this option to a higher number of pixel.

Turn pages when autoflowing Click this to allow the turning of the pages when the text flows automatically using the autoflow command.

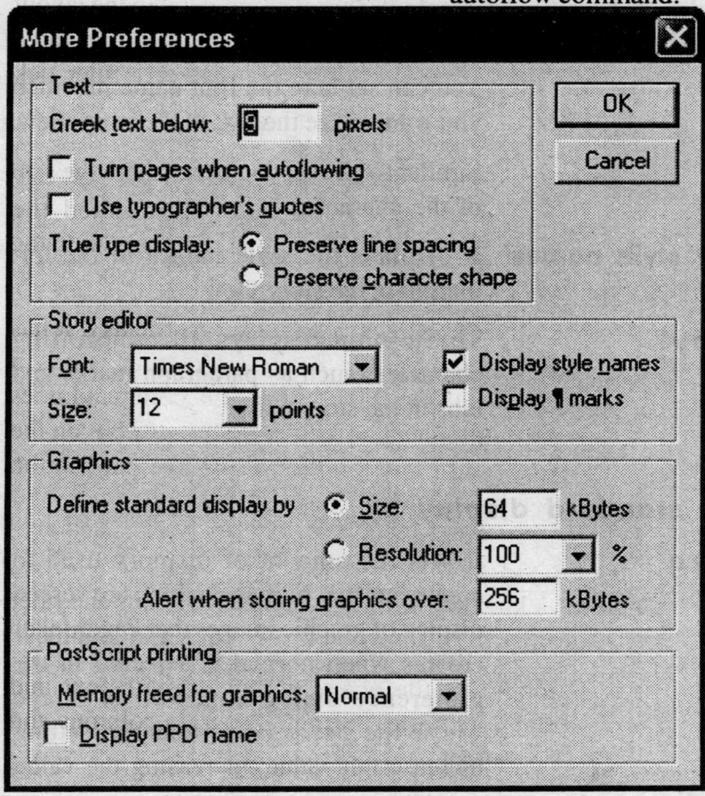

Use typographer's quotes Display open and closed quotation marks (" ") and apostrophes (' '). When checked you cannot type inch and foot marks on the keyboard without first unchecking this command.

True type

Preserve line spacing Preserves the line spacing or leading of true type fonts and adjust the character height as necessary.

Preserve character shape Preserves the character height of true type fonts regardless of lines spacing.

Story editor

Fonts You can set here the font name in which you want to see the text in the story view.

Size Similar to above, you define here the size of the character.

Display style names It displays the style names in the left margin in the story view.

Display¶ This option displays all nonprinting characters such as paragraph marks and tabs in the story editor.

Graphics

Define standard display by

Size It sets the amount of memory used to create internal bitmaps, which are screen display of graphic images that PageMaker creates when normal is selected in the preference dialog box. For an image whose file size is larger than this setting increase this value, increasing the value for this option improves the resolution of the graphic and increases the size of the publication, the amount of memory used and therefore the time it takes to display the graphic or save. To display the graphic on the screen, lower the value of save disk space, memory and redraw time but lower the resolution of the graphic on the screen. A graphic whose file size is smaller than the current setting is not affected by the setting.

Alert when storing graphics over Sets the file size of graphic image over which the PageMaker should alert you.

Postscript printing

Memory freed for graphics Default is Normal but you can make it maximum too, if you are using more graphics in the file.

Display PPD name It allows you to use the shortnames of printers instead of full name of the printer.

There are other preferences too in the PageMaker.

They are:

Online

This allows you to set specific parameters for making a PageMaker document Web active. Among these is the activating of embedded link sources when the Hand tool is selected and centering the upper-left of the anchor selection.

Layout adjustment

It enables you to set various parameters for adjusting page elements and ruler guides.

Trapping

It is used to set specific conditions for Trapping

Now, that I have covered most of the PageMaker 7.0 commands, you would not have trouble in finding them. But, how to use them would be shown in the next chapters when I take you to the tour of the software and ask you to create a publication alongwith me to learn more about the software.

3

Creating a Publication

Introduction

In the last chapter you had seen most of the commands. In this chapter you would learn to use them. As they say that the best way to learn swimming is to jump in the swimming pool. What we will do here is that we will create a book from the text which has been already keyed-in (typed) in some other word processing program. We will learn more about the commands seen earlier as and when we use them.

First of all we will start the PageMaker software without which nothing can be done.

Starting PageMaker 7.0

There are more than one method of starting PageMaker. You can start from any of the following methods.

1. Click at PageMaker 7.0 icon on the desktop.
2. Click **Start** button and then **Programs, Adobe, PageMaker 7.0**.
3. You can even start from the Windows Explorer.

Once started you will see the Adobe PageMaker 7.0's display screen as shown on the next page and alongwith the various copyright conditions. It will keep on displaying the various initializing routine it keeps on doing. It gives you some idea that it is doing something. Finally it reaches a point where it displays a blank PageMaker desktop with various templates for you to select one of them, if you want to create a business card, flyer, poster, etc.

Since our aim is not to create any one of them, we will close this windows

Adobe
Adobe® PageMaker® 7.0

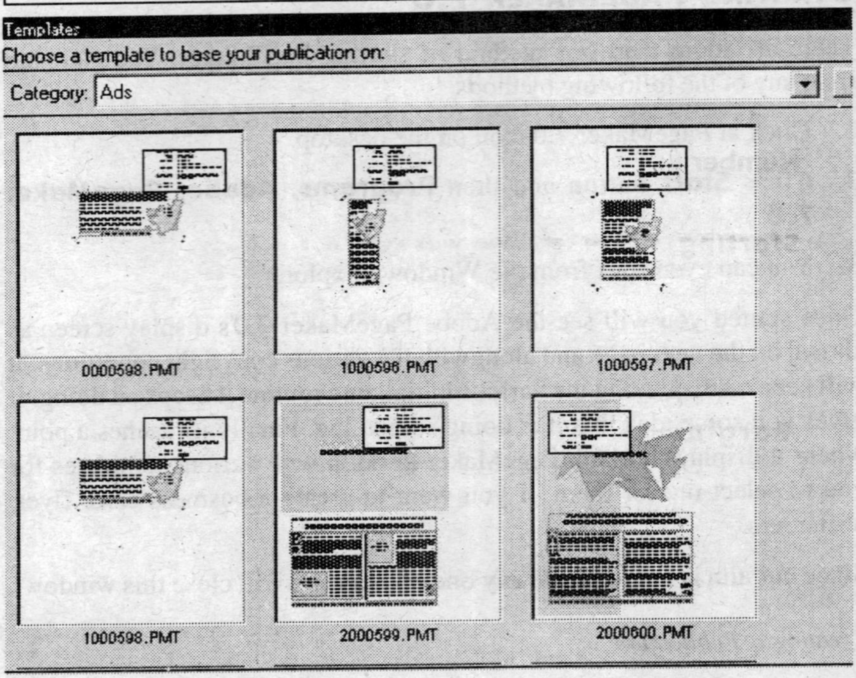
Templates
Choose a template to base your publication on:
Category: Ads
0000598.PMT
1000596.PMT
1000597.PMT
1000598.PMT
2000599.PMT
2000600.PMT

of template by clicking at the corner cross ☒ on the window. Now since we have to create a new publication for our book, we will click at New in the File menu. This will give rise to a document setup dialog box as shown here. Now, we have to fill this box, according to our specifications. We would be creating a page of size 5 inches x 8 inches and would set the details accordingly.

Page Size As said in earlier chapter, we will stick to A4 size of paper for all our work. So click at A4 here and you will see the size of the paper being reflected in the next boxes where **Dimensions** of the paper are given.

Orientation As discussed in first chapter, the orientation for this kind of page would be **Tall**. (Here it is referred as Tall and Wide instead of Portrait and Landscape).

Options Double-sided pages when selected will create left and right pages differently. You must have noticed this difference in almost all books and pages. So select it. Facing pages option will let you see 2 pages at a time on the screen. This helps in visualizing since the book would ultimately be opened like this. We would select this too.

Number of Pages You would always start with 1 and let the software fill up the pages later on.

Starting page # We will keep it 1 here. It is used for putting a number since your publication can be the 3rd chapter of the book and the first 50 pages have been consumed by the first two chapters, then you would like to put 51 here to start the 3rd chapter with page number 51.

Margins Now this is tricky. You remember the layout of various pages which were shown to you in the first chapter. It was also told that the our text page should be almost in the center of the page and the margins on all sides of the text should not less than 0.5 inches.

So let us see how the dimensions of inside and outside are measured.

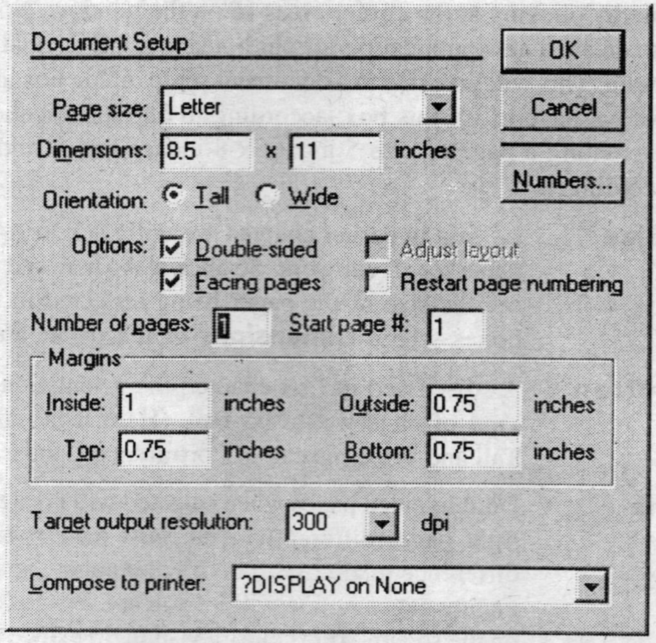

Our paper size width wise is 8.268 inches and the page size is 5 inches. This means that a total of 3.268 inches (8.268 - 5.0) of white space is left with us. This has to be divided equally (almost) on both sides of the page size. So if we divide 3.268 inches by 2, we get 1.634 inches. This much of space we have to leave on both left and right hand side of the paper to get our page in centre of the paper, horizontally.

So fill up 1.634 inches in both inside and outside margins.

Let us now come to the vertical margins. Our paper size here is 11.693 inches and the page size is 8 inches. The total margin available is thus 3.693 inches. This if divided equally into two comes to 1.8465 inches. If you want, you can truncate it to 1.846 and 1.847 respectively (an extra margin of 0.001 will not make much of a difference.)

This way you can fill up all the margins.

Target output resolution This depends upon the type of printer you are using. The usual now-a-days is 600 dpi. However, there are still printers with 300 dpi and even 1200 dpi printers are available in the market.

Compose to printer Each printer has its own set of features. The text may or may not change if you change the target printer. So it is always better to define here the printer you are going to use. If you are not sure just choose the printer attached to your computer, which is your default printer and will be shown here in any case.

So now you have all the options ready. Fill them up and your dialog box should look like this.

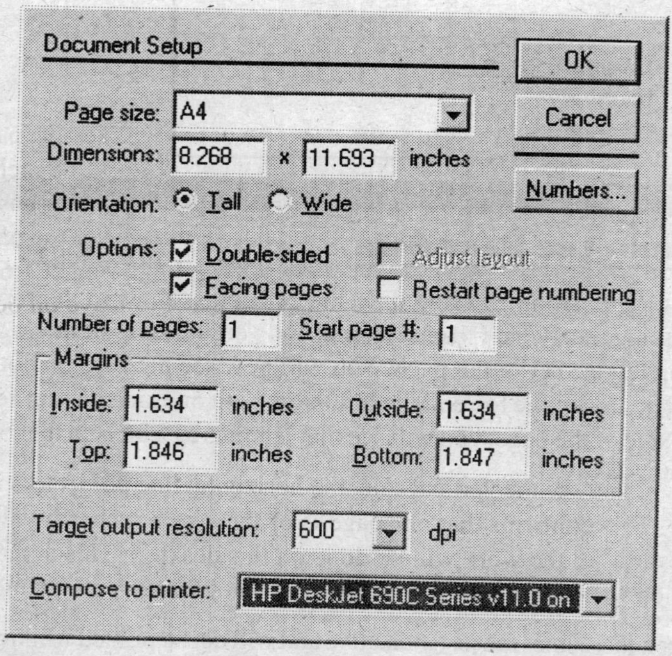

Click at Ok to get a new desktop of PageMaker to start your work. But would it not be nice to check the accuracy of the page before starting further, since if the page size is not perfect, the rest of the story will be all wrong. For this we will be using zero option. Before this you must ensure that both the rulers are on screen.

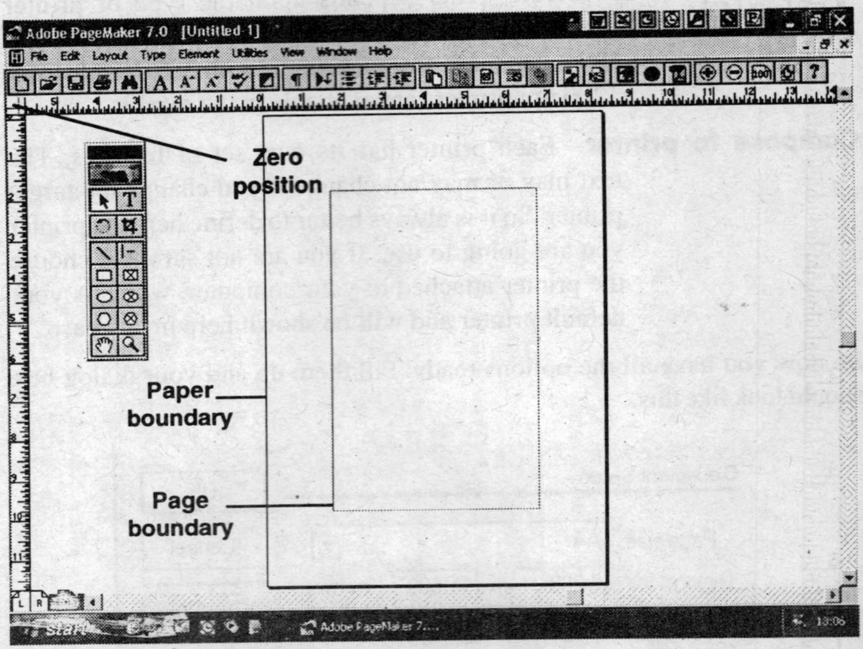

CHECKING THE PAGE SIZE

Click at zero position box and drag the zero cross lines to the top of the page crossing, i.e., where the horizontal and vertical lines of the page meet on the top left corner of the page. You will now see the zero on both sides of the ruler, i.e., on the top and the left. Now with one side having zero, see the right side of the page, you will see that it points to 5 inch on the top ruler.

Similarly if you see the vertical rule, the horizontal line points to 8 inch on the scale. This confirms that our page.is of the size 8 inches by 5 inches. Now onwards all the work will be done on this desktop. This is the actual page which will be printed as it is, once we put it through our printer.

Remember, these lines are just indicative and will not be printed while printing this page. These lines are called the guide lines and can be placed anywhere on the screen and can be drawn by dragging the mouse button on either of the ruler, i.e., on left or on top.

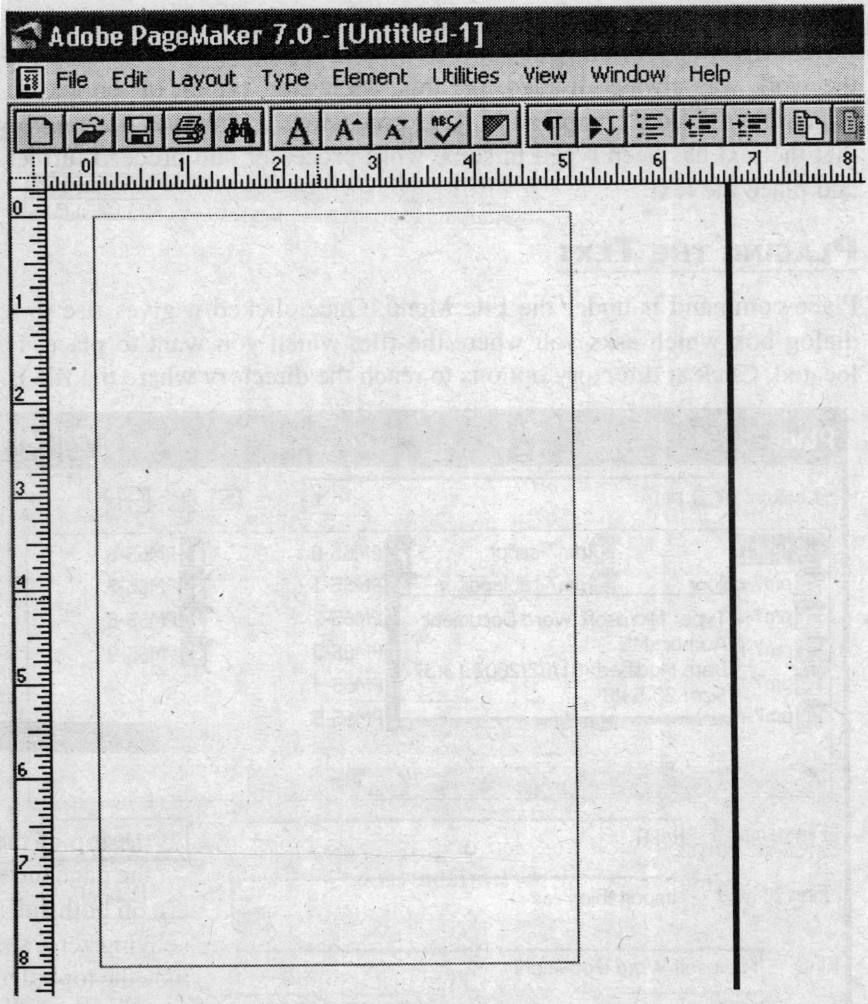

Now that we have the page ready, we would like to place some text on it. There is a convention that the text is always typed in a word processing program and then it is brought into the PageMaker. It has been there since the earlier versions of the software did not have the facilities of performing the various checks on the text, which most of the word processors have. These are: Spell checking, Find and Replace, etc. Slowly and slowly all these have been added to the PageMaker software too and can be conveniently used on the text of the PageMaker. I have a different opinion about this. Since in most of the earlier offices where it was used, there were different operators for both word processing and page making. Thus the work was always divided like this. Moreover, typing of the text in PageMaker is slow compared to word processing. Either way we assume that the text has been typed in some word processor and proceed further and place the text.

PLACING THE TEXT

Place command is under the File Menu. Once clicked it gives rise to a dialog box which asks you where the file, which you want to place, is located. Click at directory options to reach the directory where the file is

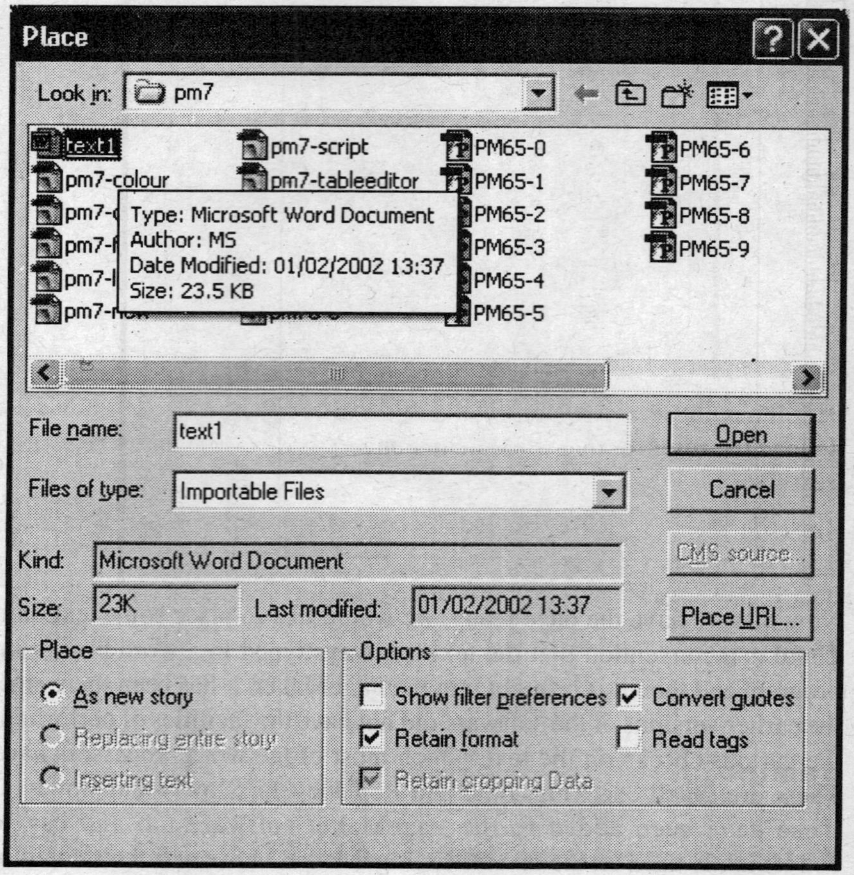

located. Double Click (or click and press Ok) to place the file in your publication.

Now this file could have been keyed in any of the word processing programs, PageMaker has the filters for most of the word processors. If the text in one of the word processors for which PageMaker has in built filters, the text will be inserted as it is. If it is not able to recognize the type of word processor, it will ask for the name of the software used for creating it, as shown here. You click at one of the software listed here.

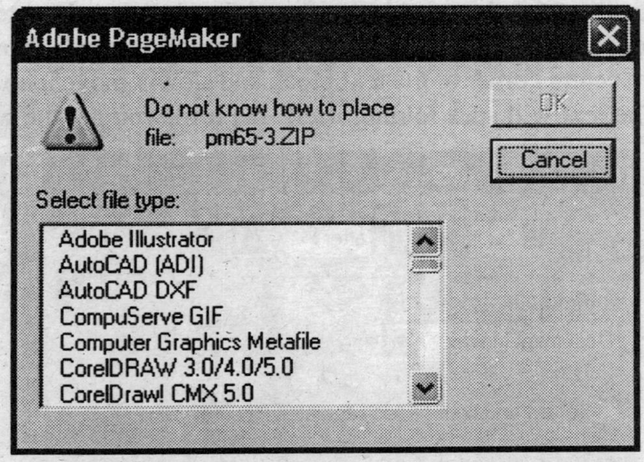

If still it is not able to recognize, then there is no option. Either you will have to load the filter for that software or convert the text into one of the known software.

Once the text is accepted, it will be available in the form of an icon. All you have to do it to place the text within the page frame made earlier by yo . There are 3 types of icons, this text can have. They are:

Manual It allows you to place the text manually, i.e., after placing the text on one page, you will have the option of placing the remaining text on the next page.

Semiautomatic You can change the text placement from page to page in this kind.

Autoflow Here the text will be placed automatically, placing all the text in one flow, creating more new pages on its own, till the whole text is placed.

Just click this icon at the starting point of the page, i.e., top left corner of the page, where we had put the zero edge earlier. In case you want the text to autoflow, you can change the option by clicking at autoflow in the layout menu.

In our case, we assume that the text is enough to last 3 pages and it has stopped after placing the text on the first page. Now at this stage you have 2 options, either click the text with pointer tool and click at the autoflow tool in the layout menu. This will make the text in autoflow mode. Now pick up the bottom centre corner of the text block and slowly move it up using the mouse. The text will start folding itself. Do it till you get the whole text

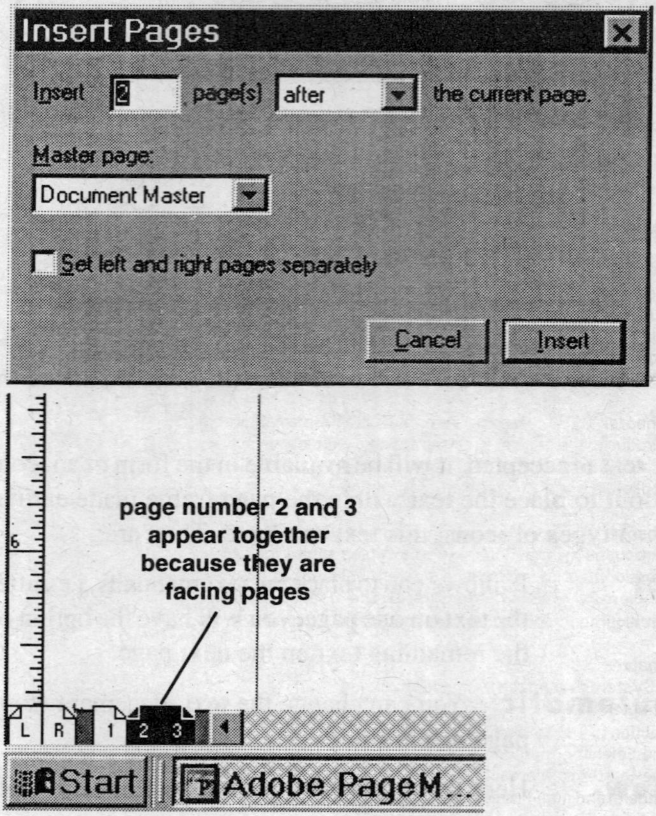

doled up. You will end up an autoflow icon. Click at the top corner of the page and see the text flow to the all the 3 pages.

Secondly, insert the pages manually, using the command, Insert Pages from the Layout menu. Click at Insert to insert 2 new pages. Then from the 1st page, pick up the text from the bottom center corner of the text block. Do not fold it this time. Instead go to the 2nd page by clicking at page 2 in the bottom box having the page number 2 and then click this at the top left corner of the page. The text will flow on the page number 2 and stop again. Repeat the same for the page number 3 too. So now we understand that if the text is big enough for more pages, it is always better to allow it to flow through. As you must have noticed that this text is just raw and need to be formatted, which is what we are going to do now.

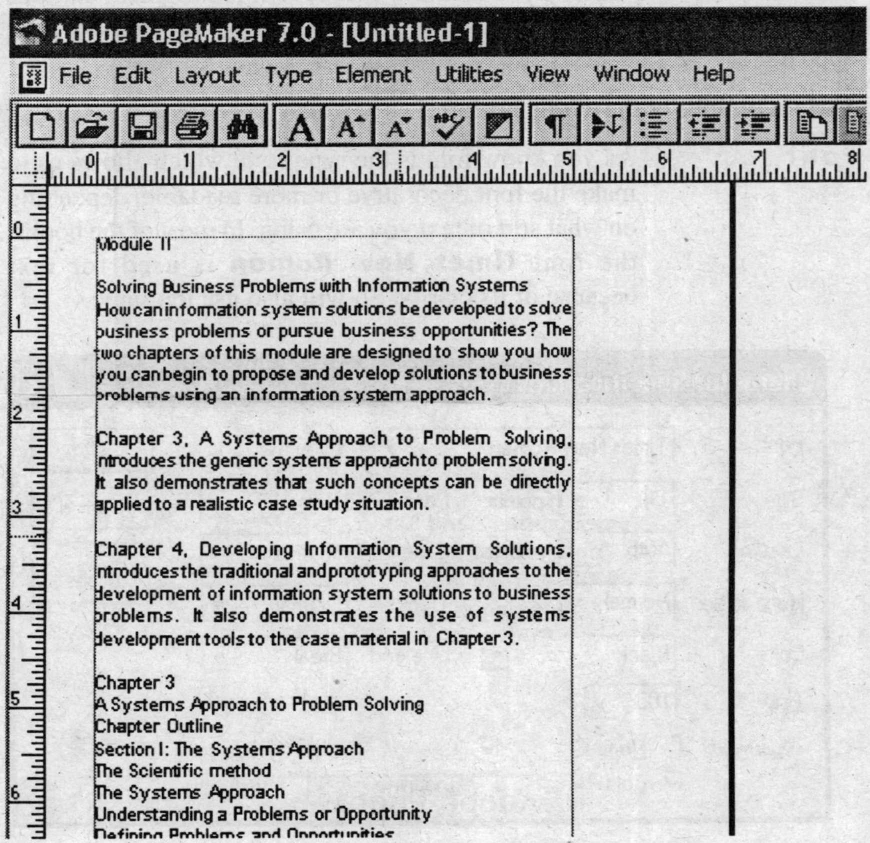

Formatting of the Text

For formatting of the text, do remember that most of the text would be similar, only few headings, sub-headings would be different, otherwise all the remaining text would be having the same specifications. So keeping this in mind what we do is that we apply the same style to all the text and then pick each heading/sub-heading manually and change them accordingly.

For formatting of the complete text, we need to select the whole text. For this we have the command called **Select All**. So place our cursor at any place within the text and call this command from Edit menu. Immediately the whole text will be highlighted from page 1 to 3. First of all we will change the font, etc., of the text. For this we have the **Character** command which is under Type menu. With the text highlighted, call this command from the type menu, a dialog box, as shown on the next page appears.

Various options of the dialog box are:

Font As you know font is the type style which allows us to make the font decorative or more readable, depending on what sort of text you are using. In most of the books, the font **Times New Roman** is used for text because of its clarity. So will also use the same.

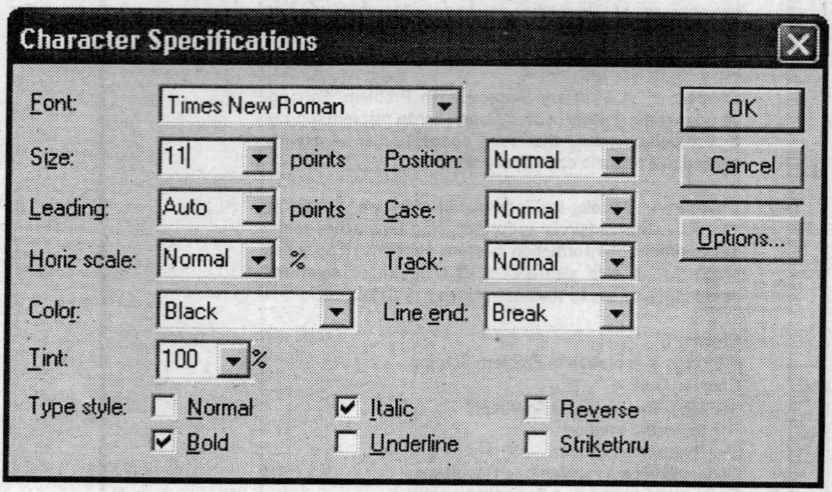

Size This signifies the weight of the character. To most of the readers, sizes 10 to 12 are quite readable. Newspapers are mostly printed in 10 points. For our book we will have 11 points.

Leading It is the space between the two lines, you can squeeze it to include more number of lines on a page if you want to. But, for our book, we will stick to Auto, meaning a space of about 2 point between the lines.

Horizontal scale This is used when you have to either squeeze the text to a line or expand it to fill the space. Neither of the condition applies to our text. So we will stick to Normal.

Colour You can choose to let you text look in a colour different from black, but, as far as our book goes, black is beautiful.

Tint If you are not choosing colour then the question of choosing tint does not arise.

Position Using this you can make your text ^{Superscript} or $_{\text{Subscript}}$. This is used for particular characters and not for the full text, as we are doing it here. So we will leave it Normal.

Case You can change the case of particular text, like making it ALL CAPS, SMALL CAPS, etc.

Track This is used for fine tuning of the text. You can make the text block loose, very loose, tight or very tight. But we will keep it to Normal only.

Line Break It is used for particular lines when you don't want the line to break. In our case we do not have to use any such options. So we will leave it Break.

Type Style Since at this stage we are using the character specifications of the whole text, we do not want to change any type style at this stage. So we will leave the whole thing as normal.

Now set the options in the dialog box, as discussed above. In this dialog box, you will notice another button called Options, click at it to get more options. These options are shown below. For our text we will not use any one of them but it is good to understand them.

Small caps size As we had seen above, there is an option of using small caps in the character settings. From here you can define how much height the small cap should have compared to full caps. Here the option is 70%, i.e., if the capital letter is of 10 mm, then the small cap will be of 7 mm.

Super/subscript size This option determines how much thick the character should become once it becomes either superscript or subscript.

Superscript position As you make the character Superscript, this option defines how much height it should go up from the normal position.

Subscript position As you make the character Subscript, this option defines how much it should go down from the normal position.

Baseline shift Here you can make the adjustment of setting the character up or down from the baseline. This command is useful when you have to align the text to the top instead of aligning it to the bottom, as is usually done.

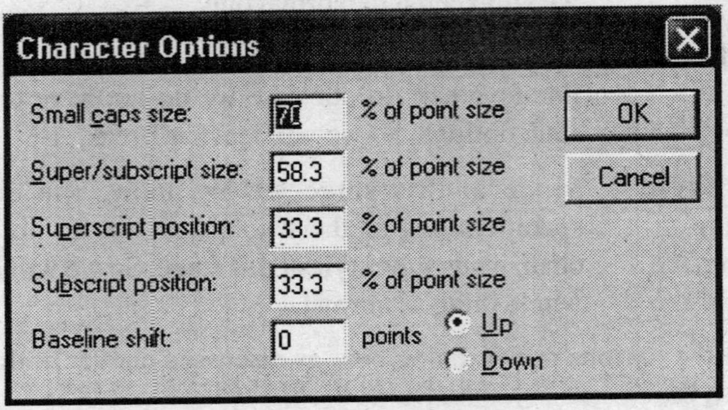

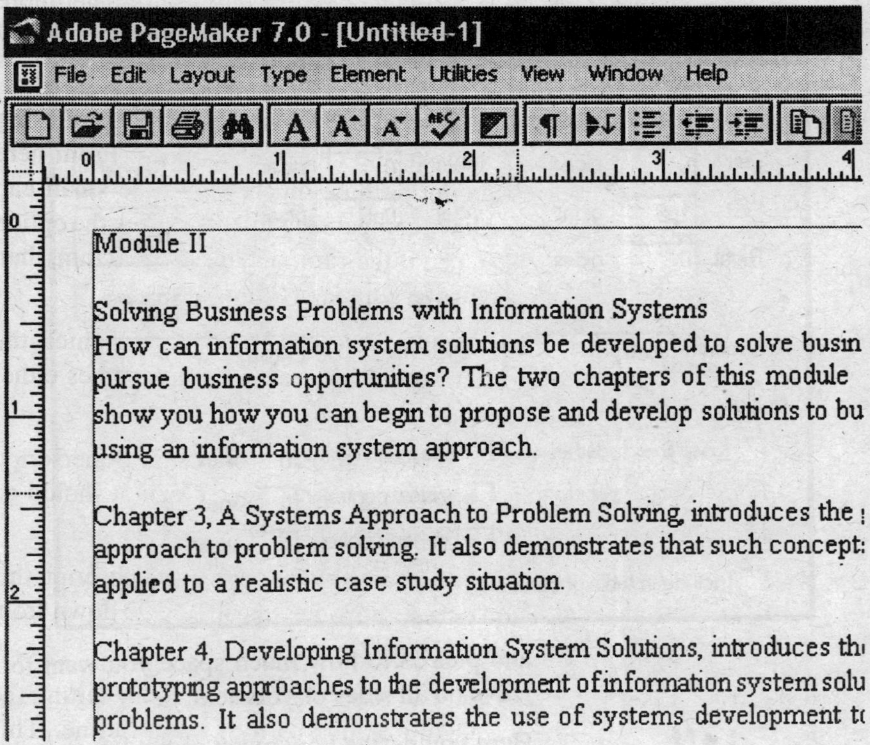

So once we have set the character specifications of the whole text, click Ok in the character dialog box to register all the changes made by you. The text will remain highlighted till you click at any place outside the text. Once done your text page would look like the one shown on the next page. Next we will do the paragraph settings.

PARAGRAPH SETTINGS

These settings are available in Paragraph dialog box which can be called by using the command **Paragraph** under the **Type** menu. As you can see from the dialog box, on next page, there are many options which can be used here. Let us see each of them. (You would notice here that the scale being used is Pica. 6 Picas make 1 inch and 1 Pica has 12 points)

Indents Here you will set the figures in terms of points

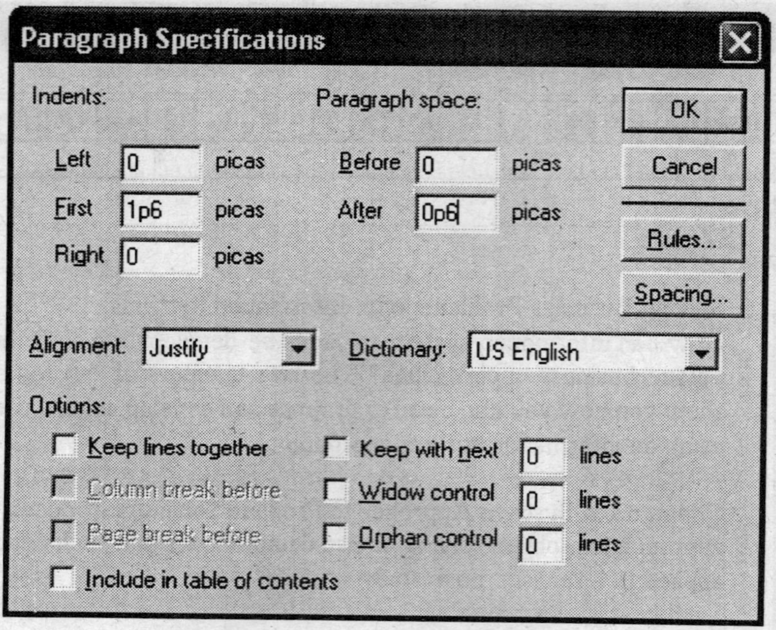

and pica as to how much space you want to leave on all sides of your text.

Left Here you define how much of the left indent you want to give to the paragraph. We do not want to give any indent here.

First The amount of space you mark here will reflect in each para being given that much of space to the first line of the para. Let us give a space of one and a half pica to it.

Right We do not want the text to shift from right alignment. So leave it at 0.

Before By putting some figure here, you will leave that much space above each paragraph. Since we do not want to give any space here, we will leave it at 0.

After We definitely want some space after each

paragraph. So we will leave 6 point space here which means that we are leaving half a pica space after each paragraph.

Alignment

The whole text is required to aligned from both sides, so we would choose the option of Justify.

Dictionary

You can choose here one of the dictionaries loaded into the system. Here we choose the US English.

Keep lines together

Once clicked it ensures that the paragraph is not split over different columns, from page to page or over graphics that have text wrap attributes defined. This option is also useful for keeping a table together when all lines of the table are in one paragraph. If a paragraph is longer than one column, PageMaker ignores this rule and breaks the paragraph at the column end.

Column break before

This option when clicked ensures that the paragraph begins with a new column.

Page break before

This option when checked ensures that the paragraph begins on a new page. This is useful if you want certain heading to always start from a new page.

Keep with next 0 lines

This when clicked ensures that the last line of the paragraph is placed with a certain number of lines of the next paragraph and specify the number of lines (1, 2, 3). This option is used to keep headlines connected to their accompanying text.

Widow control 0 lines

This command specifies how many lines (up to 3) constitute a widow, when that number of lines fall at the bottom or page range, PageMaker moves the line or lines to the next column or page to eliminate the widow.

Orphan control 0 lines This command specifies how many lines (up to 3) constitute an orphan. When that number of lines fall at the column or page, PageMaker adds one more line to the column or page to eliminate the orphan.

Include in table of contents Once this is clicked it suggests that the paragraph or heading is to be included in the Table of Contents which will be generated later.

We will use the settings shown on the page 61 (Remember to highlight the text before applying it) and click Ok. The next page figure shows the effect of these paragraph settings. But, this is not all to the paragraph settings. There is more to it. For that call the paragraph dialog box again and click at **Rules** to get a new dialog box. This is used for drawing a line over or below the text. Since we are not using these options here, we have not applied them, but, it is a good idea to understand them. Very soon we would be using them, when we come to the headings of the text.

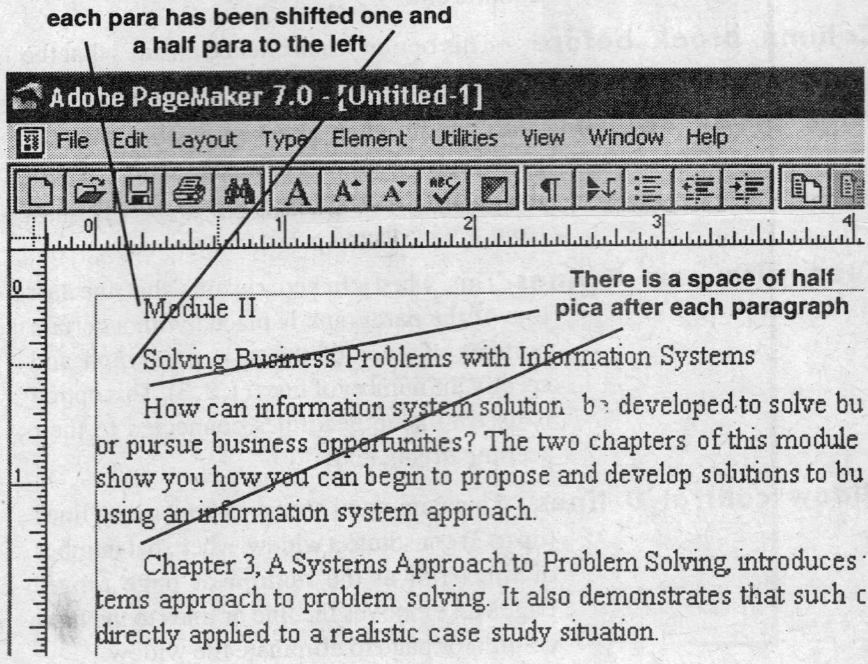

PARAGRAPH RULES

Various options here are:

First of all you have to decide which of the two options you have to choose, rule over paragraph or below the paragraph. The options is both are similar.

Stroke style You can select any of the stroke which is available here for putting above or below the text. Sorry, you cannot choose anyone beyond of the scope of the ones given here.

Stroke color Select one of the colour which you want to associate with the above stroke.

Tint Once you choose colour then you can choose the tint too.

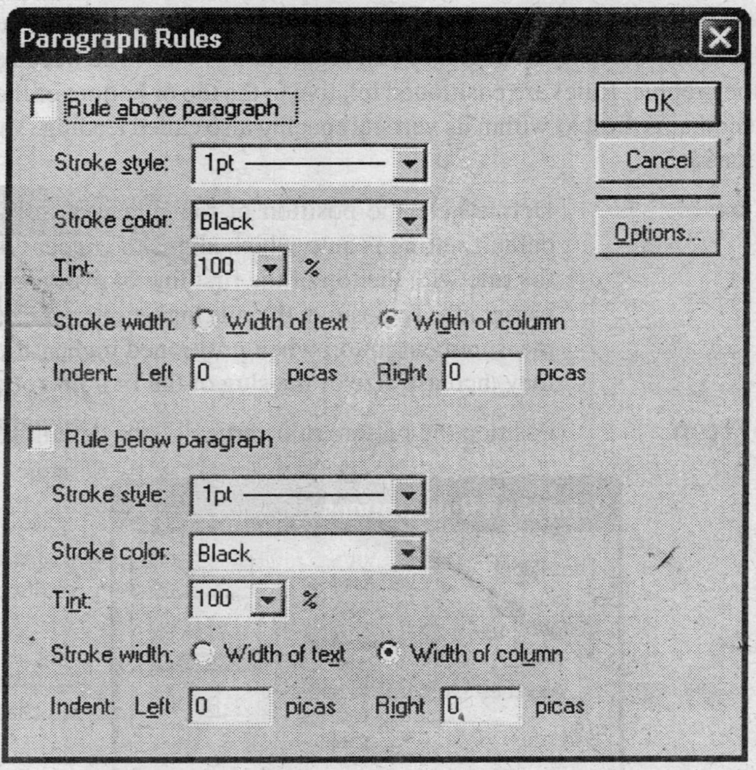

Stroke width Select here whether you want the stroke to go through the whole column or just stick to the limit where the text goes.

Indent As in paragraph, you can select how much of the space you want to leave from left or right for drawing this line. This space can again be given in picas (or you can change the preferences).

Within this rules dialog box, there is another dialog box, which allows to set the spacing above and below the lines.

Rulers Options

This displays the options of Rules and their placements. The dialog box is shown on the next page. This is used to specify the vertical placement of paragraph rules and to establish a leading grid that ensures the alignments of baselines across the column of text regardless of odd sized heading and inline graphic. Rules are positioned relative to the top or bottom of the area that contains the text within its vertical spacing also called leading. Various options are:

Top Define here the position of top rule vertically. The default setting is auto which aligns the upper edge of the rule with the top of the first line of every selected paragraph. To position the rule higher or lower, enter a measurement in top when positioned higher, the rule may increase size of the slug of the first line of text.

Bottom Position the bottom rule vertically, the default setting

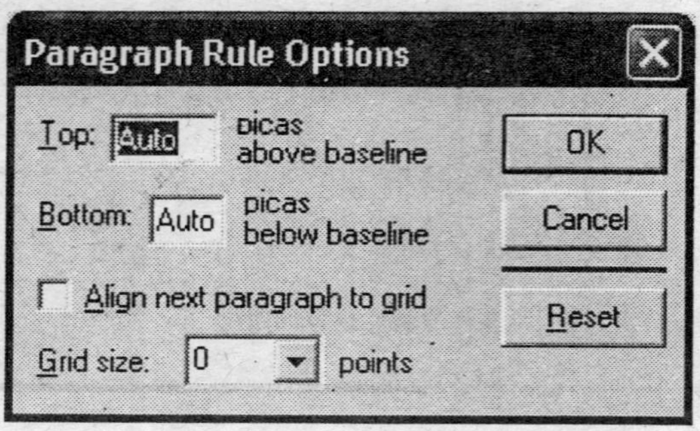

is auto which aligns the bottom edge of the line along with the bottom of the slug of the last line of every selected paragraph. When the option is set to auto the rule does not change the size of the slug of the last line of text. To position the rule higher or lower enter a measurement in bottom when positioned lower, the rule will increase the size of the slug of the last line of the text.

Align next paragraph to grid If you are creating a publication that has multiple text column you may want the baselines of the body text to align horizontally. Some attributes of heading and subheading paragraph can disrupt this alignment for the body text that follows.

Grid Size To restore the baseline alignment of body text, grid size is set. This makes the PageMaker add extra space after the paragraph if necessary to ensure that the following paragraph is positioned on this grid.

Now we come back to another option of the paragraph menu called **Spacing**. It is very important if you have to fine tune the text spacing.

SPACING

This allows you to control the spacing attributes in word and letter space, sets the pair kerning, leading method and autoleading percentage.

Word space The space between words, created by pressing the spacebar, is called the space band and is part of the font design. The default desired word spacing is 100% of the space band of the associated font, you can change the desired spacing to any percentage between 0% and 500%. When setting justifies text, you can create a range within which PageMaker spaces word by setting values for minimum and maximum. The range limits for minimum and maximum are 0% and 500% of the space band.

Letter space Each letter has a natural width that includes the space around the letter. In PageMaker a letter is measured from the left edge of one letter to the edge of the next letter. This distance is called the pen advances. The default desired letter spacing is 0% that is letter with no extra spacing added to or subtracted from it. You can change the space between letters by changing the desired letter spacing. Add or subtract any percentage up to 100% of the space band.

Pair kerning When auto is checked, PageMaker kerns, adjusts the space between a pair of characters by the amount specification in the current font. By default PageMaker kerns pairs larger than 12 points, although the effect of automatic pair kerning is less visible at small sizes. If you unchecked auto, PageMaker does not kern pairs at all.

Leading method You can select a leading method to control the vertical spacing of text within the slug (the vertical space in which a line of text is positioned). The various options are:

Baseline Select this to align the baseline of the text with the bottom of the slug.

Proportional Select this to position the baseline of the text two third of the way down from the top of the slug.

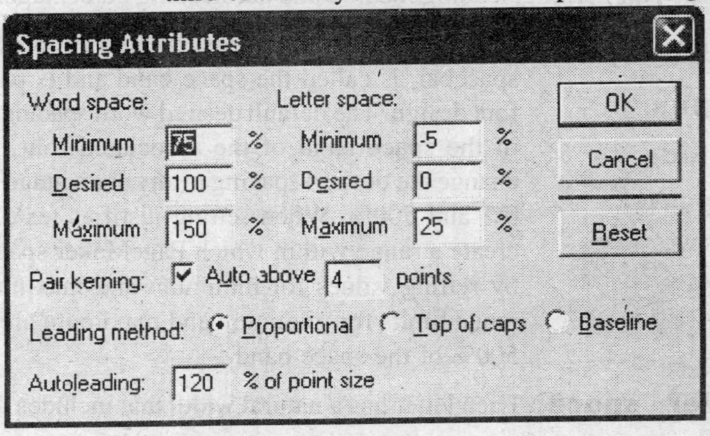

Top of caps Select this to position the baseline of the text at a distance from the top of the slug, equal to the height of the tallest ascender in the font.

Autoleading Here you can define the autoleading in terms of the percentage of the font size. PageMaker default is 120% which means that for a text of 10 points with leading Auto will have the space between two lines of 2 points.

This finishes our quest for information about the paragraph dialog box. Now that we have set the character and paragraph settings, we proceed ahead and set the various other items of the text. First of all is the chapter number.

Setting Chapter Number

As we know that whatever matter has to be changed it has to be highlighted first. So highlight "Chapter 10" in the text. So now we will do the following settings for this. I am not explaining here how you will do that. It will be a good exercise for you to do it yourself and check it later.

Font Arial

Size 24

Type Style Bold

Case Small Caps

First Indent 0

Space after 1 pica

Alignment Centre

Include in Table of Contents

With all these settings your heading should look like the one shown below. This was not very difficult, was it? In fact, all this when you practice will be very easy to follow and you would be able to do it without even referring to this book, expect for the keyboard shortcuts.

Now let concentrate on the chapter name or the title of the chapter "File System Interface". For this you do the following settings.

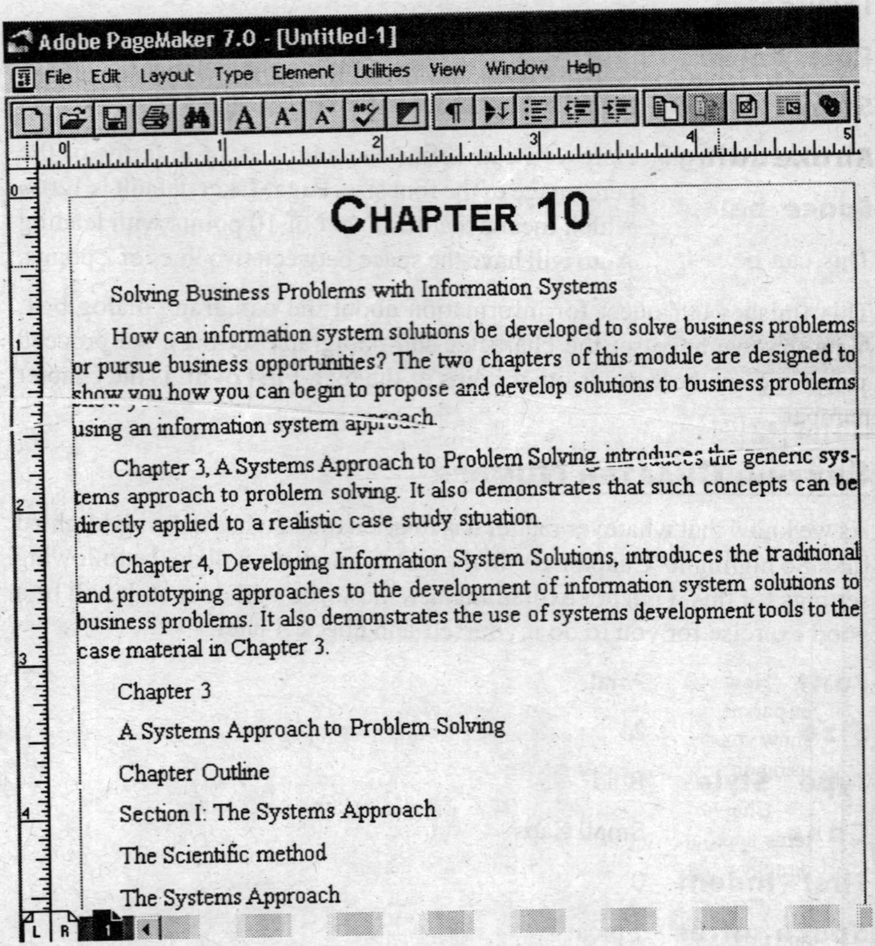

Font	Arial
Size	16
Type Style	Bold
Case	All Caps
First Indent	0
Space after	1 pica
Alignment	Centre

Include in Table of Contents

Rule below paragraph Yes

Stroke style 2 point

Stroke width width of text

Space below the Stroke 8 points

This can be seen in the figure below. Next in line is the heading called

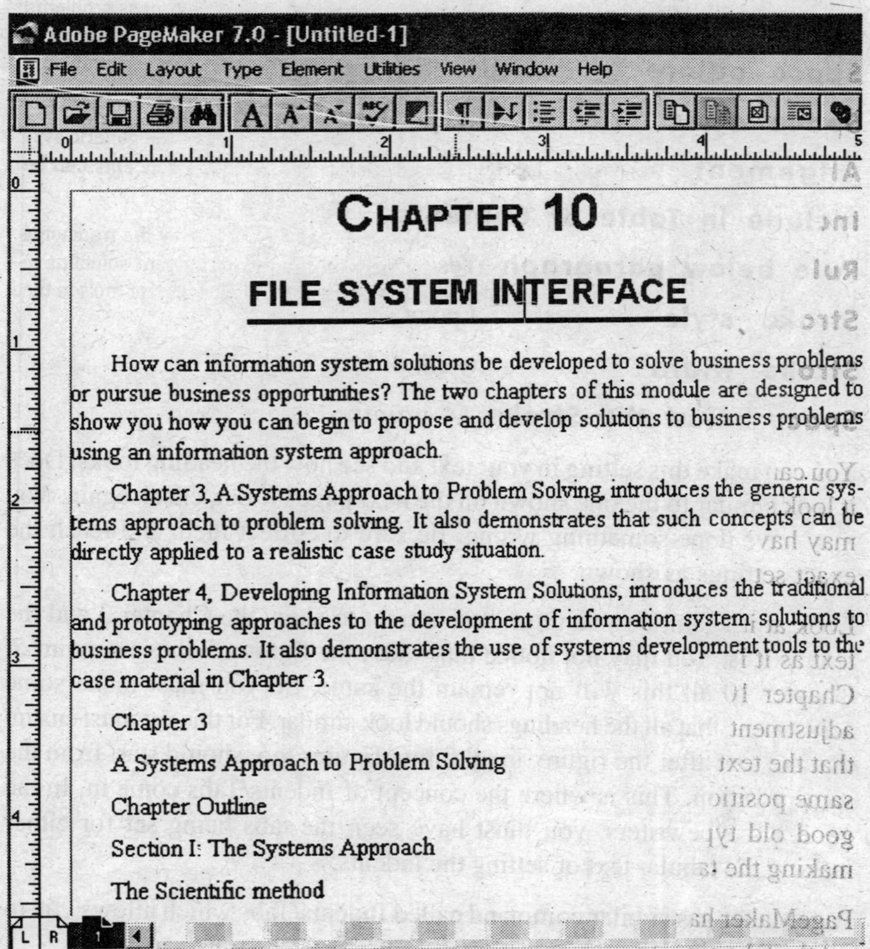

"Chapter 3 A Systems Approach to Problem Solving". For this we will be doing the following settings.

Font	Arial
Size	14
Type Style	Bold
Case	Normal
First Indent	0
Space before	4 points
Space after	8 points
Alignment	Left
Include in Table of Contents	
Rule below paragraph	Yes
Stroke style	1 point
Stroke width	width of text
Space below the Stroke	4 points

You can make this setting in your text and see how the heading looks. Does it look similar to the one shown on the next page? If not, check again. You may have done something wrong. Be sure to correct them and reach the exact settings as shown.

Look at it again, do you think it is correct to show the Chapter 3 and the text as it is. You may not notice that when the figure reaches the point of Chapter 10 all this will not remain the same. So you must make some adjustment that all the headings should look similar. For this we must ensure that the text after the figure, in all future figures too, should start from the same position. This is where the concept of Indents/Tabs come in. In the good old typewriters, you must have seen the tabs being set for either making the tabular text or setting the indents.

PageMaker has similar command called Indents/Tabs which allows you to set the tabs similarly.

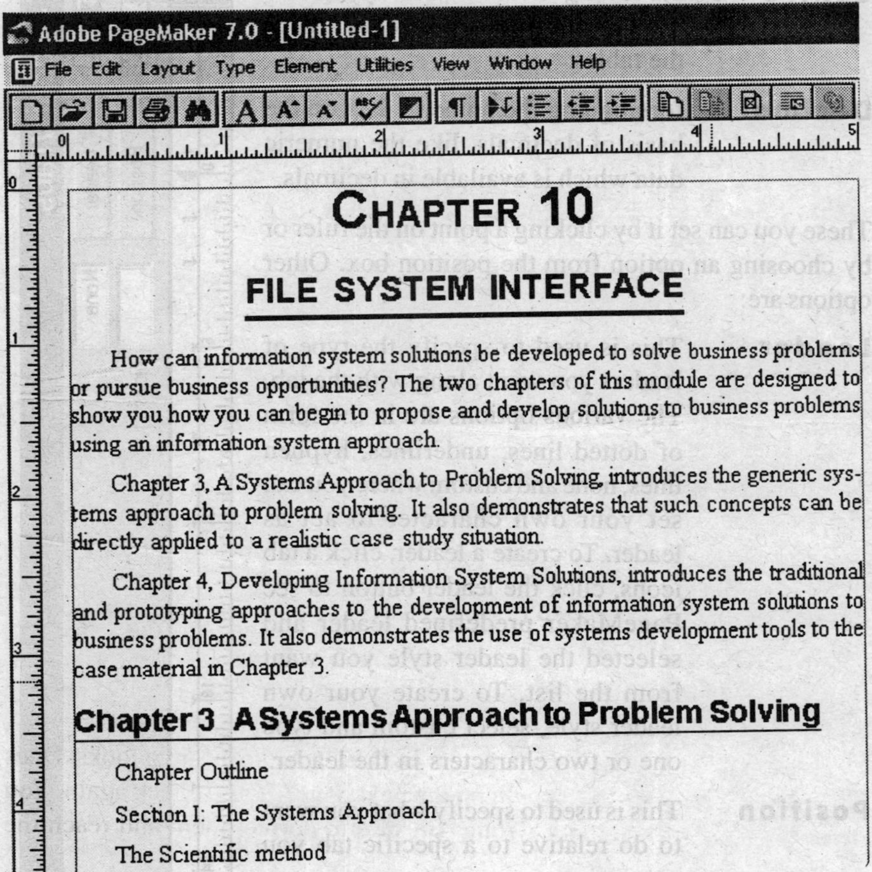

INDENTS/TABS

These are used mainly in case of tables or where you have to set the text in a tabular form. This command is also used to set the tabs at places where once pressing the text may move to that point.

You can click an icon to specify what kind of tab you want to set. The various types of tabs available are:

Left for setting the text data, like the usual text.

Right for setting the numeric data, like the amount in Rupees which you must have seen that it is allied to the right.

Centre for setting the data which you want to centralize, mainly the headings of the tables.

Decimal for aligning the numeric data on the basis of decimals, like the numeric data which is available in decimals.

These you can set it by clicking a point on the ruler or by choosing an option from the position box. Other options are:

Leader This is used to specify the type of leaders you want along with the tab. The various options are in the form of dotted lines, underlines, hyphen lines, none and custom where you can set your own character to act as leader. To create a leader, click a tab icons, click the leader button to see PageMaker predefined leader and selected the leader style you want from the list. To create your own leader style, select custom and type one or two characters in the leader.

Position This is used to specify what you want to do relative to a specific tab you can:

Add tab It adds a tab at a position specified in the edit box.

Delete tab It deletes the tab from a position specified in the edit box.

Move tab It moves a selected tab from its current position to the position you type in the edit box.

Repeat tab It repeats a tab automatically

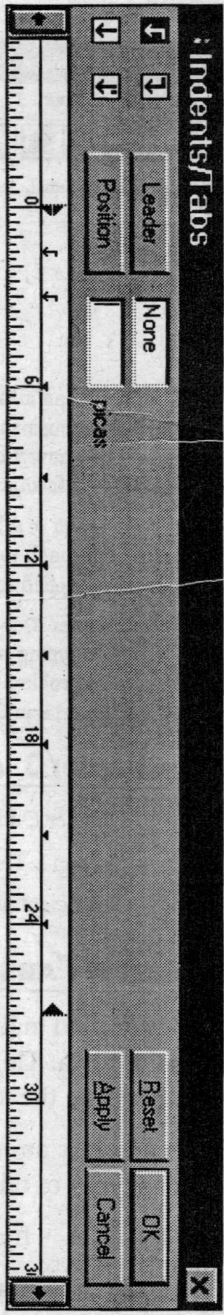

setting a series of tabs at the distances between the selected tab and the proceeding tab or the tab ruler zero point.

Reset Once clicked it resets all the tabs and returns to the default condition.

Apply Before finally saying Ok, you can check whether your tabs have been set properly by clicking at this. This will leave the **Indents/Tabs** dialog box On and you can see underneath it that the tabs have been set properly. If satisfied, press Ok.

There are two very important type of indents which I must define here. They are Hanging indent and First indent.

Hanging indent This text has been created using hanging indent. In this you select the first line to start from zero and the subsequent lines to start from the indented point. To do

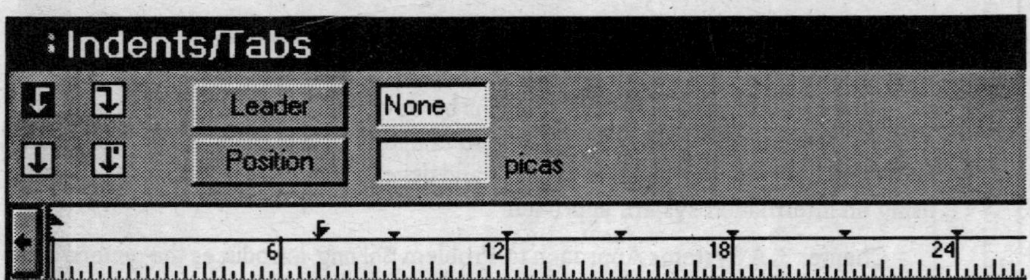

this first take the icon to the position where you want all the subsequent lines to begin, in this case 7 pica. Now pick up the upper portion of the icon and drag it to zero position. The upper portion of icon defined the first line. Put a left tab at 7 pica too, for the setting of the first line tab. This is called Hanging indent.

First indent You must have seen that in some cases the first line of each para starts from a particular distance, this is called first indented para. To set this take the icon to the zero point. Pick up the top half of the icon and drag it to the point where you want to set the first line indent.

Coming back to our problem, we will set the indents in our heading using these options. Incidentally, Indents/Tabs dialog box can be generated by

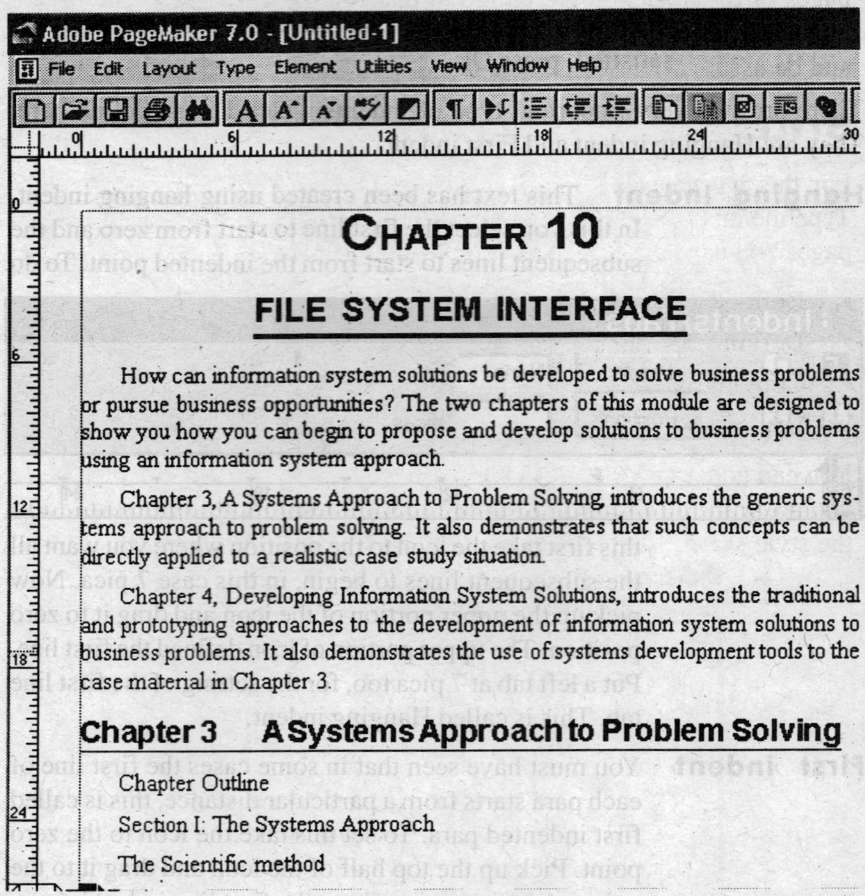

clicking at Indents/Tabs under the Type menu. Since the Chapter 3 to say 3 or more will not take more than one and a half pica, we will for the safe side put the left indent at seven pica on the heading.

Set this indent on the heading "Chapter 3 A Systems Approach to Problem Solving". Now press tab between 3 and the text "A System......". Notice the change. But first see the tab set at three pica in the Indent/Tab dialog box.

But all we going to do this for each and every headings. You think it is possible to remember all these settings of the headings for full 200 to 300 pages of the text. You are bound to make some mistake somewhere. To avoid this kind of thing, we have what are called as Styles. You set styles and be assured that all the chapters have the same kind of styles.

STYLES

For this we have the command called **Define Styles**, available under Type menu. Once called it gives rise to a dialog box as shown on the next page. You can add new style sheet to a publication by:

- Define style from scratch using the formatting of a selected paragraph.
- Defining a new style on one of the active publications existing styles.
- Copying an existing style sheet from another publication.
- Importing word processed document with style sheet attached.

You can add a new style to your publication style sheet at any time while you are working on your publication. Once you have added a new style to the style sheet, that style appears on the style palette.

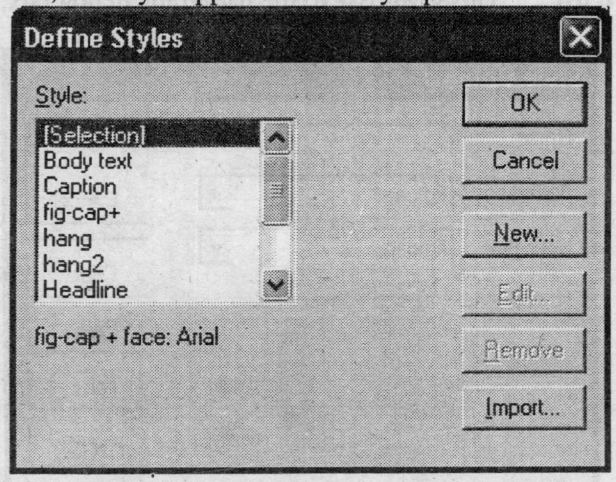

Style sheet dialog box has the following commands:

Style PageMaker initially supplies a list of styles which can be used. You can select any one of the same by clicking it and changing its parameters.

New/Edit Choose one of these depending upon whether you want to edit the existing one or create a new one. A quick way to create a new style is to base it on an existing one. This style will have to be selected before you click new.

Remove Select the style which you want to remove and press remove, this particular style is deleted.

Import You can copy all the styles of a particular publication from another PageMaker publication or template.

Once you select one of the them, New or Edit. It gives rise to a new dialog box, as shown here. In the case of new, you have to give a name here. It also shows you the settings already made, to give you a brief idea of what is stored under this style. On the right hand panel, you have the 4 settings:

Character Clicking at it gives rise to the character dialog box, which we had discussed earlier. You can set the various options here like, Font, Size, Leading, etc.

Paragraph This gives rise to the paragraph dialog box, where you

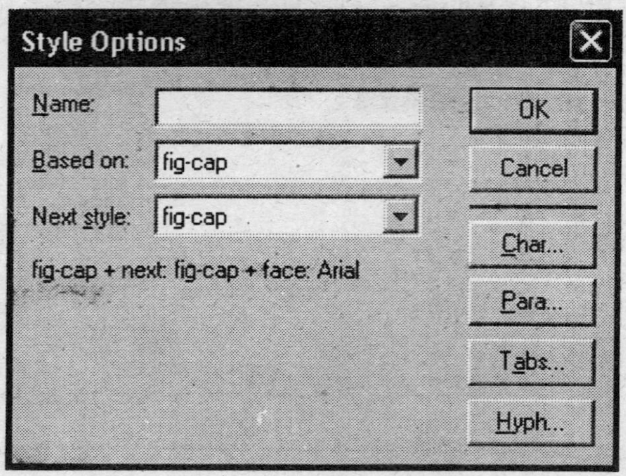

can set the paragraph settings like indents, para spacing, alignment, etc.

Tabs You can set the Indents/Tabs from here.

Hyphenation Now this is what has not been discussed before. Let us discuss this first.

HYPHENATION

The hyphenation command permits two separate operations. Its main purpose is to determine how words should be hyphenated in a selected paragraph or paragraphs of a particular style. You can also use it to add words and hyphenation instruction to your user dictionary.

When you click at the hyphenation the dialog box appears which has the following options.

Hyphenation Select to have the hyphenation ON or OFF. If off, select one of the following option.

Manual only Select this option if you want a discretion hyphenation. A discretional hyphen is that which you insert manually where you want a word to break, if it falls within the hyphenation zone. To insert discretional hyphenation in story editor or layout view, press **Ctrl + Shift + hyphen** window where you want the word to be hyphenation.

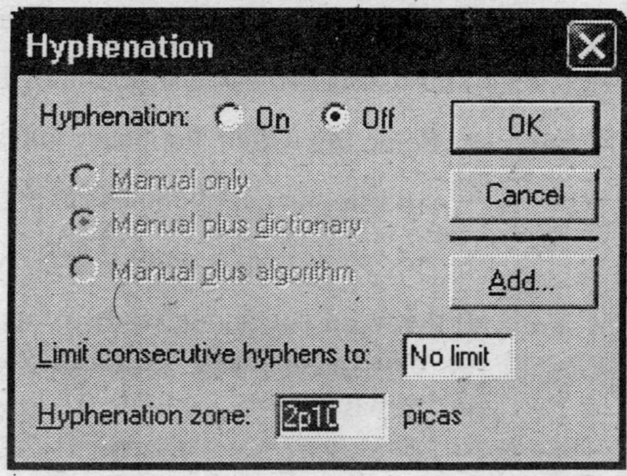

Manual plus dictionary Select this option to hyphenate words containing discretionary hyphens as well as words in the online dictionary, raking of possible hyphenation breaks. In case we have both the discretional hyphen and dictionary one, the discretionary hyphen prevails over.

Manual plus algorithm This provides for greater flexibility for hyphenation. Words may be hyphenated by discretionary hyphens, dictionary or by the hyphenation algorithm. This algorithm permits hyphenation break in words not found in the Page Maker dictionary or the user dictionary.

Limit consecutive hyphens to You can define the limit of hyphenated words that occur in consecutive lines in a paragraph by using this command. You can enter number from 1 to 255 or type nolimits.

Hyphenation zone Determines the amount of space in which hyphenation can occur at the end of each line for unjustified text. Page Maker applies the desired word spacing and built-in letter spacing. If the last word in the line does not fill and that word starts to the left of the hyphenation zone, PageMaker tries to hyphenate that word. In general, the larger the hyphenation zone, the more ragged the right margin of text will be. The smaller the zone, the more hyphenation will occur. This option has no effect on justified text.

Add This displays the add word dialog box for:

- Selecting which dictionary you want to modify.
- Add or change hyphenation breaks for a word.
- Add word to or remove words from the dictionary.

If the word you add, already exists in the dictionary, the new hyphenation breaks and capabilities replace the previous ones.

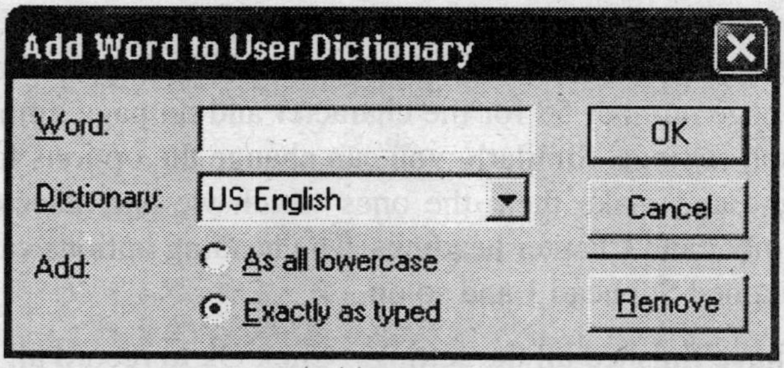

This finishes our introduction to the Hyphenation command. Now we know how to use it. If you want that no word should break in your text, choose the option of OFF.

Now we know about the all the options of the Styles dialog box. Click each

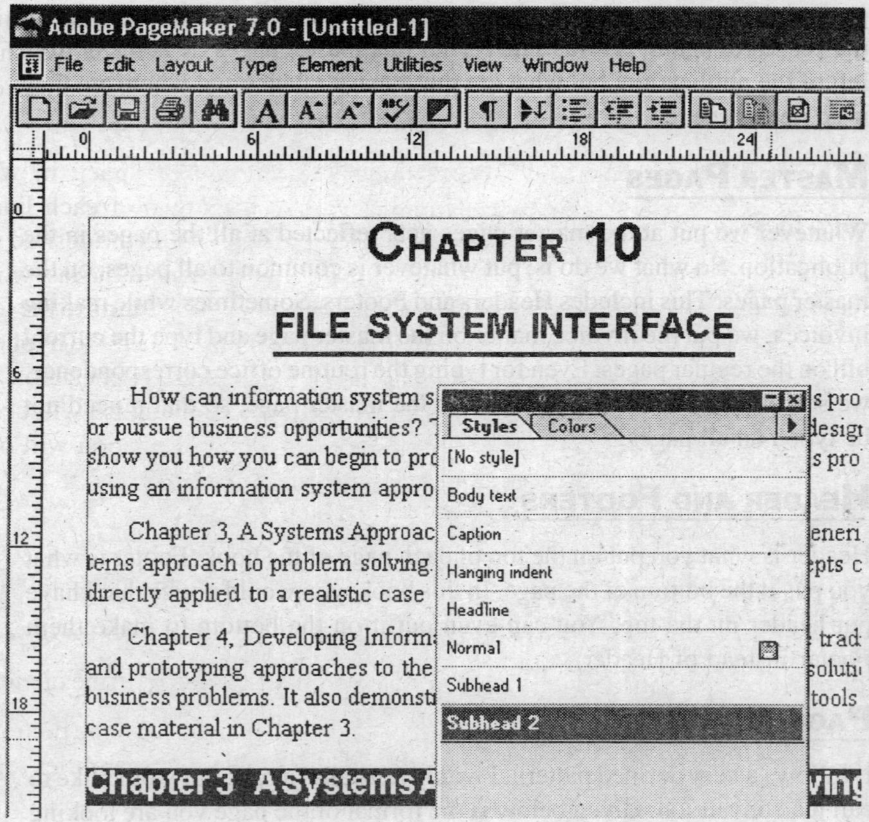

one of them, one by one and fill up their respective data. For example, for the Body text, you fill the details, which you had filled up for the complete text, as on page number 58 for the character and on page number 61 for the paragraph settings. Similarly you can change the options for Caption and Headline and make them the ones which we had selected for the Chapter number and Chapter headings. The heading options can be set in the option named Subhead 1 and so on.

When you have finished all the settings. Click Ok to record all the styles. Now all you have to do is to apply them. Call the styles sheet on the screen from the Window menu. By picking up paragraph one by one, you can apply the styles as shown here.

You must have noticed that we have not given any folio number to our pages in the publication. For this we have to understand the concept of master pages again. As was said earlier that master pages lie at the bottom left of the publication, but what are these master pages and where are they used, let us see

Master Pages

Whatever we put at the master pages gets reflected at all the pages in the publication. So what we do is, put whatever is common to all pages, on the master pages. This includes Headers and Footers. Sometimes while making invoices, we put the invoice matter on the master page and type the current bill on the regular pages. Even for typing the routine office correspondence, we sometimes make the letterhead on the master page, so that it need not be typed on all pages.

Header and Footers

Header is what you put on the top of each page of the book. Footer is what you put at the bottom of the page. In this book, you would notice that I have put header on the top. You can even put it on the bottom to make them Footer instead of Header.

Page Numbering

It follows a very defined pattern. I would not call it a rule, but would like to call it a convention. Given below is the format of the page you are looking

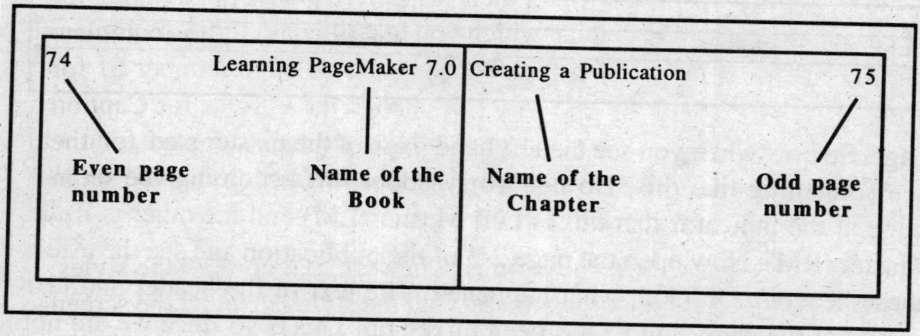

at. Now you know what comes where, but how to create it, is the problem. For this click at the master page location, to see the master pages on the screen. You will see a blank page format side-by-side as seen above. With the help of the mouse click at any place in the page format and type the name of the chapter. Click this with the pointer tool and drag its corner to the left top of the right hand page format.

Click it with the text tool and format it according to the requirements. For a book whose text is of the size of 11 points, the folio text can be of 9-10 points. So you can choose it to be in 10 points. Again using the pointer tool click at the text to form a block of text. Drag the right corners of the text block to make it half of the page size, as shown above.

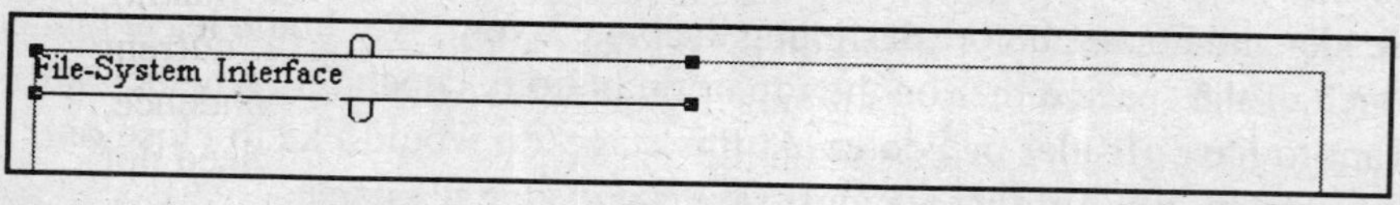

Again click at any place inside the page block to get cursor for typing. Type **Ctl+Alt+P**, to get a symbol **PB** on the page. This is the indicator of the page number on the master page. Make it 10 points Times New Roman as above but make it right aligned by **Ctrl+Shift+R**. Now drag it to the right corner of the right hand side of the master page, as shown below, after making the block as half.

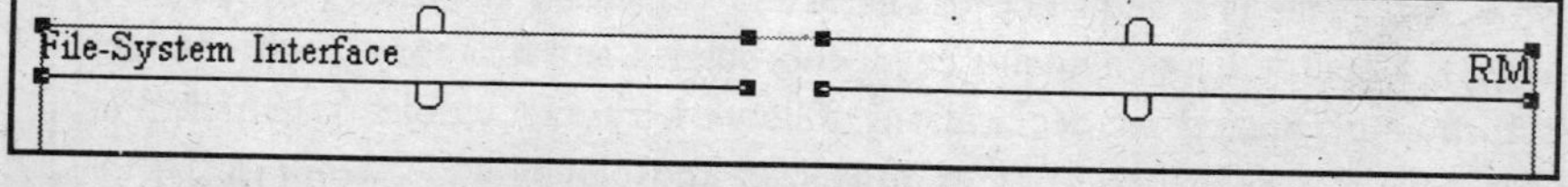

Similarly for the left hand page, type Ctl+Alt+P for the page number on the left hand corner and the book name for the right hand side of the left hand

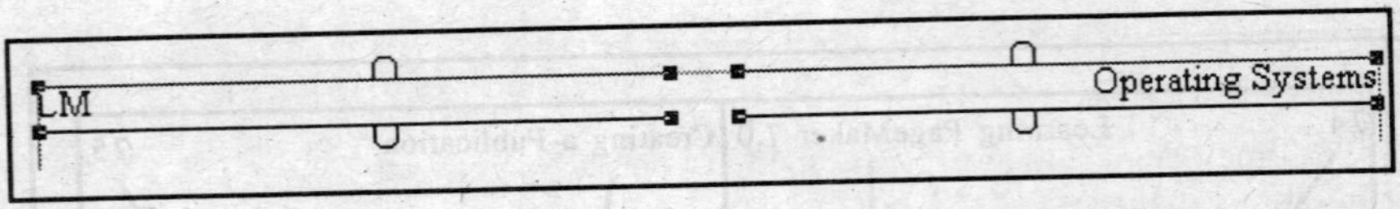

page. So now when you see the left hand page of the master page, you will see something like this. Do not worry about **RM** becoming **LM** on this page, it the indicator that this is Left Master (LM) and the other is Right Master (RM). Now open the page 2-3 of the publication and see the effect these headers. Oh God, what happened. The text of the header and text matter of the page 2 and 3 has been mixed up. This is so since we did not make provision for having the header on the top of the page. So we have to leave about one and a half pica space on the top of the each page to accommodate the headers. So lets see how it is done.

On the master page put a guide at one and a half pica from the top. This is our indication that the text would start from this line downwards. Now what you will have to do is that you will have to drag the text on page number 2 and 3 downwards by one and a half pica to make the header look like the one shown here. Due to constraints in page size, both pages are shown one by one. It is not possible here to show both the pages together on this and next page.

So now what do we gather. We should always make provisions for the Header and Footer, before designing the page layout. We should leave that much of the space either on the top or on bottom, depending whether we want to have Header or Footer. At this stage we would like to close our publication. But, for that we must save it and give it a name.

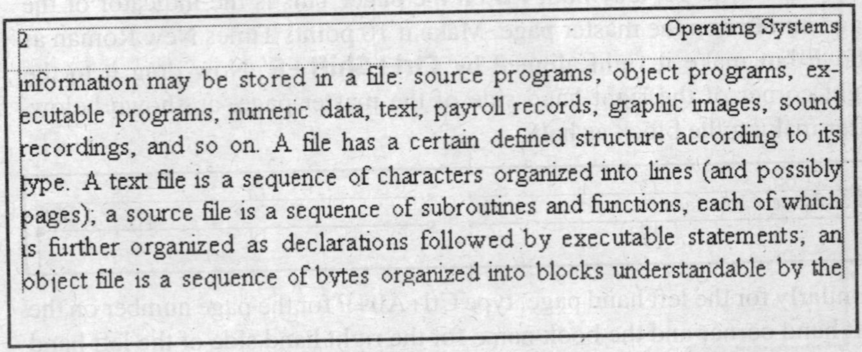
2 Operating Systems

information may be stored in a file: source programs, object programs, executable programs, numeric data, text, payroll records, graphic images, sound recordings, and so on. A file has a certain defined structure according to its type. A text file is a sequence of characters organized into lines (and possibly pages); a source file is a sequence of subroutines and functions, each of which is further organized as declarations followed by executable statements; an object file is a sequence of bytes organized into blocks understandable by the

> File-System Interface 3
>
> Time, date, and user identification. This information may be kept for (1) creation, (2) last modification, and (3) last use. These data can be useful for protection, security and usage monitoring.
>
> The information about all files is kept in the directory structure that also resides on secondary storage. It may take from 16 to over 1000 bytes to record tnis information for each file. In a system with many files, the size of the directorv itself mav be megabvtes. Because directories. like files. must be

SAVING

It is a natural command, since whatever you do on computer, you must save it to preserve for the future. So first time when you give the save command **Ctrl+S**, PageMaker will ask you to give a name to your file. It is totally optional, where you want to save the file in your directory.

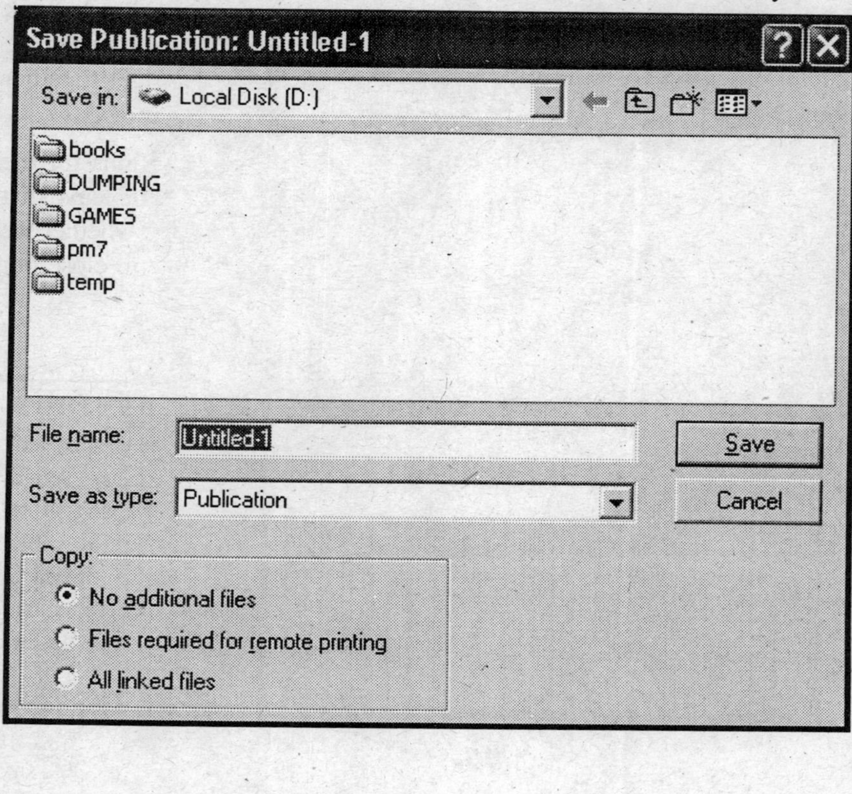

Select the name which you want to give to your publication, its location, etc., before giving the save command, to get the save dialog box, as shown here. Once saved the file would be stored in the hard disk and can be called whenever required.

CLOSING OF THE PUBLICATION

When you feel that you have finished your work with the file, close the publication using the **Close** command from the File menu.

So now that we have saved and closed the file, we take a step backward and see how much we have done on the file. But, there is more to be done. So take a break and in the next chapter, I will tell you more commands of PageMaker.

4

Editing Publication

Introduction

In the last chapter you had created a document. In this chapter we would learn more commands and edit it to make it more accurate and appealing. But, first thing first, let's open the file.

Open

PageMaker's **Open** is no different from various other open commands. It is available under **File** menu. Once clicked it gives rise to a dialog box, as shown here. You click at the file you want to open. This file will be opened

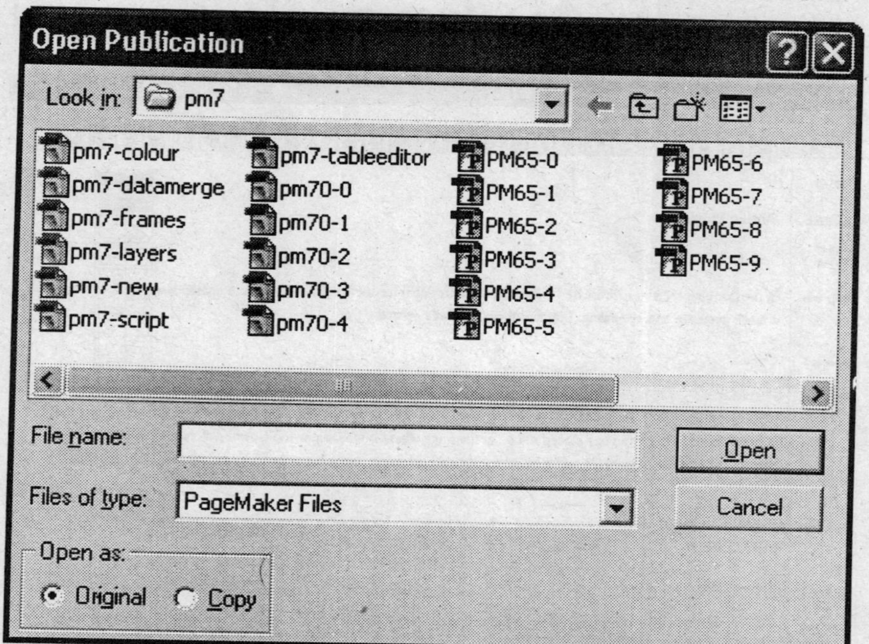

in the position, where you has closed it, i.e., at the page where it was when you closed it. Remember, you can even open a copy of the original file and then save it with a new name. Now let us perform our various other commands on this file.

PageMaker has its own word processing, which is built-in. This is called **Story Editor** in PageMaker. You can perform the various word processing operations using these commands.

STORY EDITOR

Click your text with text tool anywhere in the text and press **Ctrl + E** to get into the story editor mode. As you can see from the figure below, changing to story editor, the **Layout** menu has become the **Story** menu. It has commands which are applicable to story editor only. Not only this, the text is also displayed with the style name on the left hand side for easy reference.

Now we will perform the various word processing options on this text while still in the story editor mode. The first and foremost is the **Find** command.

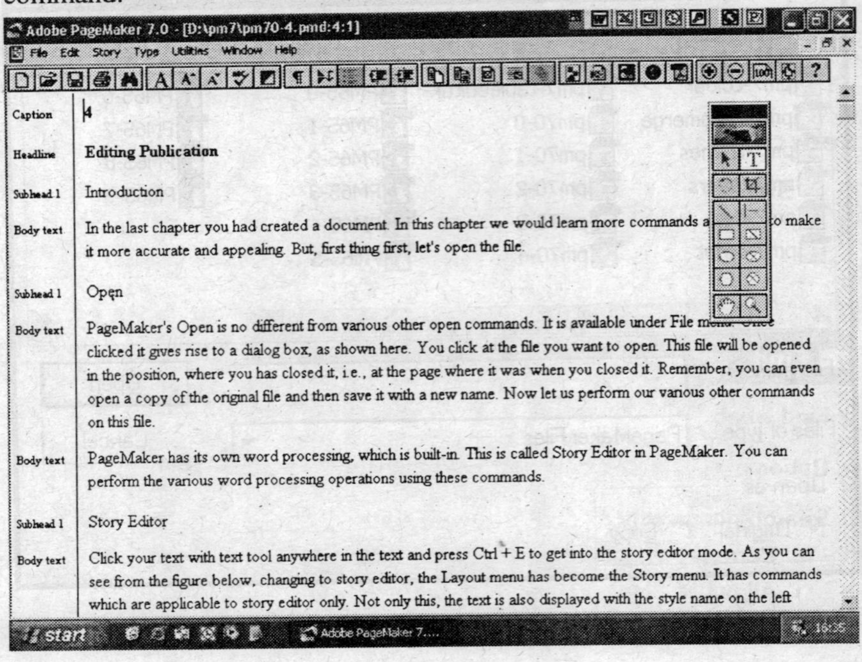

Find

This command is used to find a particular word in the text. This command can be called from the **Utilities** menu. Once the dialog box, as shown here, comes on the screen, you can type in the word which you want to search. Then by clicking at **Find**, you will be able to start the search.

Various options of the dialog box are:

Match case This command is used when you have the word which exactly matches the case of the word typed in the box.

Whole word Sometimes you are looking for a word maybe "Ta" as a single word. If you do not click this then all the words starting with "Ta" will also be selected.

Search document

- **Current publication** The search will be performed in the current open publication only.
- **All publications** The search will be performed in all the publications which are open.

Search story

- **Selected text** It is possible that you may have highlighted some text from which you want to find this particular word.

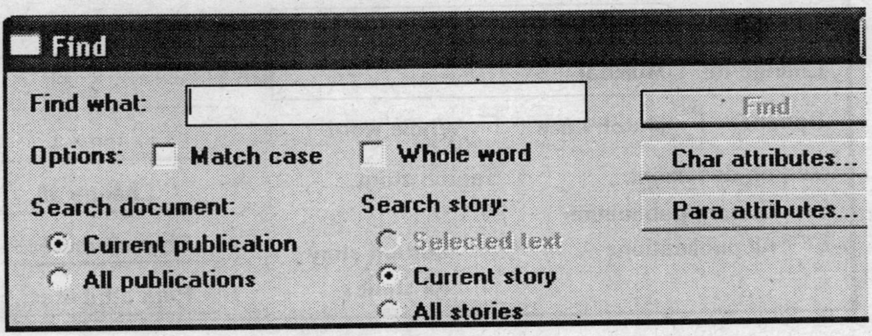

Current story Instead of highlighting some text, you can search for the word in the whole story.

All stories There may be more than one stories in the publication. This option will search in all the stories of the publication.

The second part of this command is **Change**, where you find something and change it with another.

CHANGE

This command is used when you have to replace one word with another. Supposing due to the change of name of the city called *Bombay* to *Mumbai*, it has become necessary to make the same change in your publication which has the word extensively used. Now, it is not possible to find out each occurrence of the word and change it manually. So, this command comes in handy. All the various options of the **Find** command and valid here too, like the options of match case, whole word, etc.

You have the option of changing all at one go by clicking **Change All**. Otherwise click at **Change** and it will change one by one. Le me discuss here the two other options which I had not discussed under Find. These are **Char attributes** and **Para attributes**.

Change Character Attributes

This dialog box helps you in changing character properties using the other

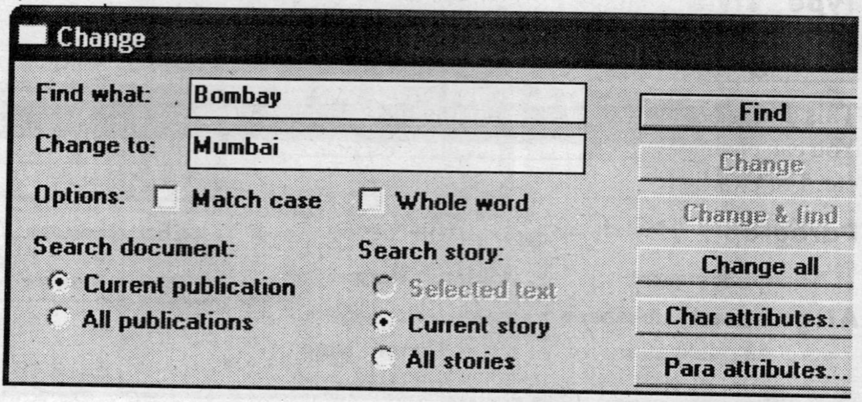

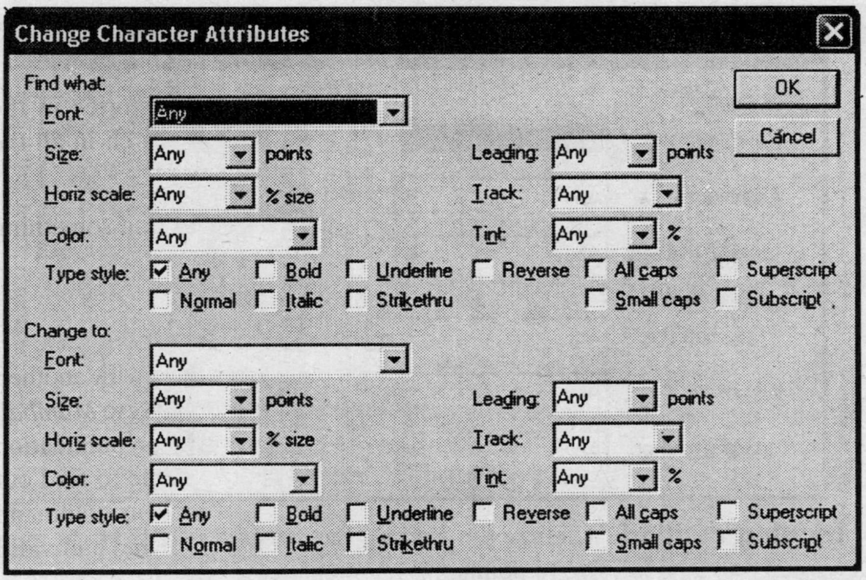

options as well. You can change with respect to fonts, sizes, types, etc. But remember for this both your fields of **Find what** and **Change to** in the opening **Find** dialog box should be blank. For example,

Font Change all **Arial** font to **Times New Roman** font. For this change **Find what Font** to **Arial** and **Change to Font** to **Times New Roman**.

Size Change all occurrence of 14 points size to 12 point size.

Type style Change all occurrence of **Bold** to **Normal**.

Change Paragraph Attributes

This dialog box helps you in changing the various options of the paragraph. You can change with respect to paragraph styles, alignment, leading method, etc. For example,

Paragraph style Change all the occurrence of maybe **Heading 1** to **Heading 2** as the case maybe.

Alignment Change the alignment of **Body Text** maybe from **Justify** to **Left** alignment in the selected text.

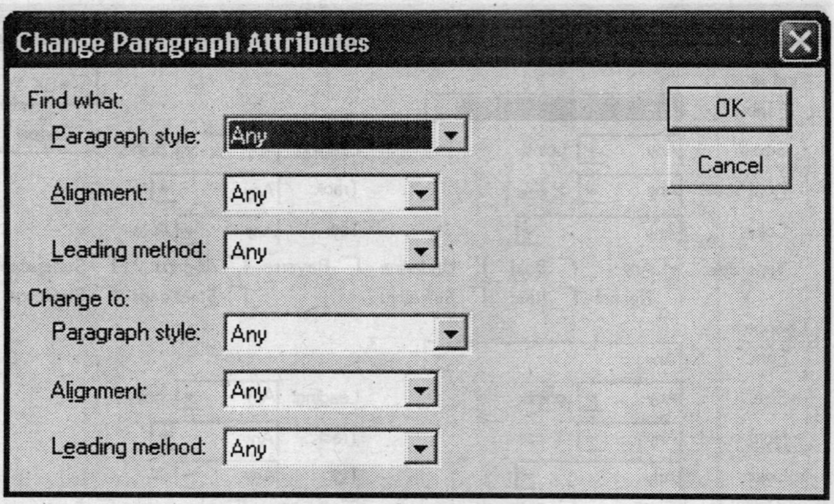

Leading method Change the leading the selected text from Auto to 15 points.

This way you can change the paragraph settings of your liking.

Now we come to the most important part of the story editing, i.e., spell checking.

SPELL CHECKING

PageMaker supports two main dictionaries. One of them is called **UK English** and the other one is called **US English**. While installing the software you have the option of installing either one of the two or maybe you can install both of them. But, preferably for a publication, you will use either one of them.

When you spell check your document, each word of your document is compared with the corresponding words in the dictionary. If not found in dictionary, it is pointed out as an error. Then the choice is yours whether to accept the word as it is or make the change according to the changes suggested by the software.

For checking the whole document, your cursor should be at the starting point of the text. However, if you want a particular part of the text to be spell checked, then select this text before entering the story editor and then

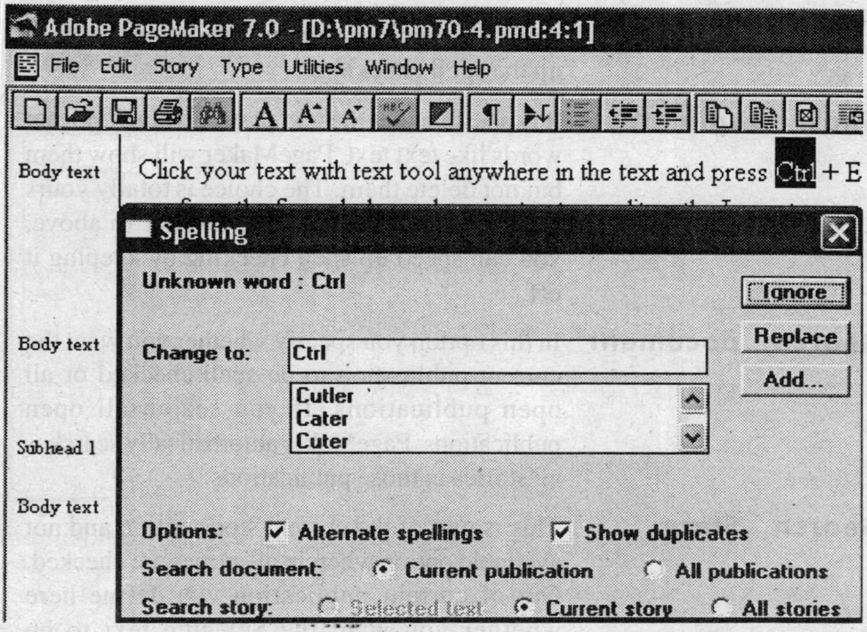

start the spell checking. The **Spelling** command is available under the Utilities menu. Once initiated it will give rise to a dialog box, where you just have to click **Start** to start the spell checking. Once a wrong word is found the spell checking dialog box, as shown here, will be displayed.

This dialog box has the following options:

Change to PageMaker displays the word which is not there in the dictionary with which it is comparing. In this box either you type the word you think is the corrected version of the word not found or alternatively, you can click from the possible words given in the box below for suggestions. After selecting, click it twice to make sure that the word fills the box of change to before replacing.

Alternate spellings These words are provided from the dictionary to give suggestions regarding words. If however, you do not want them to appear, select the options accordingly for this can definitely speed up the spell checking.

Show duplicates It is possible that the text may contain duplicate words like text text. PageMaker will show them but not delete them. The choice is totally yours to drop one of them or not. Similar to above, you can speed up spell checking by keeping it off.

Search document In this option you specify whether you want the current publication to be spell checked or all open publications. If you search all open publications, PageMaker automatically searches all stories in those publications.

Search Story This is part of the current story option and not available option wherein all stories are checked. Out of current publication you define here whether you want the Selected text to be checked or Current story to be checked or All stories are to be checked. Select one of these which is applicable.

Start/Ignore This will show Start when you begin to spell check otherwise during the checking it will show Ignore. Supposing there is a word in the text which is not there in the dictionary, you have two options, either to replace with a new/same word with new spelling or accept it as it is. To accept it as it is click at Ignore. For replacing see the next para.

Replace As discussed before, you can either type a new spelling of the word or select from the option given as alternatives. Select one of them and press Replace

Add Opens the add word to user dictionary dialog box in which you specify the word you want to

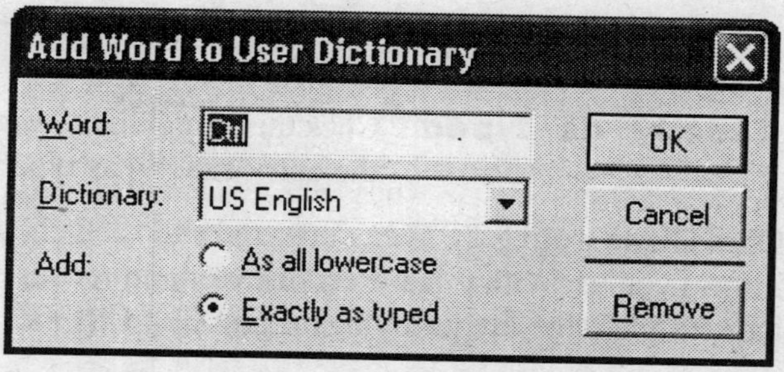

add to or remove from the dictionary. If a word is displayed in the Change to edit box PageMaker displays it in the word edit box otherwise the word box is empty, ready for you to type in the word you want to add.

Word This box displays the word which come from the previous menu of being not there in the Dictionary.

Dictionary PageMaker adds the word in the word edit box to the dictionary you select.

Add all lowercase Click this to add the word to the dictionary in a generic form that will match that word with any ordinary capitalization pattern, so PageMaker

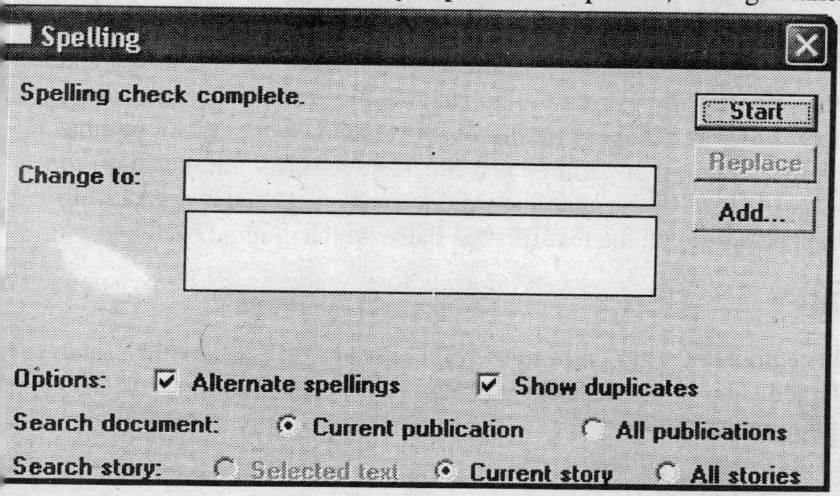

will highlight only spelling errors not capitalization errors.

Exactly as typed Click this to highlight words if they do not match the entry exactly as typed.

Once all the word have been corrected and spell checked, PageMaker will inform you so. With this we end the story editor session, so you can come back to the page layout by again pressing **Ctrl+E**.

But, this is not the end of editing. There are other editing commands which are very commonly used in all the word processors. These are **Cut, Copy, Paste**, etc. Let us see how these commands are used.

CUT

This command is used to cut the selected text or graphics from your file and keep it available for pasting it later to any other place in the same file or any other file or even any other software which supports the clipboard text.

To select an independent graphic to cut, use the pointer tool. To select text or an inline graphic, use either the pointer tool or the text tool, keeping in mind the following guidelines:

— Use the pointer tool to select an entire text block, maintaining its type specifications and line length. Cutting and pasting a text block by text tool turns it into a separate story.

— Use the text tool to select a range of text to cut.

When you use the pointer tool to cut an entire text block from a page, the space that was occupied by the block remains blank. When you use the text tool to cut all or part of a text block, PageMaker automatically closes the gap. When you cut an inline graphic or an independent graphic with text wrapped around it, the text fills the space which graphic occupied.

COPY

This command is also used to copy the selected text or graphics from your file and keep it available for pasting it later. Only difference it has from **Cut** command is that it leaves the original text as it is whereas in the case of **Cut** the original text is lost.

When you have more than one publication open, you can copy objects between publications without using the **Clipboard**. Select an object in one publication, drag it to position in the other publication window and release the mouse button to create a copy.

PASTE

This command is used to place the selected text or graphics from clipboard, where the text using the above **Cut** or **Copy** command has been kept. You can paste text and graphics using either the pointer tool or the text tool, depending on how you want the pasted object to be incorporated into your publication.

When you use the pointer for pasting, the location of a pasted object is determined by its original position on the screen, if it is visible. The object is pasted at a slight offset from that position, if it is not visible, PageMaker places the object in the centre of the visible page. To paste an object at its original position, press **Shift** as you choose paste from the edit menu.

Text pasted using the pointer tool becomes a separate text block. This text is not thread to the other text in the publication and it retains the formatting it had when cut or copied. A graphic pasted with the pointer tool is independent and is not tied to the text surrounding it.

PASTE MULTIPLE

This command is just an extension of above mentioned **Paste** command wherein instead of pasting from the clipboard matter once, you can paste it as many times as you want by defining the number of copies you want and their placement too.

Method of pasting is also similar to paste command, i.e., when to choose the pointer tool and when to choose the text tool. Various options available under this dialog box are:

Paste You can specify here the number of copies you want to paste.

Horizontal offset You can specify here the horizontal distance between each of the pasted objects or group of objects. This option is not available when multiple pasting with the text too.

Vertical offset You can specify the vertical distance between each copy of the paste object or group of objects. This option is also not available when multiple pasting with the text tool.

You can even enter positive or negative value in horizontal offset and vertical offset. Positive number offset copies from left to right and from top to bottom relative to the original object. Negative number offset copies from right to left and from bottom to top. You cannot undo this command.

WORKING WITH COLUMNS

You can divide the page of the publication into different columns of equal size. You can create columns of unequal length by pulling guides to the required place. However, the text flow from previous page, i.e., **Autoflow** does not recognise this option and does not flow the text in unequal columns. The maximum number of columns that you can create on a page are 20.

If not defined the page is counted to have 1 column, so that the number of column which you should mention here using the column guides should be minimum 2.

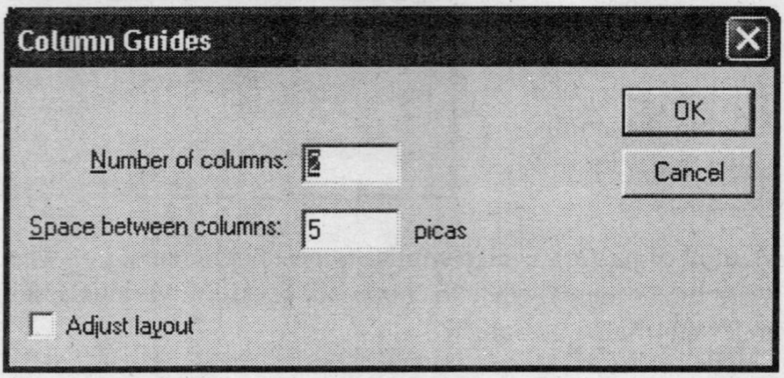

Number of columns Specify here the number of columns you want on the page.

Space between columns Specify the amount of space you want to leave between the two columns.

If you have to have a full publication divided into the columns, it is advised to have the columns made on the master page itself so that you do not have to set the guides on all pages.

This is where I come back to the page layout of setting two pages on one A4 paper, which was briefly introduced to you on page 15 of this book. In this case too, we will divide the A4 page into 2 columns each forming a page. As you would remember the paper size of A4 is 11.693 inches by 8.268 inches. Out of this we will make two pages of 7 inches by 4 inches and leave enough space for cutting on all sides.

We will select out **Document Setup** as follows:

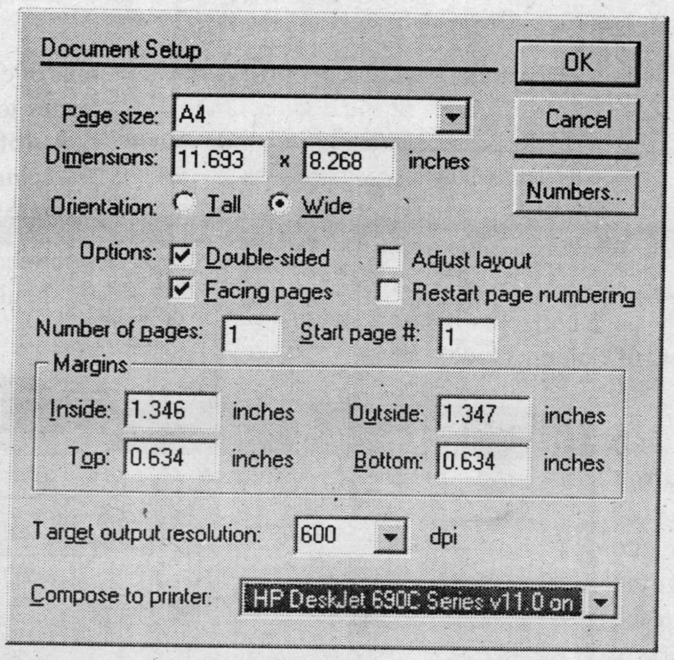

As you would have noticed that we have left space of 1.346 inches and 1.347 inches on both sides respectively. This would leave you with a space of 9 inches on the horizontal side. On the vertical side, the space of 0.634 inches on both sides would leave the vertical page size of 7 inches.

Once clicked the above document setup would leave you with a page layout as shown below.

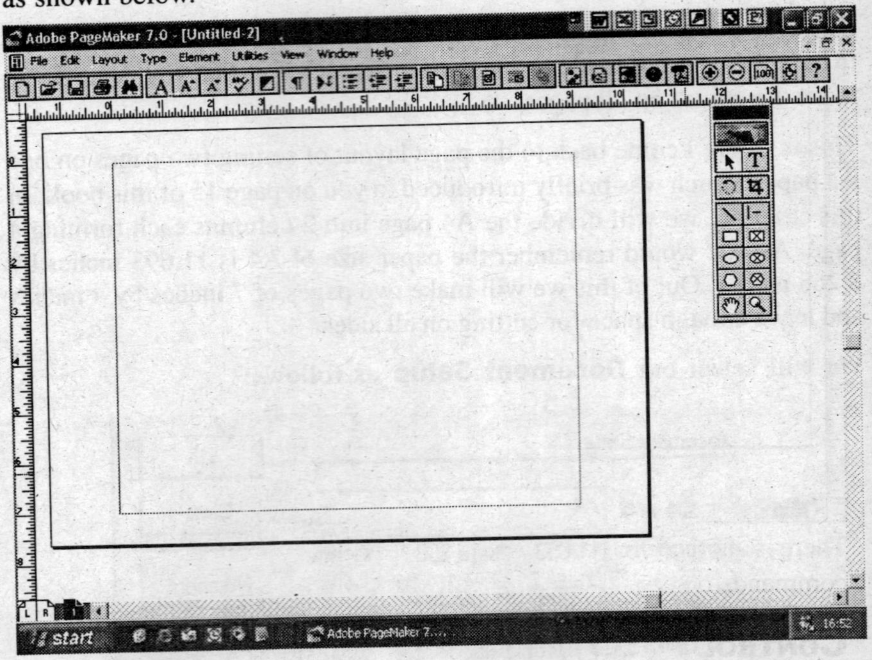

Now that you have a page size of 9 x 7 inches. All you have to do is to divide the page horizontally into 2 and this can be done easily by using the command of Column guides.

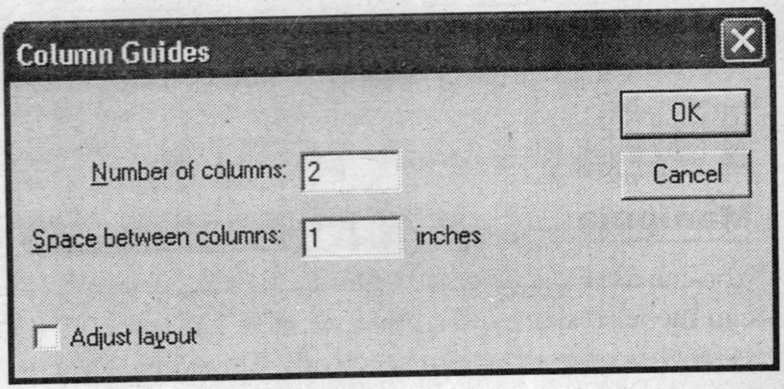

Just call **Column guides** and divide the page into 2 column with 1 inch space between them. You have now 2 columns each of 4 inches and 1 inch space in between them. This can be then be applied in the master page and you have the page with two independent pages of sizes 7 inches by 4 inches.

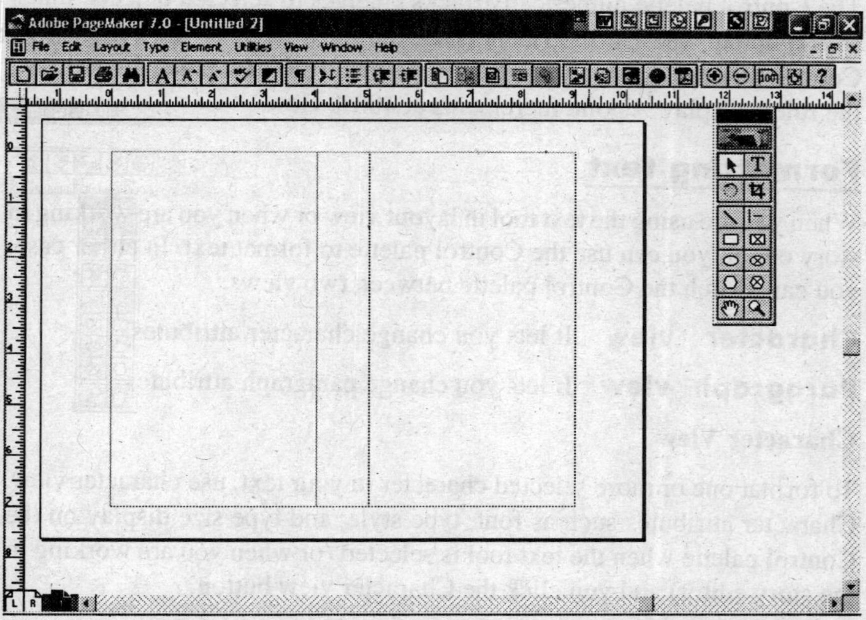

There is another method of working which helps you in putting most of the commands on the screen. This calls for Control Palette on the screen.

CONTROL PALETTE

This command available under Window menu displays the control palette, as shown here. This can be used to format text & graphics and to trace the movements of the cursor & positions of objects on publication pages. The Control palette displays different options depending on the object or the tool selected.

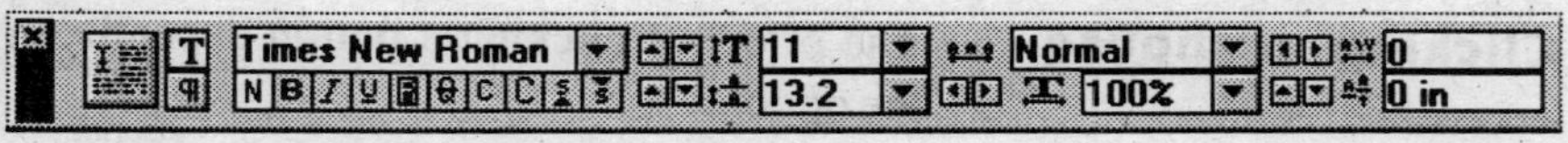

Manipulating objects

You can use Control palette options to manipulate objects on the page. You can move, resize, rotate, skew or reflect graphic objects and text blocks and crop imported graphics, as well as measure their size and position on the page.

The Control palette numerically tracks changes to selected objects, much as the dotted lines in the rulers track the movement of the cursor. The Control palette displays values accurately to 1/20 of a point. In contrast, the rulers display ¼ point increments at 400% view.

Formatting text

When you are using the text tool in layout view or when you are working in story editor, you can use the Control palette to format text. In either case, you can switch the Control palette between two views:

Character view It lets you change character attributes.

Paragraph view It lets you change paragraph attributes.

Character View

To format one or more selected character in your text, use character view. Character attributes such as font, type style, and type size display on the Control palette when the text tool is selected (or when you are working in the story editor) and you click the Character view button.

Paragraph View

To format one or more selected paragraph, use paragraph view. Paragraph attributes such as styles, alignment and indents display on the Control palette when the text tool is selected (or when you are working in story editor) and you click the Paragraph view button.

Changing and applying palette settings

You can change settings on the Control palette in several different ways. Depending on the option, you change settings by:

Clicking a mouse The effect of clicking a button depends on the option.

Typing an entry When you change a Control palette setting by typing a number, PageMaker displays an alert message if the number is invalid. For example, you can't rotate an object more than

360 degrees. When you change a setting by typing a word, for example, a font or paragraph style, PageMaker compares the available options to match the characters you are typing. When you change a setting by typing an entry, you must click the **Apply** button or press **Enter** to apply the change to the selected text or object.

Performing arithmetic You can add to, subtract from, multiply or divide any existing value for an option by typing a mathematical expression into the edit box.

Selecting from a list When you change a setting by selecting a list option, PageMaker applies the change immediately.

Using the Nudge buttons Nudge buttons are located next to most options on the Control palette that have a numerical value. Clicking a nudge button increases or decreases the value for an option by a set amount. When you change a setting by clicking on a nudge button, PageMaker applies the change immediately.

You can set the horizontal and vertical nudge amount for the **Position** and **Sizing** options and the vertical nudge amount for shifting the offset of an inline graphic using **Preferences** on the File menu, but for all other options, the nudge amount is fixed. Hold down **Ctrl** as you click a nudge button to increase the nudge amount; this is called the power nudge. Power nudge is the nudge amount multiplied ten times.

Changing the options By default, options on the Control palette use the measurement and vertical ruler defaults set for the publication. However, you can use a different unit of measure for a particular measurement, such as paragraph indents or the dimensions of an object. Activate a numeric option, and then **Shift + F11** (Windows) to cycle through the units of measure available for the option.

Using the keyboard You can use the Control palette to modify graphics and text blocks without removing yours hands from the keyboard.

Control palette options available with an object selected

Apply button Click to modify selected objects after you type numeric values for one or more options. Clicking a button or selecting an option from a list automatically applies your changes. PageMaker implements all changes entered on the palette that are not yet applied. The appearance of the Apply button changes depending on the selected object. If you have no object selected, the button displays the icon for the tool currently selected. If you have several objects selected, the Apply button displays an icon representing several objects.

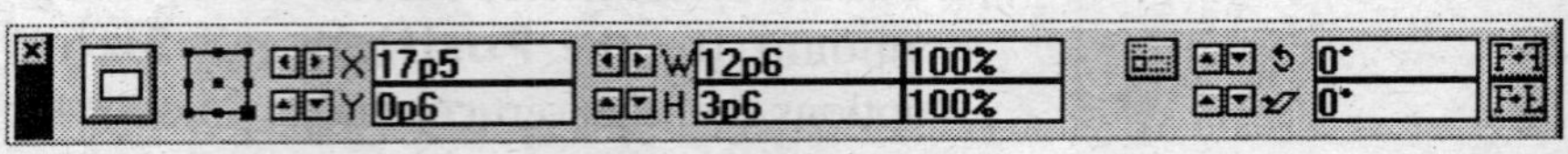

Proxy The Proxy represents the selected object. The reference point on the Proxy represents the point you are manipulating on the object; the X and Y coordinates displayed in the position option are those of the active reference point. You can change the reference point by clicking a different reference point on the proxy or by clicking or dragging a different handle on the object.

When the reference point is a box, the reference

point remains stationary and modifications are measured from it. When the reference point is an arrow, the reference point moves as the object is modified. To change between a box and an arrow, click the active reference point.

To select a reference point, activate the proxy and then press the arrow keys. Alternatively, select a reference point by pressing a number on the numeric keypad. When NumLock is on, the numbers 1-9 on the numeric keypad, each correspond to a point on the proxy. The 5 key corresponds to the center reference point and the 7 key corresponds to the upper-left reference point.

Position Displays the X and Y coordinate values of the reference point on pointer, relative to the current rulers. If your reference point is the upper-left corner and you are positioning a rectangle, X and Y reflect the coordinates of the upper-left corner of that rectangle. If you are drawing a rectangle, X and Y reflect the coordinates where you pressed the mouse button when you began to draw. When you select multiple objects, X and Y reflect the reference point for the rectangular area defined by the outside edge of all selected objects. You can also move or resize a selected object by changing the values in Position option. Nudge amount is 0.01 inches or as set in the Preferences dialog box.

Allowable values You cannot enter a value that positions any part of an object outside the pasteboard. When resizing, you cannot enter a value that creates a horizontal or vertical dimension that is zero or negative.

Sizing option Displays the width W and height H of the

selected object or cropping rectangle. PageMaker displays only one size for lines, which is line length L. When the reference point appears as an arrow, the specified values resize the object or cropping rectangle by repositioning the reference point. Nudge amount is 0.01 inches or as set in the Preference dialog box.

Allowable values Maximum size of a graphic is 45.51 inches (116 cms). Maximum size of a text block is 2.75 inches (58 cms). You cannot enter a value that positions any part of an object outside the pasteboard or that creates a horizontal or vertical dimension that is zero or negative.

Percentage scaling It displays the percentage changed from the original size. This option is available for scaling objects drawn with the PageMaker drawing tools or images placed on the page.

When the reference point appears as a box, the specified values resize the object from the reference point or when the reference point appears as an arrow, the specified values resize the object by repositioning the reference point.

If you scale an object drawn in PageMaker, the percentage of original size reflects the original size only during the current editing session. If you deselect the object and then select the object again, 100% is displayed for both options. PageMaker always remembers the original size of imported graphic objects.

When the reference point appears as a box, the reference point remains stationary and PageMaker applies the specified percentages from the reference point outward. When the reference point appears as an arrow,

PageMaker applies the specified percentages by repositioning the reference point to stretch or shrink the object.

Allowable values You cannot enter a value that positions any part of an object outside the pasteboard or that creates a horizontal or vertical dimension that is zero or negative.

Scaling and Cropping This option indicates the way you are resizing a graphic. When you select an imported graphic using the pointer tool, PageMaker highlights the Scaling button. When you select an imported graphic using the cropping tool, PageMaker highlights the Cropping button. Whichever tool you select, you can click either button to determine how to resize the graphic.

Proportional scaling When you scale an object, use this option to specify whether you want to change an object's height and width independently or maintain its original proportions. When the option is turned on, PageMaker maintains the original proportion of height to width when you resize a graphic. When you resize proportionally, the values for the percentage options change in tandem, regardless of which one you enter values in. When this option is turned off, you scale the object's height and width independently.

Printer resolution scaling When you scale a bitmap graphic, i.e., with TIFF extension and so on, turn this option on to scale the image so that its resolution is compatible with the target printer resolution in the Document Setup dialog box to be same as magic stretch.

Rotating Rotates the selected object using the reference point on the proxy.

When the reference point is a box, the option rotates an object around the reference point. When the reference point is an arrow, the option rotates an object by moving the reference point.

Positive numbers rotate the object counter clockwise; negative numbers clockwise. When you rotate an object more than 10 degrees but less than 350 degrees, the proxy rotates to approximate the rotation of the object and the reference points on the proxy remain the same in relation to the selected object.

Skewing It skews the selected object horizontally in relation to the selected reference point on the proxy. When reference point is a box, the object is skewed from the reference point. When the reference point is an arrow, the object is skewed by moving the reference point. Positive numbers move the top edge of the object to the right and negative numbers move the top edge of the object to the left.

Now we know how to use the Control palette. We come back to our book for which we had placed text and done some editing on it like spell checking etc. Now we perform more commands on it. One of them is called Book and is used to combine the various publications of a particular book.

Book

Use this command to create a list of publications to be treated as a single document called a **Book**. You can work with each publication in the book separately too or you can tell PageMaker to perform certain tasks showing or creating an index, creating a table of contents, or printing the entire book in one go.

This command can be called from **Utilities** menu. Book publication list dialog box lets you create a book list and control the page numbering of the publication in that list. The options of the dialog box are discussed below:

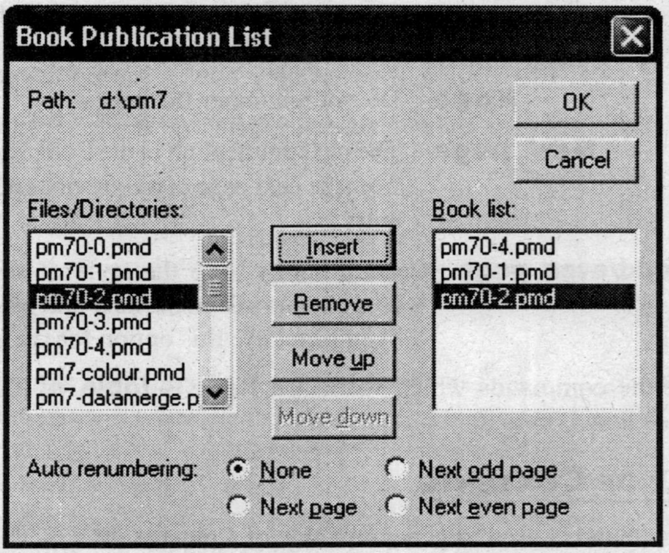

Insert Add the publication selected in the list box on the left to the book list on the right. You can also double click the publication name in the left list box to add it to the book list. To update this list you rename a publication or move it to a new location on your hard disk. Remove the publication you renamed or moved and insert the new version into the book list.

Remove Use this to remove the selected publication from the book list.

Move up/Move down The command moves the selected publication up or down one position in the book list. This becomes necessary when you have to make sure that the page numbering in the publications is not to be disturbed and their sequence remains the same.

Auto renumbering PageMaker repaginates and prints the publication of the book in the order they appear in the book list. You can choose the options as following:

None Do not renumber the pages.

New page The next publication in the Book should start from the next page of the previous publication entry.

Next odd/even page Certain books have the style of starting all new chapters from the next odd page or next even page, use this option for the same.

One of the commands which works on Book is **Table of Contents**, let us see how it uses it.

TABLE OF CONTENTS

This command is used to generate Table of Contents (TOC). This can be created for a single publication or a number of publications if the book list is used. The created TOC is in the form of a new text story which can be placed on any page of the current publication or can be placed in a new publication for printing.

The main 3 steps involved in creating a Table of Contents are as following:

1. Open the style sheet and mark the style which you want to appear in

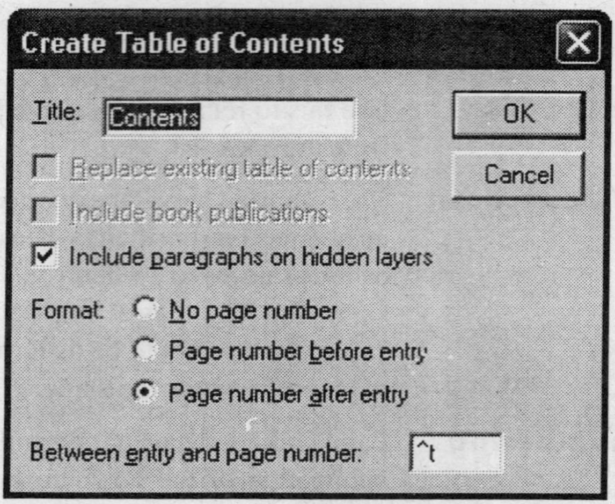

TOC by going through paragraph command and clicking at the bottom where it says whether to be included in TOC or not.

2. Generate the table of contents as defined above by using the TOC command from the Utilities menu.

3. Place the text created in current publication or a new publication for editing/printing.

The Table of Contents dialog box has the following options:

Title In this box you type the name of TOC which you want to give, PageMaker suggests the name of Contents when you open the box. However, you can change the same by typing a new one.

Replacing existing...... It will be off if there is no table of contents created before. However, in case you have already created one before and are now replacing it with a new one, click it into this. Also you can create a new one to compare with the old one by not clicking this.

Include paragraphs.... When you read about layers you will come to know about the layers which are not visible to you. These can be included for creation of table of contents.

Include book publication It will be off in case you have not created a book list. Click this to include all the publications of the book.

Format Various options available under this dialog box are as under:

No page number Specify if you do not want page numbers to appear in the table of contents.

Page number before entry Specify if you want page numbers to appear before the entry in the table of contents.

Page number after entry Specify if you want page number to appear after the entry in the table of contents.

Between entry and page number This column is used to specify whether you want tab to appear in between the entry and page number. Other options are that you have a carriage return or a number of tabs, etc. The choice is totally yours. You can even have ^tVol-1^t, to make Vol-1 appear alongwith all the page numbers. This can also be defined in the Preference column in the File menu.

Another command depending upon the book command is **Index**. Let us see how it works.

CREATE INDEX

This command is used to Create index for a single publication or for all the publications in your book list. The index becomes a new story that you can place in an existing publication or in a new publication you create just for the index.

Creating of index is done in 4 steps.

1. Create index entries by using command Create Index entry.
2. Create the index using Create Index command.

3. Review or edit the index entries by using Show Index command.
4. Place the index story on a publication.

Let us start with create index, which can be called from the Utilities menu. Various options here are:

Title You can give the title to the Index by typing in the box provided for, up to a maximum of 30 characters, PageMaker proposes Index as title for your index, which you can change according to your choice.

Replace existing index This command is used to replace an existing index which had been created earlier. You can even retain the earlier one and create a new one to compare the two, for this you will have to uncheck this command.

Include book publication You can generate index for a combined book if the book list is active else you can create the same for a single publication.

Remove unreferenced topics There maybe few topics which are not cross-referred. You may like to remove them. An unreferenced topic may be a topic which:

- you imported the topic for cross-reference but did not use.
- for which all index entries were deleted.
- left in the topics list after you have removed an index marker in the publication.

Checking this option does not remove

the entries in which you selected to Suppress page reference. Uncheck this option if, for example, you are generating a rough index for view and you want to retain the imported topics from a large book list can make your publication file very large, you may want to remove the unreferenced topics when you generate your final index.

Format Click this option to obtain **Index Format** dialog box in which you can format certain elements of the index.

This box is used to include section headings in the index, to determine whether index entries will be indented (nested) or in single paragraph (run-in) format and to specify which characters will separate parts of an index entry.

Include index section headings Index which is being created can have the section headings in the form of A, B, or C, etc., if you click this. Else you can uncheck this.

Include empty index sections Supposing a section has no entry may be in section X, then it will create entry for that too with a message no entries.

Format This is used to select one of the two options available in Page Maker, i.e., Nested and Run-in.

Nested In this option the text of index appears in an indented format in which each level of an entry is a separate paragraph.

Run-in In this option the text of index appears

in the form of a single paragraph having all levels of each entry.

The following options give you the control over the formatting of the characters which use can be used to form separate parts of the index. These include commas, tabs, semicolons, colons, etc.

Following topic Specify here the character you want to be inserted between the text and the first entry of page number. The default is two spaces.

Between page #s Specify here the character you want to get inserted between two page number entries. The default is a comma and en space.

Between entries Specify here the character you want to be inserted between second and third level entries. The default is semicolon and en space.

Page range Specify here the character you want to be inserted between first and last number in a range of pages. The default is en dash.

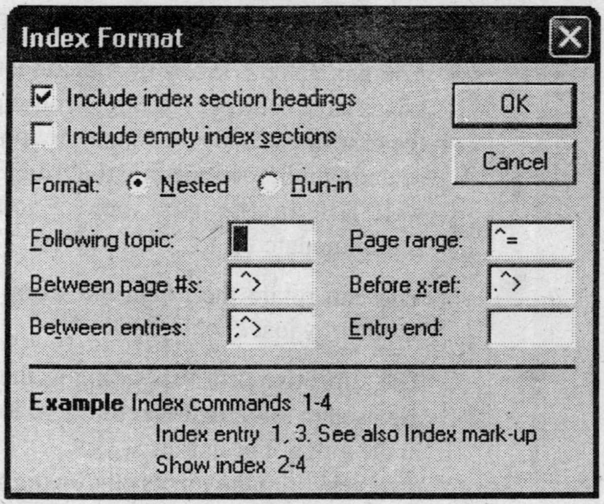

Before x-ref Specify here the character you want to be inserted before a cross-reference. The default is a period and en space.

Entry end Specify here the character you want to be inserted between at the end of every referenced entry (in nested format) or to follow the last cross-reference in the topic (in run-in format). The default is no character.

Nest step is to add index entries. This is done by command called **Index Entry** available under the **Utilities** menu.

INDEX ENTRY

This command is used to create index in a publication file and to edit the index entries. When you click at Index entry the add index entry dialog box appears, the options of which are discussed below:

Type It has two options, **Page reference** or **Cross reference**. When you click page reference it gives you the page number as the reference. Whereas if you select cross-reference then instead of page numbers you get the cross reference such as See, See also, etc.

Topic You can have 3 levels of indexing. For it, three boxes have been provided for. You should provide the text in each level of index by typing or even selecting it before opening the Add index entry, it will fill up the first box. Each level can accommodate up to 50 characters.

You can rotate the topic text from one level to another by just clicking in the box.

Sort The sort boxes corresponding to the topic levels are used to tell PageMaker how to sort each entry in the index. The entries are spelled in the index as they appear in the topics edit boxes but are sorted

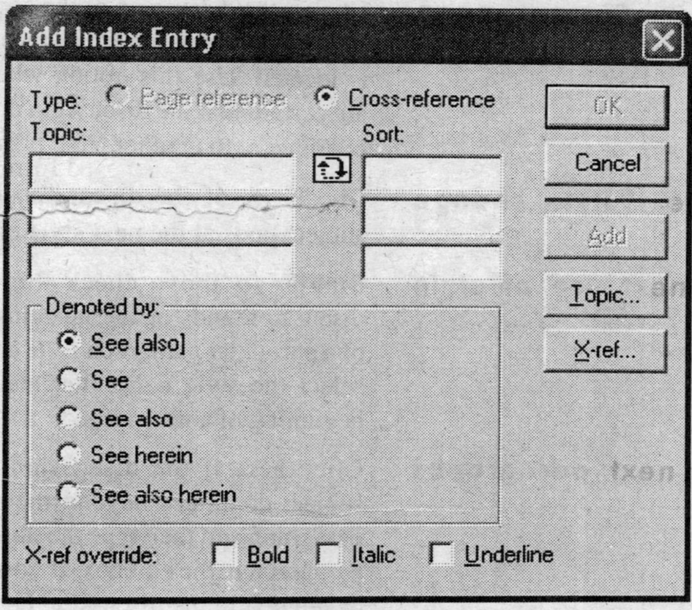

alphabetically according to the spelling in the sort edit boxes. For example, if the topics references is PM and you want it to be sorted in the index as PageMaker, then type PageMaker in the sort box against the topic box of PM.

Add Click to add another index entry at the same location after you add an entry, PageMaker puts off this button until you make a change, so that you do not mistakenly add an entry twice. To add another entry, type over existing text in the topics edit boxes and click add or Ok.

Topic Click this to view the topics already selected and for which the index has already been created. You can also use this option to add topics to the topics listed directly.

Page range These options are used to define where the discussion of the subject ends, so that PageMaker can supply page number for the references.

Current page Click if the discussion of the subject is limited to the page on which the marker is located. Use this option when you are certain that the discussion does not continue onto another page/pages.

To next style change Check this if the discussion on the subject ends at the next style change.

To next use of style Similar to above check this if the discussion ends at the next instances of a particular paragraph style and then select the style name that marks the beginning of a new subject.

For next paragraphs Click here if the discussion of the subject continues beyond the current paragraph and then type the number of paragraph in the edit box. If you add or delete text in the discussion be sure to adjust the number of paragraph specification for the page range.

Suppress page range Click to create an index without a page references. This is useful when you are in the process of revising an index and you want to create entries as placeholder to index later.

Page# override PageMaker provides 3 options Bold, Italics and Underline for emphasizing index entry page numbers. Selecting any one, two or three option causes the style of the page number to be printed as selected.

PageMaker keeps the setting for page# override—for all new entries until you change it consequently. If you want all cross reference or page reference to be italics, only selected italics the first time you create an index entry.

This way you will be able to create the index entries. Now the next step is to check them. For that we have the command called **Show index**.

SHOW INDEX

This is used to see index before it is printed. Here you can edit entries but you cannot add an entry in this. To show the complete index on screen, PageMaker goes through the process of renumbering pages, updating book references and then it shows the complete index. But, this is so when the book list is active, if not it will show the index of the current publication only. In this book list also you can see the index of current publication only by pressing **Ctrl key** while opening **Show Index** command.

The **Show Index** dialog box lists all index entries in your publication or book stored alphabetically into sections. Topic level are shown as well as all pages of references and cross references.

The dialog box contains:

Index section PageMaker arranges index entries into sections. Select the section you want to display from the index section list.

Next section You click this to display the next alphabetical section which is not empty or has at least one entry.

Accept After you have made the changes to the entries, click this to accept.

Add x ref Click this to display the add index entry dialog box in which you can add a cross-references to an index entry. If you select an index entry before clicking, add x-ref fills the topic edit boxes.

Edit This is used to display the edit index entry dialog box in which you can edit any portion of index entry.

Remove This is used to delete a selected entry from the index. Only the index entry is deleted but the topic reference remains.

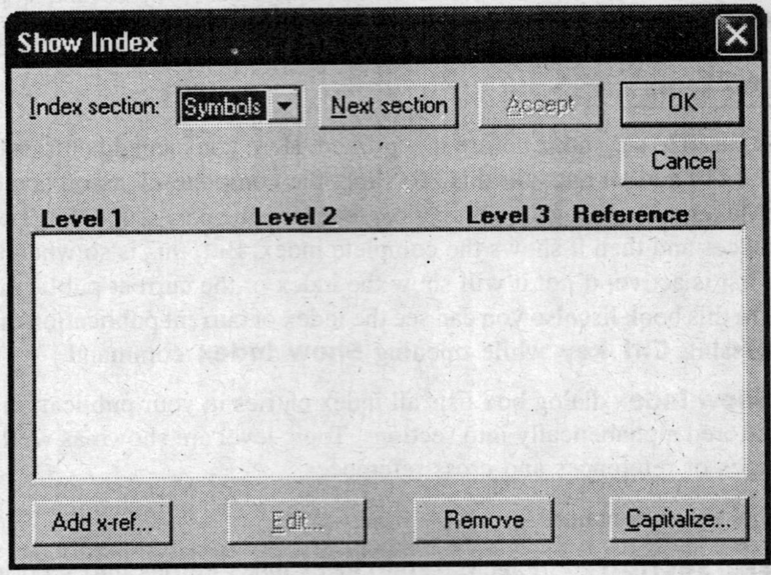

Capitalize Opens the capitalize dialog box described below. Capitalize button is available only if you generate index from a single publication.

This selected topic Captalizes the first letter in level 1 of the selected index entry.

All level 1 entries Capitalizes the first letter in level 1 for all entries in the index.

All entries Capitalizes the first letter in all level (level 1, 2 and 3) of all entries in the index.

Now that the index is ready, it can be printed. So let us understand the options of printing.

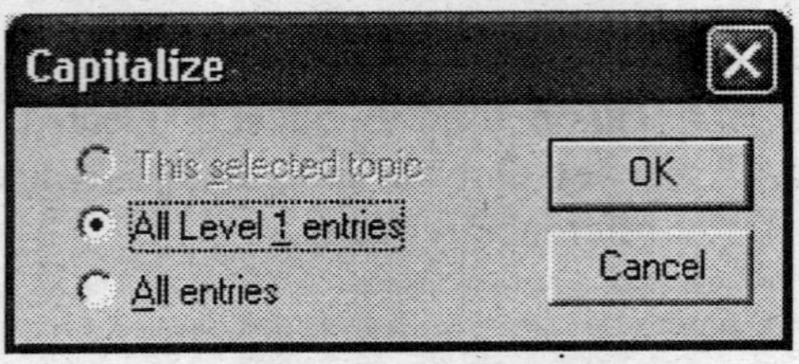

PRINT

This command is dependent on the type of printer you select to print. The options usually change with the printer driver that is loaded. The print dialog box has the following options:

Printer Under the normal circumstances, the default printer which you have selected is shown here. If you have loaded the drivers for more than one printer, you can choose to select any one of them by clicking here.

Collate This option collates the printed output. This is useful when you are printing multiple copies. Normally when you print pages 1 to 10 with 5 copies, the PageMaker will print 5 copies of pages 1 to 10, starting with 5 copies of page 1 and so on. With this command, it will print page number 1 to 10, 5 times over in a collated form.

Reverse order By choosing this option, you can print in the reverse order, i.e., while printing 1 to 10 pages, it will print 10 first, then 9 and so on.

Proof By choosing this option you can print the pages as lower quality proofs.

Copies Type here the number of copies you want to print.

Pages Select here the selective pages you want to print, the various options are:

- **All** Select this to print all pages.
- **Ranges** Select here the particular pages, you want to print. You can choose to print non-consecutive pages by typing their numbers with a hyphen each and followed by comma (,), e.g., 45-56, 67-78, etc.
- **Print** You can select to print either **Odd** pages, **Even** pages or **Both** pages
- **Ignore 'Non-Printing'** Click this if you want to print the non-printing characters too.

Reader's spreads It allows for the evaluation of two-page spreads.

Book This command is valid if you have the publications lined up in Book. The options here are that you can print all the pages of all the publications in the book or choose otherwise.

Orientation PageMaker automatically selects the option for you, but, you can choose to be different.

Setup dialog box This depends totally upon the printer you are using and differs from printer to printer.

Options This dialog box has the following options:

Scale

Percentage You can scale the pages to any size before printing.

Reduce to fit If the page which you have designed is bigger than the paper on which you are printing. With this command you can make it print on the same paper.

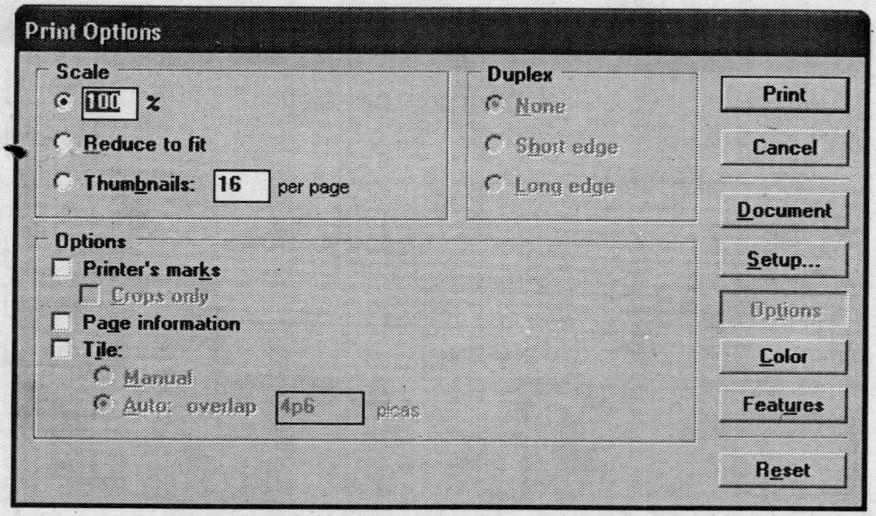

Print as Thumbnails You can print miniature editions of the pages as icons with a maximum number of 16-pages per sheet of paper.

Duplex The various options here are **None**, **Short edge**, and **Long edge**.

Options Here are the various options which can be printed on the page itself, i.e., Printer's marks, Page information and if you have used the tiling option, print with a defined overlap option.

Color This dialog box has the option to print the colour which the printer supports and if not whether to print them as black or else. Also the way the colour separation is to be done.

Features This again depends on the type of printer you are using.

Now that we have edited the publication and have created Index, Table of Contents of the publication, Spell checked and have made the other formatting of the text. Finally we have printed the publication according to our needs. This finishes the complete process of creation of a book for publication.

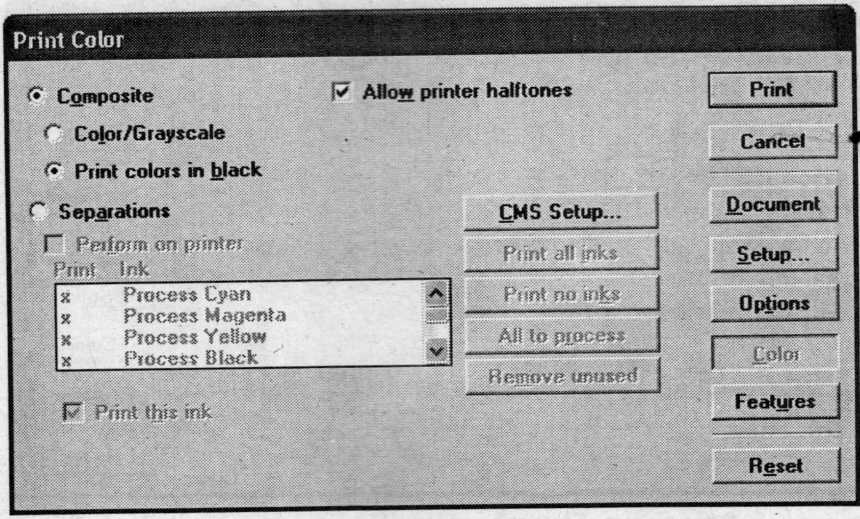

But so far we have done nothing with respect to Graphics and their placements in the text. This we will discuss in the next chapter.

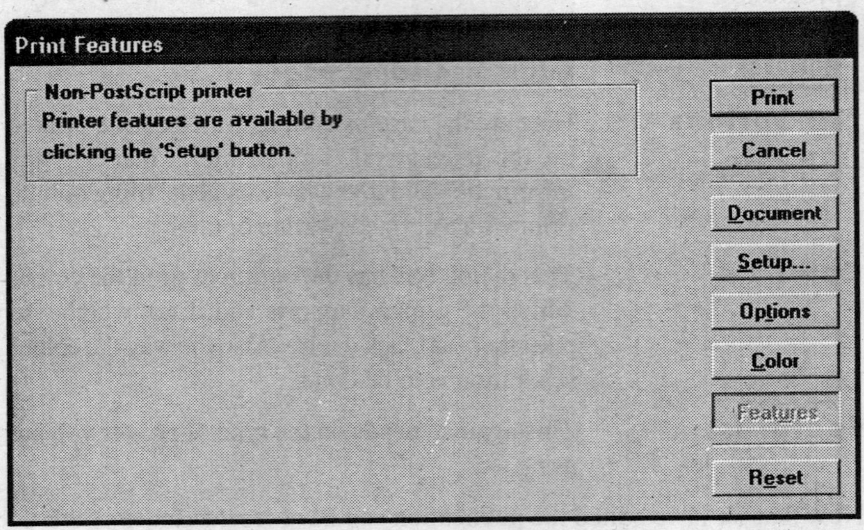

5

Working with Graphics

Introduction

So far we have talked about text only in the context of PageMaker. It is not that the software is not capable of anything else but text. In this chapter we will see how the graphics are handled in PageMaker.

Insert Objects

This command is used to create an object in another program and insert it as an **Object Linked Embedded** (OLE) within a PageMaker publication. The **insert object** dialog box, shown here, lists the object type available from the OLE compatible program (including source or server program) on your system. Once you select an object and click Ok, the program that creates the object type gets started or is brought to the

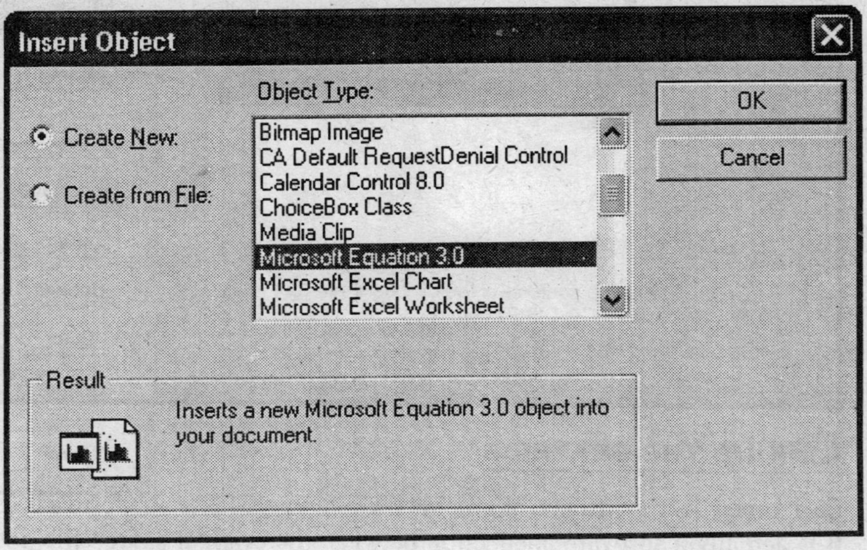

foreground and opens an untitled document. You can then create an object (such as a graph or chart or even copy a clip art). When you finish creating the object, choose update from the program file menu and then close the program. The object you created is imported into your publication as an OLE embedded object and you are transferred back to PageMaker.

Paste Special

The other way of inserting object into the publication is via **Paste Special**. You create the object in the program of your choice and copy the object from the program. Now come to PageMaker and use the command called **Paste Special** available under the **Edit** menu.

Depending upon the type of object that you have copied, this dialog box will give you the options for pasting. Remember, these are on the basis of best capabilities of the object or how it will be suited to be inserted. Click Ok to have the object inserted into publication.

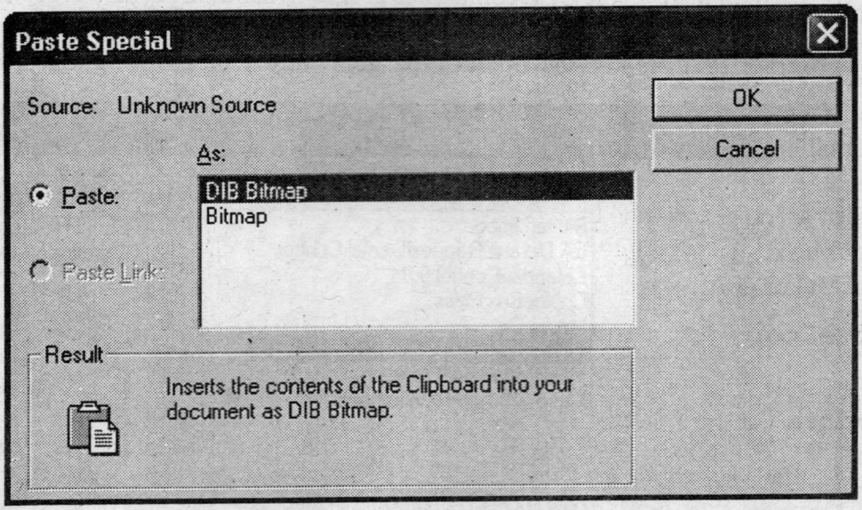

Linking the Graphics

Each time you import a text or graphic file into PageMaker you form a link. It is actually a software connection between the original source file and your publication. Generally there are 2 ways of forging different kinds of links between the two:

1. You can use the original PageMaker proprietary linking method (probably the best).
2. Object Linking and Embedding (OLE) method.

Both these methods have been discussed above. But, what is the need for linking. There are few distinctive advantages of using PageMaker links.

1. To share your work with someone else who is also using this graphic.
2. To update it regularly.
3. To use less disk space.

These can also be done by using the Link Options.

Link Options

You can choose to have PageMaker update the linked object automatically each time you open the publication. If you are worried about this type of automatic modification of your internal linked material, check the **Alert Before Updating** checkbox to have PageMaker provide a safe dialog box for update control.

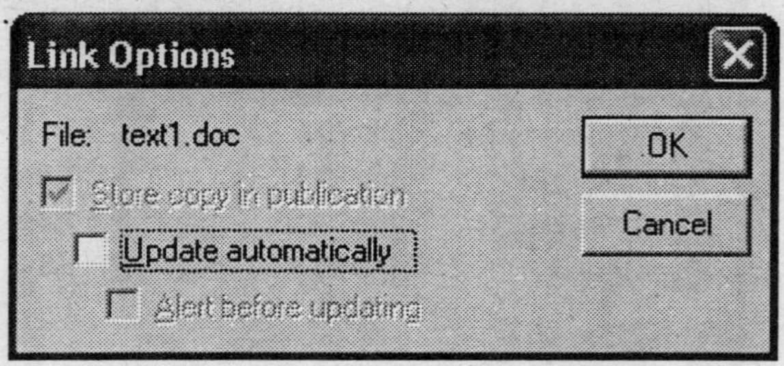

Store copy in publication This command stores a complete story of the object in the publication.

Update Automatically Updates your publication automatically upon opening or printing, if external copy of the linked file has been modified. If when opening or printing a publication, PageMaker encounters a link for which automatically is checked but for which it cannot locate the external file, PageMaker displays the cannot find dialog box.

Alert before updating This command always confirms with you before updating your publication.

LINK INFO

This command is used to view additional information about a linked object selected in the publication. The **link info** dialog box, shown on this page, has the following options.

Location Specifies the location and the name of the externally associated file.

Kind This describes the type of file.

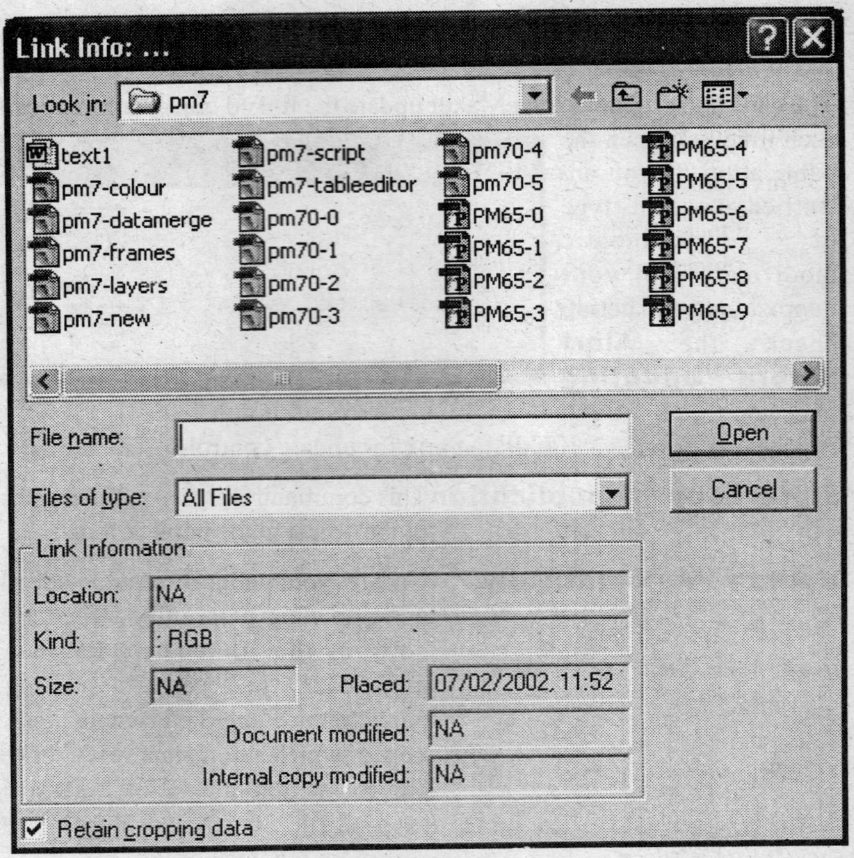

Size	Describes in terms of hard disk space how much space this file is using.
Placed	Describes the time and date when the file was placed into the publication.
Document modified	Describes the time and date when the document was last modified.
Internal data modified	Describes the time and date when the linked object or text was last modified in the publication.

EDITING ORIGINAL

No matter what linking method you choose, the resulting link gives you instant access for editing your imported object. This command is available under the Edit menu.

This is how it works.

1. Once clicked on the object it will easily and quickly open a linked object for editing in its original program.
2. When you finish editing, save the original file.
3. Exit the application and you end up back in PageMaker with the linked object updated by your editing sessions.

This is as far the linking and placing of objects/graphics is concerned. But, how about mingling text with graphics. Well, for that we have the command called **Text Wrap**. This is how it works.

TEXT WRAP

This command is used to define how the text should wrap around the graphics. The way the text wraps around a graphic is determined by the graphic boundary. A graphic boundary can be rectangle or you customize its shape by selecting the graphic and dragging the diamond handle that surrounds it. You can add new handle by clicking on the dotted line.

The text wrap dialog box has the following options:

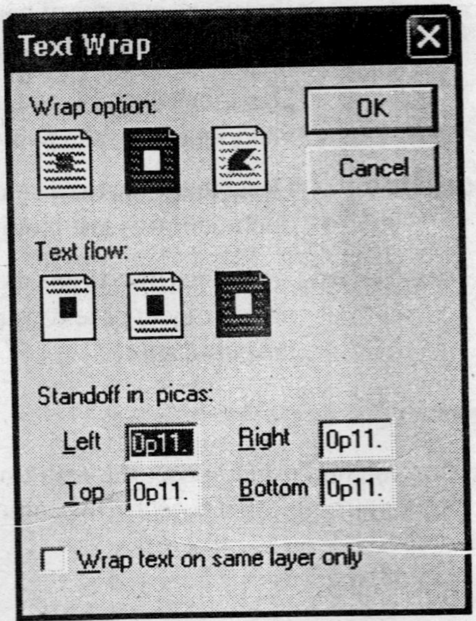

Wrap option — Select one of the first two options either to flow text over the graphic or to create a rectangle graphic boundary. If you have already customized the graphic boundary the third icon is highlighted.

Text flow — There are 3 different icons which determine how the text flows around a graphic.

- **Column break icons** — Stops the text flow above the graphic and then continues the text flow at the start of the next column.
- **Jump over icons** — Stops the text flow above the graphic and then continue below it leaving white space on either side.
- **Wrap all sides icons** — Flows the text around the graphics on all sides.

Standoff in — Define the space in a selected measurement for space to be left around the graphic. If you want text to overlap parts of the graphic specify a negative standoff value.

Bring to Front/Send to Back

Use the **Bring to front** and **Send to back** commands to change the stacking order of overlapping text and graphics on the page.

When you choose to Bring to front, the text/graphic/pattern whichever is selected comes to the front taking everything else to the background. Similarly, Send to back sends the selected item to the back, bringing to the front others. These commands are mainly used in case of reverse highlighting.

Reversing the Text

Supposing you have to make some text in **Reverse**. This is how you will do it.

1. Type the text which you want to make as reverse.

   PAGEMAKER

2. Draw a box around the typed text.

   PAGEMAKER

3. With the box selected, click at **Fill** in the Element menu. From the available list, select **Solid** to make the box filled with solid black.

4. Now the text beneath the solid box is hidden, you have to highlight it. Select the text by text tool and make it **Reverse** from the **Type** style.

5. You can see the text in reverse. But, it may not be permanent. To make sure that it does, select the box and click at **Send to back** to make the text in front and box in back permanently.

Another interesting features have been included in the version 7.0 of the software. These are called frames, lets see how they work.

Working with Frames

There are 3 frame options given in the toolbar. These are:

Rectangular

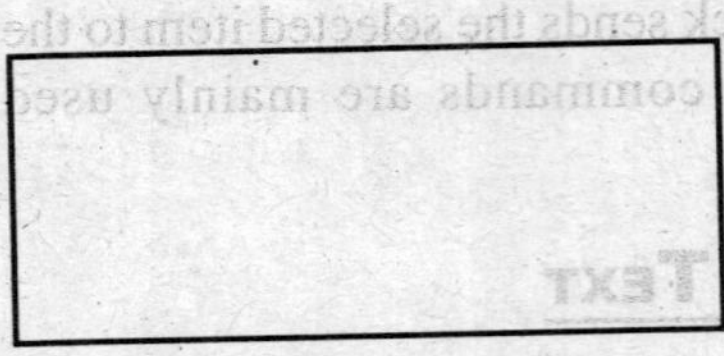

Oval

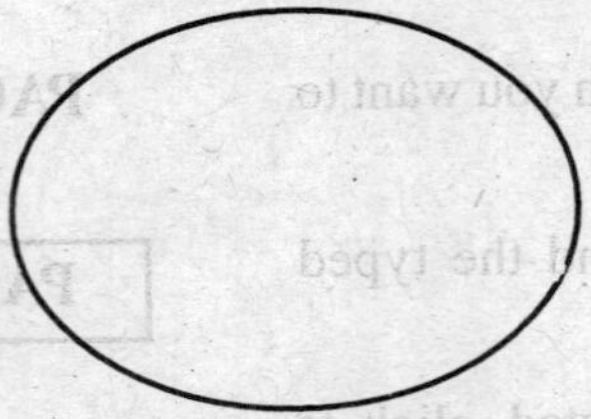

Polygonal

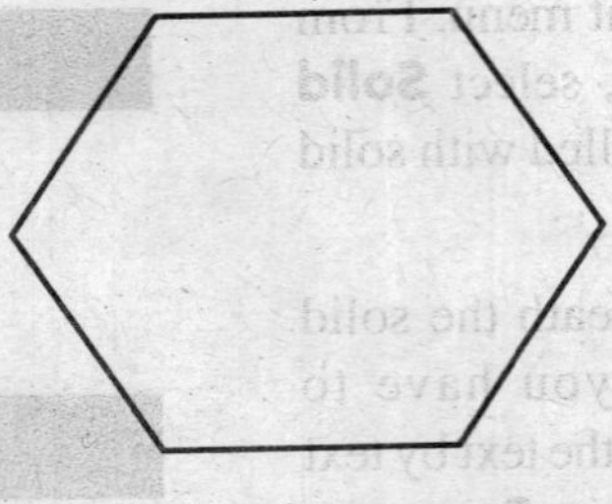

These frames help you type in the text directly into the shape of your choice. Creating them is very simple. Just click at the required shape in the toolbar and draw the shape in the publication.

Let us see what are the options available for the frames.

Attach content Supposing you have drawn a frame and on the other side you have typed a portion of the text. Now you want this text to fit into the frame. This option is used for this.

1. Type the text and draw the frame, as shown here.

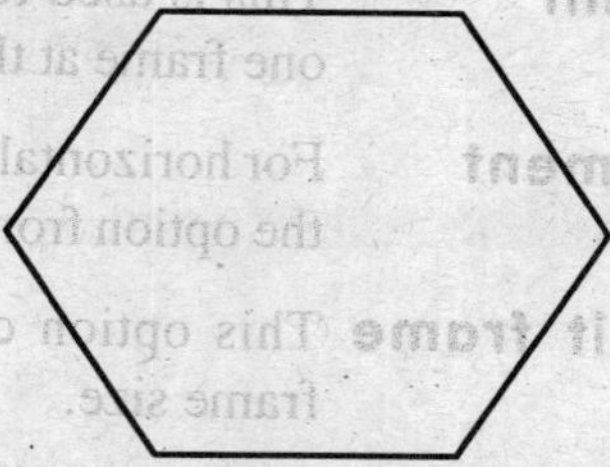

These help you type in the text directly into the shape of your choice.

2. Select the polygon and select the text with the pointer tool. With both selected click at Element menu and Frame option of **Attach content**. See the result, the text has gone into the polygon.

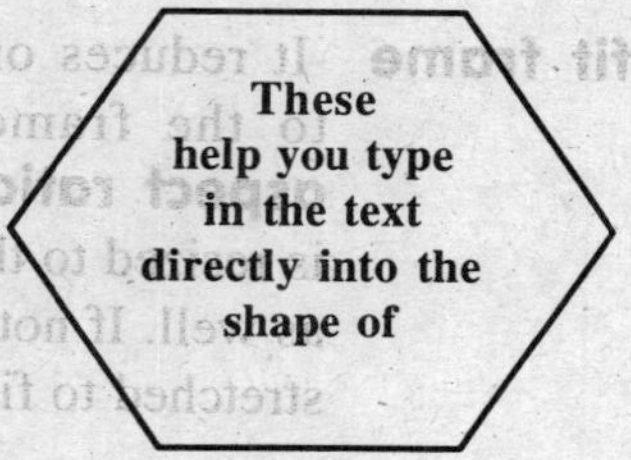

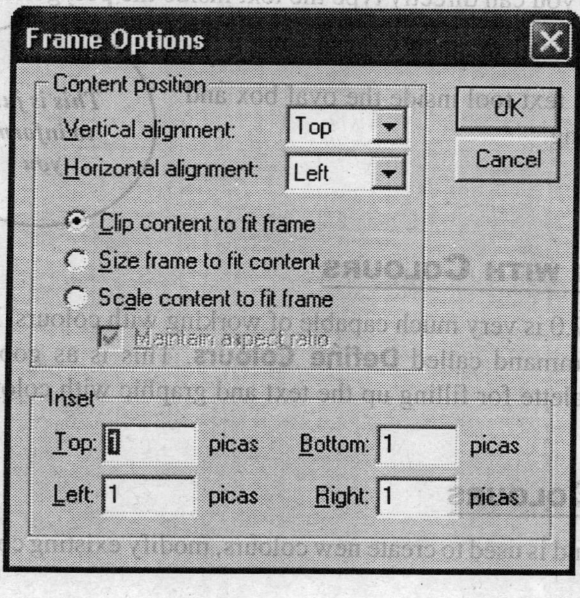

Next you have the **Frame Options**, which are:

Vertical alignment This is used for aligning of more than one frame at the top, centre or bottom.

Horizontal alignment For horizontal alignment, select one of the option from Left, Right and Centre.

Clip content to fit frame This option clips the graphic to the frame size.

Size frame to fit content This option expands the frame to fit the exact size of the graphic.

Scale content to fit frame It reduces or enlarges the graphic to the frame size. If **Maintain aspect ratio** is selected the frame is resized to the graphic's aspect ratio as well. If not selected, the graphic is stretched to fit the frame.

Inset Here you give the amount of space that you have to leave on all the sides.

What's more you can directly type the text inside the polygon too.

1. Draw the oval shape of your choice.
2. Click the text tool inside the oval box and start typing.

Working with Colours

PageMaker 7.0 is very much capable of working with colours. For this we have the command called **Define Colours**. This is as good as using the colour palette for filling up the text and graphic with colours of your choice.

Define Colours

This command is used to create new colours, modify existing colours, copy

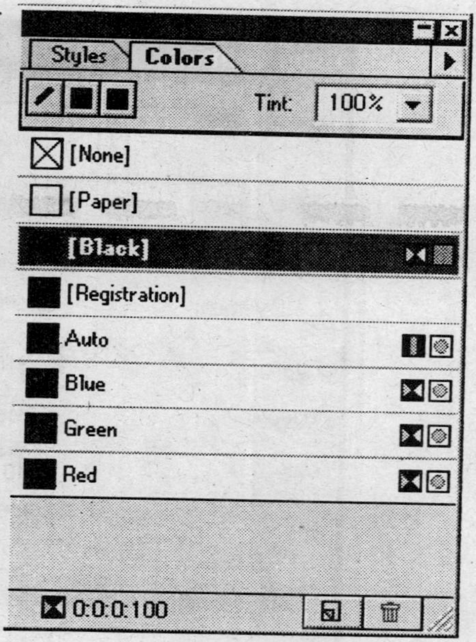

colours from other publications, or delete colours from your publication. When you create a colour, its name and a colour patch appear on the Colour palette. The colour name appears in the **Dialog box** and **Fill** and **Stroke** dialog boxes. You can then apply colours to text and graphics.

Here you can even change the Tint of the colour in terms of the percentage. Each colour has its own set of icons for changing its options. If you click in it, you get another dialog box, as shown on the next page, which has the following features:

Name Type a name for a new colour or edit an existing colour name (up to 31 characters). Assign colour names that help you easily identify those colours when you select them from the colours palette.

Type There are three options to choose from **Spot**, **Process** and **Tint**. Select Spot or Process to create a colour using one of these two basic colour types. Select **Tint** to create a lightened tone of a spot or process colour or a lighter tone of another tint.

Model Select any colour model to specify a spot colour out of the three options available

RGB	Red, Green, Blue
HLS	Hue, Lightness, Saturation
CMYK	Cyan, Magenta, Yellow, Black

As a rule, however, select the CMYK model to specify a process colour.

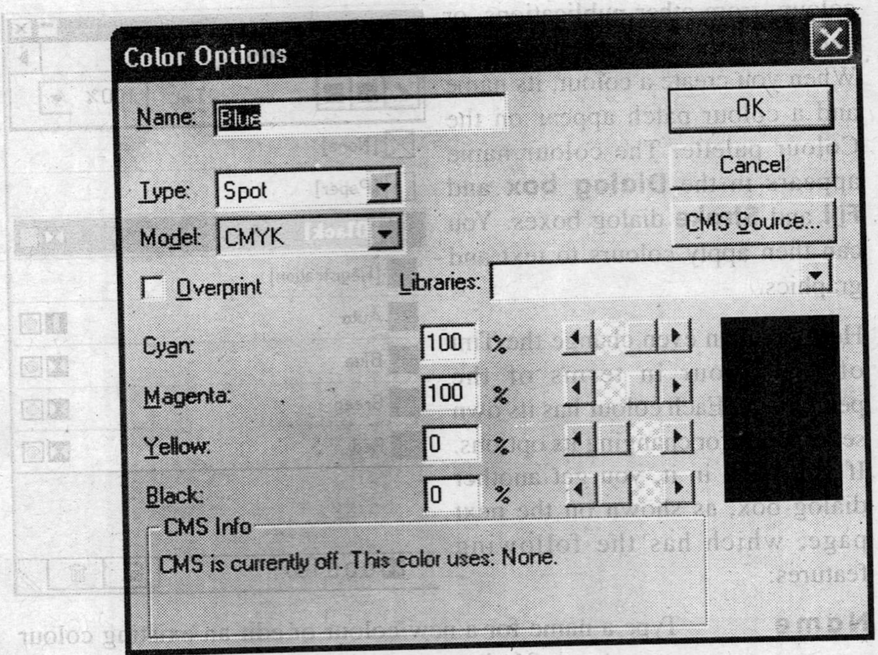

Overprint Select **Overprint** to specify that the colour you are creating will print over any colour that appear behind it. By default, when you print a colour, the colour knocks out colours behind it—which means that the top colour prints and the colour behind it do not print where the top colour overlaps them.

Libraries Select the name of a colour library to open that library. These are the standard ways for designers, ink manufacturers, and commercial printers to specify and print colours. PageMaker includes colour-matching systems from which your can choose colours: Crayons, Dic Colour Guide, FOCOLTONE, Greys, Online, PANTONE MATCHING SYSTEM, TOYO Colour Finder, and TRUMATCH.

When you select a colour library name, a dialog box appears that displays color swatches and names. To select a colour, do one of the following:

- Use the scroll bars to locate the colour you want. Click to select it.
- Use the arrow keys on your keyboard to move among the colour swatches.
- Type the name of the colour in the edit box to select the colour quickly.

Click Ok after you select a colour. To select multiple colours from a library, hold down the **Ctrl** key as you click the colour swatches.

Base colour Select the name of the spot or process colour on which to base the tint. You must specify a spot or process colour before you can specify a tint of it.

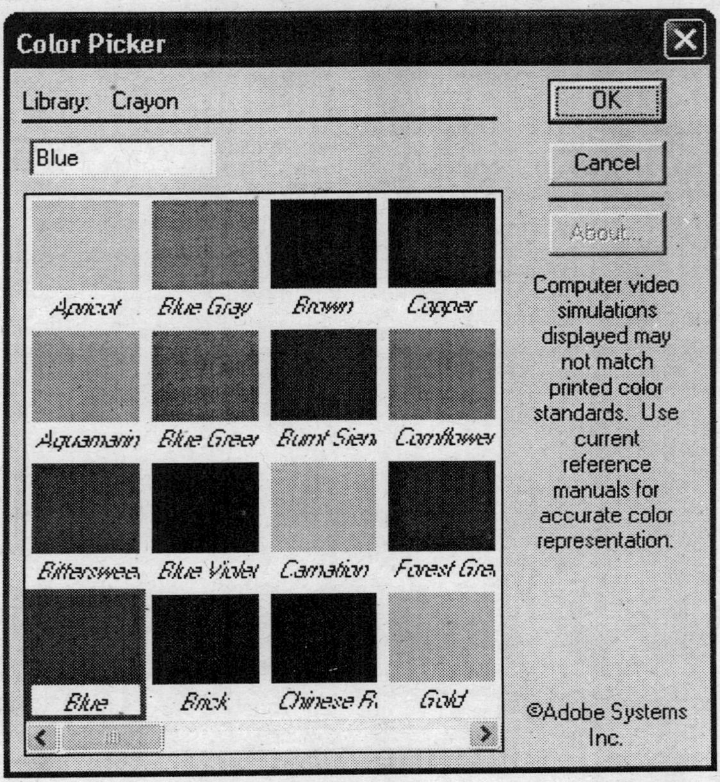

Tint Enter a percentage or adjust the colour value slider bar to specify the percentage of the tint. PageMaker lets you specify tints in 1% increments, but many commercial presses only print tints in 5% increments.

In the next chapter, we would learn about another new feature of PageMaker 7.0. It is called Layers.

6

WORKING WITH LAYERS

INTRODUCTION

Use of layers is a new concept in PageMaker, though it has been in use in software like Photoshop and Illustrator. In a publication you can have as many layers as your RAM allows you to have. Each page of the publication can have a layer. It is easy for you to hide one layer while working on another on the same page of the publication.

This way you can have the image and the text on the same page but sharing the different layers. This helps you in working with text without disturbing the image and vice versa.

NEW LAYER

To create a new layer, we have to do the following:

1. Call the layer palette on the screen by **Ctrl + 8**.

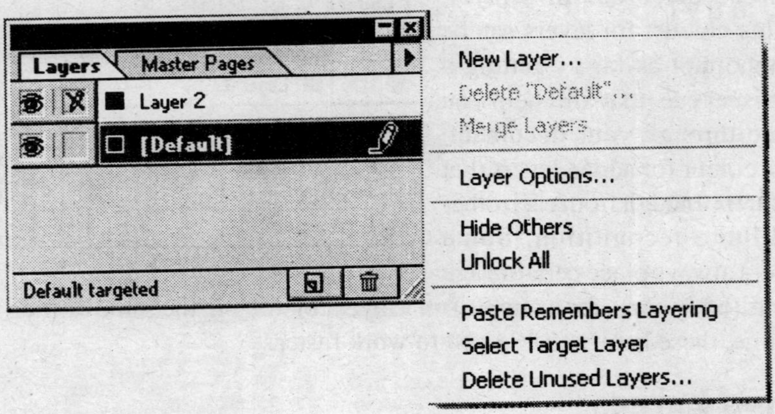

2. Click at right most corner button to get another menu, to click at **New Layer** to give rise to another menu.

3. In this **New Layer** dialog box, give the name of this new layer and select the colour for it.

4. You can also choose whether you want this layer to be seen or hidden by clicking at **Show layer**.

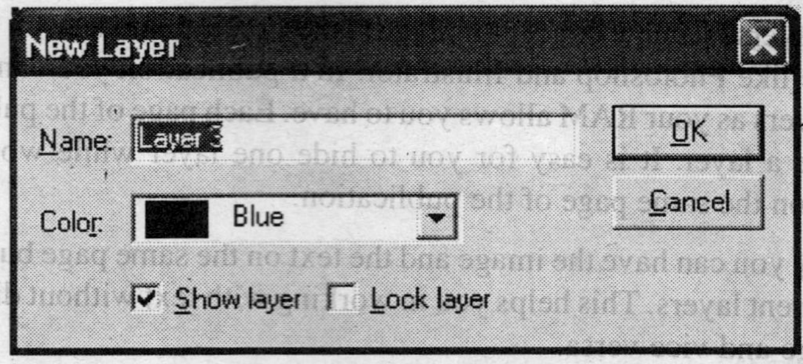

Once you have created a new layer, this layer will be shown on the layer palette as shown.

So now you have the second layer named as Layer 2 which you just created.

Let me add here the significance of the choice of colour in a layer. Choosing colours for layers can be very important as far as getting a quick visual cue that will help you navigate through your document. Choose colour for added layers that are different enough from each other to facilitate recognition. Some designers always place certain page elements (body copy, for example) on a layer coloured in the same fashion. Over time, these habits enable you to work faster.

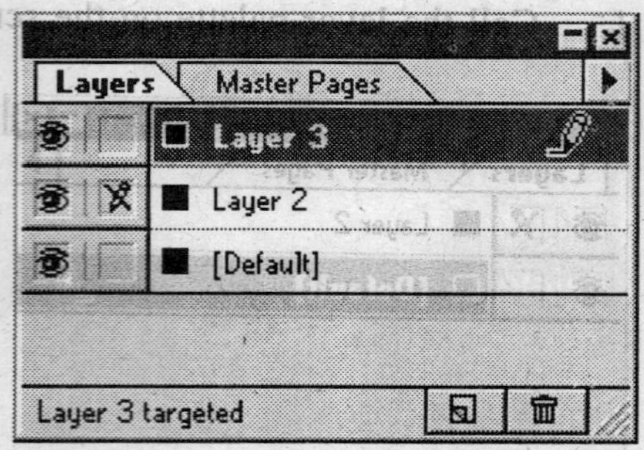

MOVING LAYERS

Using mouse click at the layer which you want to move. All the layers of objects move in accordance, placing them in a new order relative to objects on other layers. Pressing **Shift** and then selecting will help you in selecting more than one layer. When you drag two or more layers to a new position, they maintain their layer order relative to one another.

Hiding Layers

To hide a layer, click the icon to the left of the layer name. Drag up or down to affect other layers above or below the layer you first clicked. This turns off the **Show** option in the **Layer Options** dialog box for the selected layers. Click again to turn the option back on and redisplay a layer.

Deleting a Layer

To delete a layer, you can do the following:

1. Select the **layer name** which you want to delete in the layers palette.
2. Choose **Delete Layer** from the **Layers palette** menu, or click the **Trash** icon in the palette. You can also drag the layer to the Trash icon located on the Layers palette.
3. In the **Delete Layer** dialog box, select an option:
   - Click **Assign Items From Deleted Layer To**, and choose the name of the layer to which you want the objects moved.
   - Click **Delete Items on All Pages From Layer** to remove all objects throughout the publication assigned to that layer.

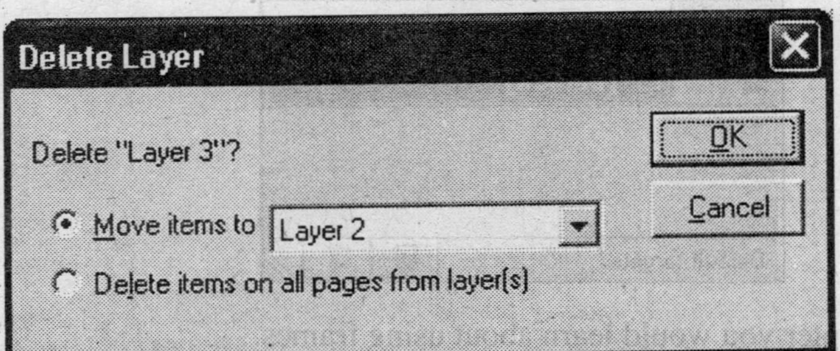

Deleting Layers without Objects

When you close the **Layer Options** dialog box, it checks for blank layers and point out the same and asks whether you want to delete that

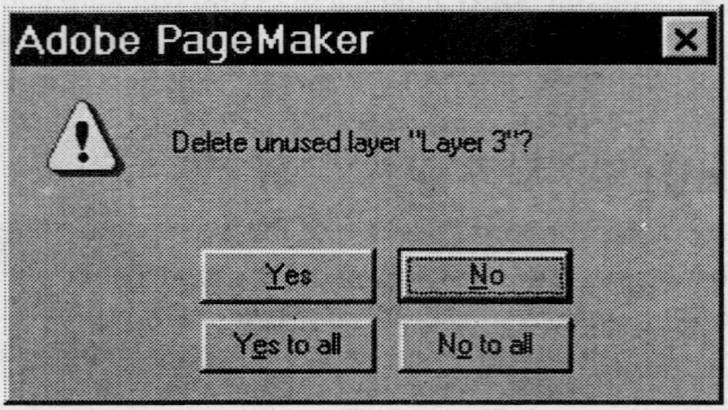

layer. If you want to delete that layer or all the other unused layers too, click at the required button for deleting and close the dialog box.

Locking a Layer

To lock a layer, you can do the following:

1. Click the **Pencil** icon to the left of the layer name.
2. Drag up or down to lock other layers above or below the first layer you clicked. This turns on the **Lock** option in the Layer Options dialog box for the selected layers.
3. Click again to turn off the option and unlock a layer.

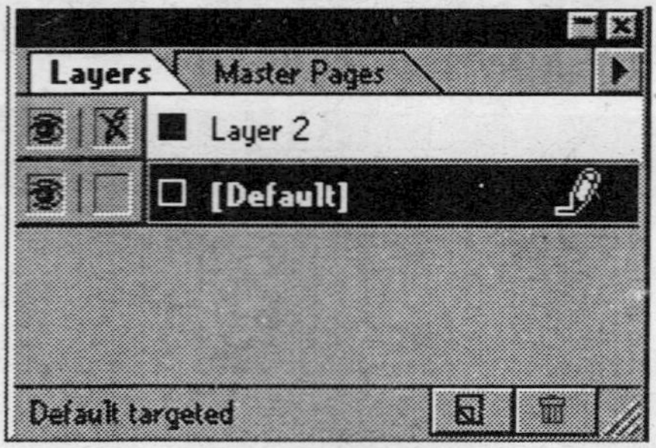

In the next chapter you would learn about using frames.

7

USING FRAMES

INTRODUCTION

PageMaker's frames option is brand new and it gives the professional user an expanded list of page composition possibilities. To begin with, it's important to understand the difference between frames and strokes, because the two are often confused.

A stroke is a border around a surrounded text block or selected graphic. PageMaker's strokes are configured in the Stroke and Fill and Stroke dialog boxes. A stroked area is sometimes called a "framed" area in common parlance and this is exactly where the confusion comes in. A frame in PageMaker means something quite different. A frame is an area that acts as a receptacle for text of a graphic. It may or may not have a stroked border. The most common use for a frame where graphics are concerned is to allow the page designer to adjust the cropping of a selected graphic as it is placed in a frame.

PageMaker enables you to configure three types of frames:

Rectangular

Oval

Polygonal

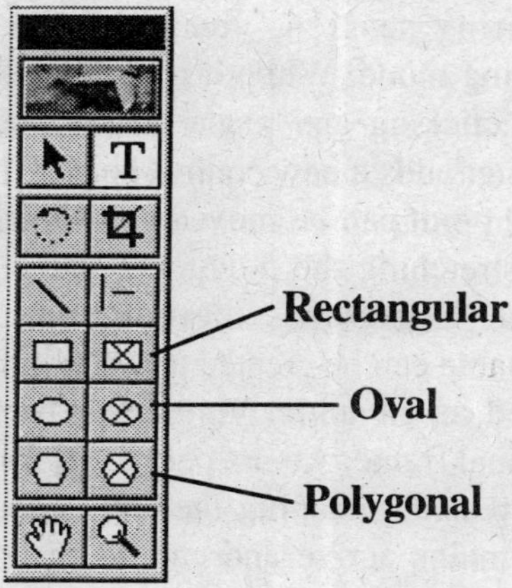

The three frame icons in PageMaker's Toolbox (Rectangle, Oval and Polygon) have an "X" drawn through them to distinguish them from their non-frame shape counterparts. When a frame is placed on a page it continues to have an X drawn through it (blue by default) so that frame shapes can be distinguished from similar non-frame shapes.

CREATING FRAMES

Polygons (whether standard polygons or polygonal frames) can be created by a click-and-move method. Instead of clicking a point and then dragging out a polygonal shape at the start, a clear rectangular box appears around the point of the cursor. Clicking at that point finishes the shape. Either method (click then drag than edit or click then move) can produce very complex polygonal shapes. If this is a polygonal frame, the resulting shape can be used as a shaped environment for attached text or graphics.

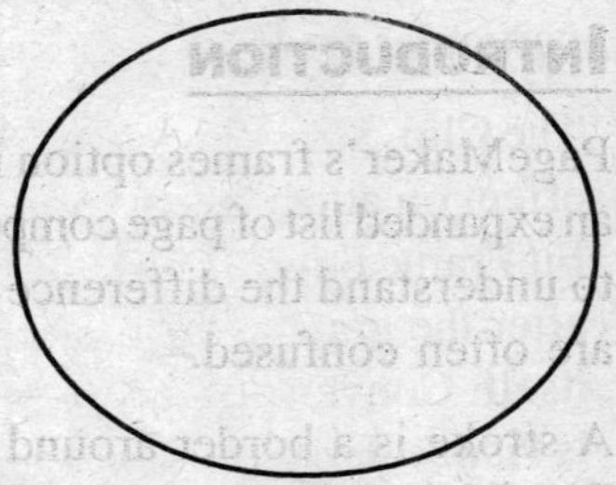

EDITING FRAMES

The Rectangular and Oval frames maintain their general shape proportions no matter how they are resized. The Polygon frame is the only one of the three that is adjustable. By double-clicking any side of the polygon frame at any time during an editing session, you can activate its reshaping mode. While it is in the reshaping mode, clicking any place on the polygon's perimeter adds a new control point. This new control point can be moved anywhere on the page, stretching the polygon's shape as it is moved. Using this method, any shape imaginable can be created and any image can be used as an underlying from for a new polygonal frame. After a polygonal frame has been created, attaching the text is easy. The text remains active and can be resized and manipulated even after it is attached to a frame, as long as it doesn't become so big that it breaks the bonds of the frame.

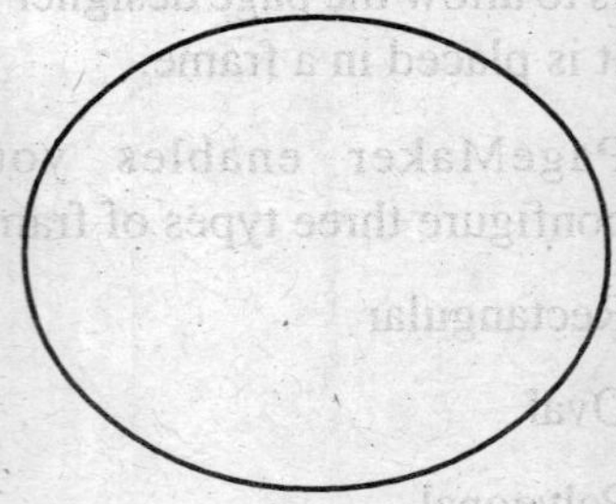

THE FRAME OPTIONS DIALOG BOX

The Frame Options dialog box is opened by selecting Frame Options from the frame submenu in the Element menu. If you alter the settings here before any frame is drawn onscreen, the settings will apply initially to all frames. If a frame is selected first, the settings will apply to only that particular frame. Frame settings can be altered at any time.

The Clip, Sizing and Scaling options found in this dialog box have little or no effect on attached text and refer to attached graphics. The Clip Content to Fit Frame option clips the graphic to the frame size. If you resize the frame after the graphic is attached, the attached graphic displays a larger part of itself. Conversely, if you shrink the frame, a smaller portion of the graphic is visible. Even after the graphics are in the frame, you can use the Cropping tool to move them around to achieve the best composition.

The Size Frame to Fit Content option expands the frame to fit the exact size of the graphic. Resizing the frame afterward displays either the blank space around the graphic or cuts off part of the graphic display. Scale Content to fit Frame reduces or enlarges the graphic to the frame size. If Maintain Aspect Ratio is checked, the frame is resized to the graphic's

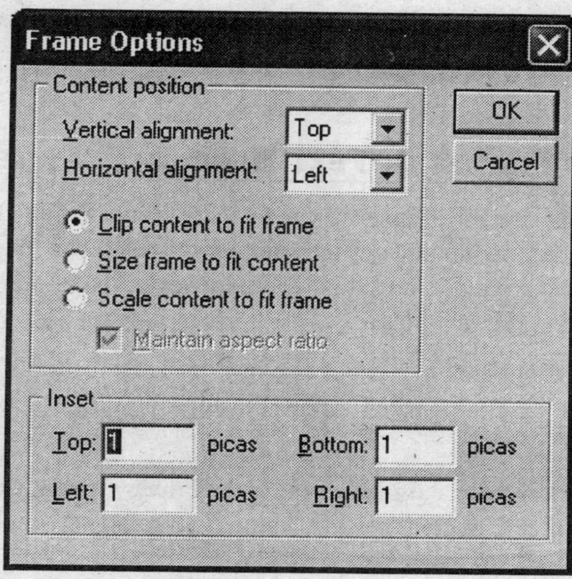

aspect ratio as well. If it is not checked, the graphic is stretched to fit the frame.

The insert distances and the alignment for Vertical (Top, Bottom, Center) and Horizontal (Left, Center, Right) also can be adjust. This has no effect on attached text, but is targeted to attached graphics. The Fill and Stroke options can be applied to any selected frame.

Frames with Tighter Text Fits

Follow the following steps to do this.

1. Attach your text to a rectangular frame and adjust the frame to get the right general alignment. Set the stroke (border of the frame) to "Paper Color" so that it becomes invisible.
2. Copy the frame with the text to the Clipboard.
3. Choose Paste Special from the Edit menu and paste the frame and text back to the screen as a WMF graphic.
4. Draw a new frame and attach the WMF graphic to it. Now when you adjust the frame, you will be able to get the frame borders much closer to the text.

Text placed in a frame can always be restyled or resized with the Text tool. Just select the text area by dragging the text cursor over it and apply the necessary changes.

Combining Frames in Text Blocks

PageMaker requires a little maneuvering to place frames as inline graphics in a text block, because all that are accepted for inline use are true graphics formats. There is a way around this taboo, however, using the tools that PageMaker offers. Here's how:

1. Bring your text block to a page. Use one of the frame tools to draw a frame and set it aside. Place (import) the appropriate graphic and set it aside.
2. Double-click the place frame, opening the Frame Options dialog box. Make sure that Clip content to fit frame is selected and click OK.

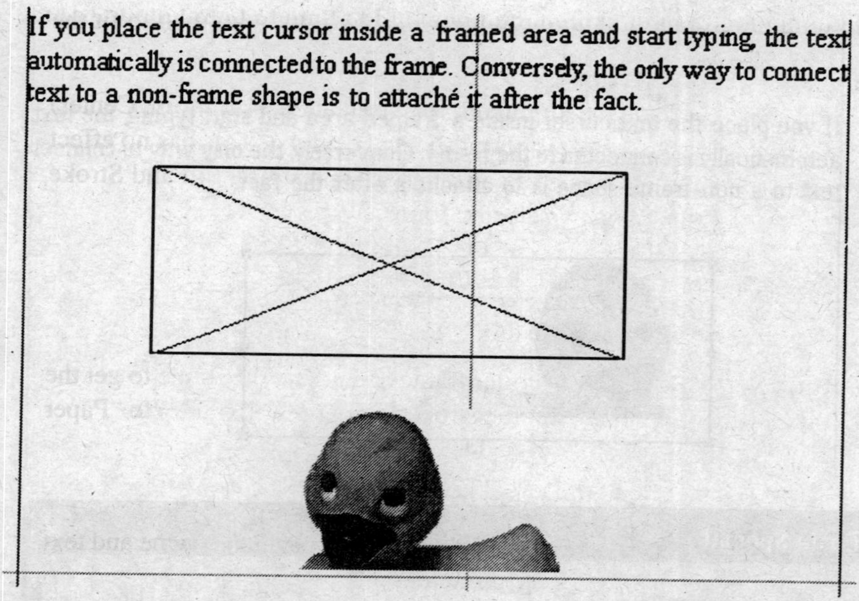

3. Select the frame and then press Shift while selecting the graphic. Choose Attach Content. The graphic becomes part of the frame.
4. Copy the framed graphic to the Clipboard .
5. Notice that the graphic fits the frame proportionately.
6. Choose Paste Special from the Edit menu. In the dialog box that appears, select WMF and click OK.
7. The pasted graphic now appears on the screen. Select it and copy it to the Clipboard. Place the text cursor at any place in your text that you would like the inline graphic to appear and select the Paste command. The graphics that are placed in the text are inline graphics and are now a permanent part of the text block.

TEXT FRAMES

Although you can use any of the frame shapes to enclose attached text, the most common choice is the rectangle. This imposes the least surprises on the text when you reconfigure the shape of the frame. The least common is the oval, because this frame shape of the frame. The least common is the

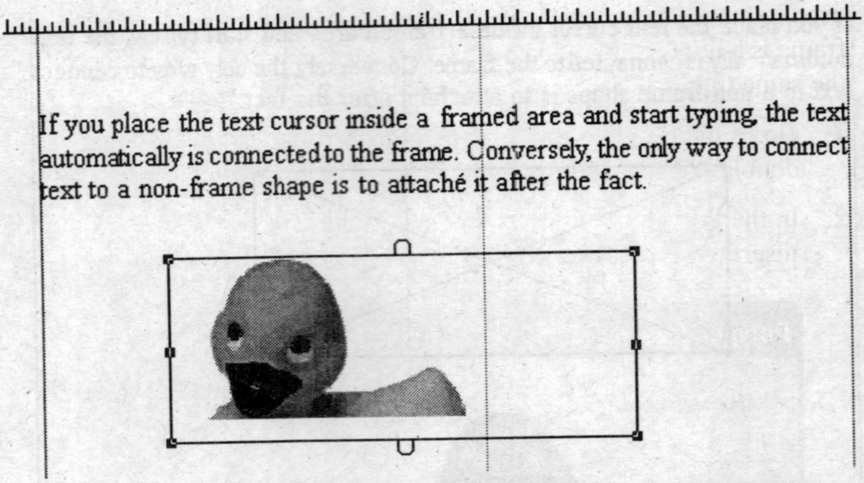

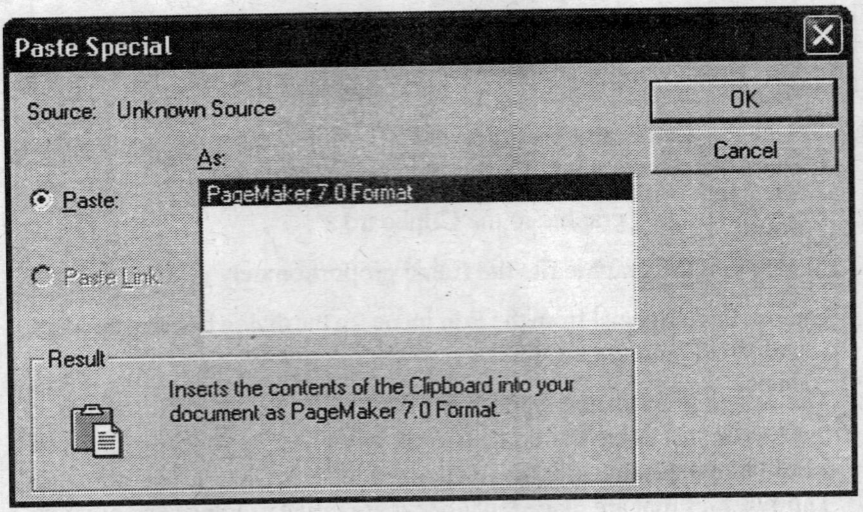

oval, because this frame shape imposes unexpected changes on the incorporated text. The polygon frame is a special case. By attaching text to a polygonal frame, the text can be altered in ways that make this a possible substitute for wrapping text around an image. If the polygonal frame's border is changed to the paper color (rendering it invisible), the reconfigured text inside takes on the altered shape of the polygon without you or your audience being able to see the frame. In this way, the polygon frame can be used to control text without it being obvious. Reconfiguring a polygonal frame is a little simpler than using the PageMaker text wrap process to do the same thing. Here's how to proceed:

1. Go to the Polygon tool in the Toolbox (not the Polygon Frame) and double-click it. This opens the Polygon Settings dialog box.
2. In the Polygon Settings dialog box, set the sides to four and the Star Insert to 0%. Click OK.

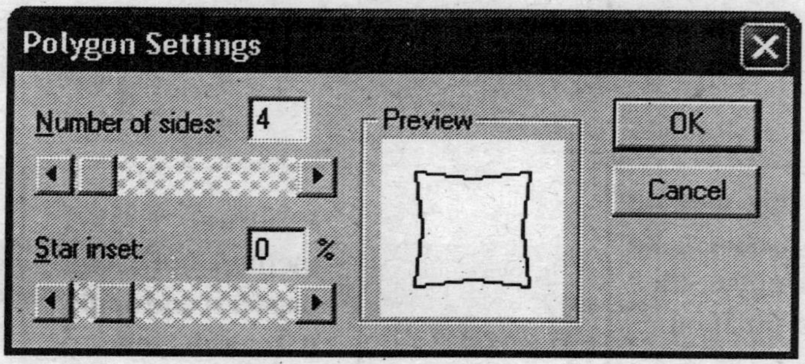

3. Select the Polygon Frame tool from the Toolbox and draw a shape on the page. Notice that it looks like a simple rectangle, which is the best frame to start with when working with text. Select both the frame shape and your text block and Attach the text to the frame (Attach Content command found in the Frame submenu in the Element menu).
4. Adjust the frame as needed, which moves words in your text to alternate lines.
5. Double-click the frame, activating the Polygon Reshaping operation. Click one on any side of the polygon frame, which places anew control point at that spot. Adjust the polygon shape and watch how the tex responds. Explore this method until you master it and apply it to any needed text wrap situation.

Explore this method until you master it and apply it to any needed text wrap situation.

Explore this method until you master it and apply it to any needed text wrap situation.

Explore this method until you master it and apply it to any needed

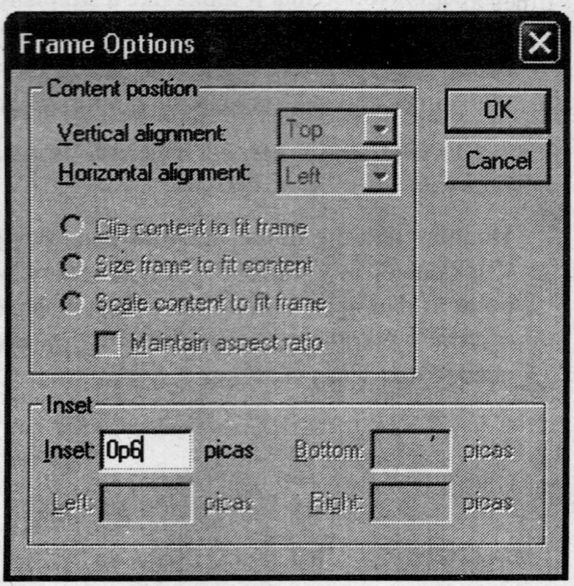

8

WORKING WITH DATAMERGE

INTRODUCTION

To create form letters, envelopes, or mailing labels, you merge a data source file with a target publication.

The *data source file* contains the information that varies in each version of a merged publication, such as the names and addresses of the recipients of a form letter. A data source file can be a text file or a comma-delimited file created in a spreadsheet or database application.

The *target publication* is a PageMaker document that includes the data field placeholders and the text and other items that remain the same in each version of the merged publication.

The *merged publication* is the resulting PageMaker document that contains the boilerplate information from the target publication repeated as many times as it takes to display each record from the data source.

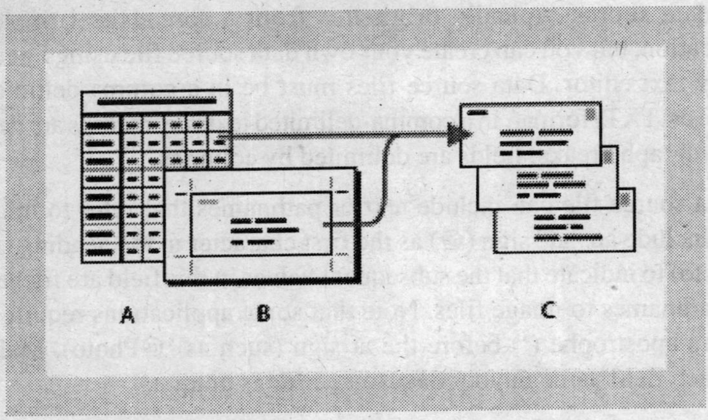

A. Data stored in a spreadsheet or database

B. Boilerplate information in a target publication.

C. Merged Publications

In the data source file, *data fields* are the columns of specific information, such as "First name" or "Address." *Records* are the rows that contain a complete set of information for the target publication.

PLANNING A DATA MERGE

Before you set up your target publication, determine what you want the final publication to look like, so that you know which fields are necessary to accomplish the merge. For example, if you are creating a postcard that will be mailed to customers, you may want to use the following data fields:

<<First Name>> <<Last Name>> <<Company>> <<Address>> <<City>>, <<State>> <<Postal Code>>

Make sure that your data source file is structured in such a way that you can include the appropriate fields in your target publication. For example, the top row of a spreadsheet should contain the field names, such as Company and Address, that you'll use in the target publication.

WORKING WITH DATA SOURCE FILES

The data source typically originates from a spreadsheet or database application, but you can create your own data source file using PageMaker or any text editor. Data source files must be in a comma-delimited text (.CSV or .TXT) format. In a comma-delimited text file, records are delimited by paragraph breaks; fields are delimited by columns.

A data source file can include text or pathnames that refer to images on disk. Include an "at" sign (@) as the first character in the heading (such as @Photo) to indicate that the subsequent values in this field are filenames or full pathnames to image files. Note that some applications require you to type an apostrophe (') before the at sign (such as '@Photo). Make sure that each field name in your data source file is unique.

To save an existing data source file as a comma-delimited file:

1. Open the data source file in its original spreadsheet or database application.

2. Make sure that the file is organized for the merge to occur. In spreadsheet files, the names in the top row will become the data field names you add to your target publication. In database files, the table field names will become the data field names.

3. Use the Save As feature to save the file as a comma-delimited file.

SETTING UP THE TARGET PUBLICATION

Once your data source file is created, you need to set up the target publication and insert the fields from the data source file. The target publication contains boilerplate text and graphics—such as the design that you want to appear on every postcard—as well as the fields from the data source.

The target publication includes fields from the data source.

When you merge data, PageMaker creates a new publication that replaces the fields with the data you designated in the data source file.

MERGING RECORDS

After you format the target publication and insert fields from the data source file, you're ready to merge the information from the data source with the target publication.

When you merge, PageMaker creates a new publication and replaces the fields in the target publication with the appropriate information from the data source file.

To merge records:

1. With the target publication open, choose Merge Records from the Data Merge palette menu, or choose Utilities > Plug-ins > Merge Records.

2. For Record Range, select All Records to merge all records in the data

file, select Current Record to merge only the currently previewed record, or specify a Range of records to merge.

3. For Records Per Page, do one of the following:
   - Select One Record Per Page so that each record starts at the top of the next page.
   - Select Manual Layout, and then specify the spacing between columns and rows to determine how many records will be tiled on a page.
4. Select Remove Blank Lines for Empty Fields to remove lines on which empty fields appear by themselves. This option is especially useful for optional fields such as <<Company>>. In this example, if the data source file does not include a company name in any record, a blank line may appear in the middle of an address.
5. Select Embed Images to embed placeholder images rather than linking to them.
6. Select Start New Publication After X Pages to allow additional publications to be created, and then specify the maximum number of pages allowed in a merge publication; click OK.

Remember the following:

- You can edit and save the data source file in its original application while the source file is still open in the Data Merge palette. After updating and saving the data source file in comma-delimited format, the changes will be reflected in the Data Merge palette. However, it's a good idea to turn off Preview.

  If the data source file has any unsupported image filenames or if the image files are not accessible by Data Merge, then merging will terminate at that point to prevent erroneous data in the merged publication.

  Data source files created in Windows may not always work in Mac OS, and vice versa. For example, the full pathname for an image in a data source file created in Windows will not be recognized in Mac OS.

9

Using Scripts

Introduction

PageMaker includes a number of scripts in a Scripts folder. You can use the Scripts palette to run these scripts as they are, customize them for your specific needs, create your own scripts, and trace scripts command by command.

The Scripts palette displays the contents of the PageMaker Scripts folder, including any subfolders. When you add a script to the Scripts folder, it automatically appears on the Scripts palette. Find the Scripts folder in the following location:

Program Files\Adobe\PageMaker7.0\RSRC\<language>\Plugins

Running scripts

Scripts that you want to run from the Scripts palette must be stored in the Scripts folder. The Scripts palette can automatically copy scripts to this folder.

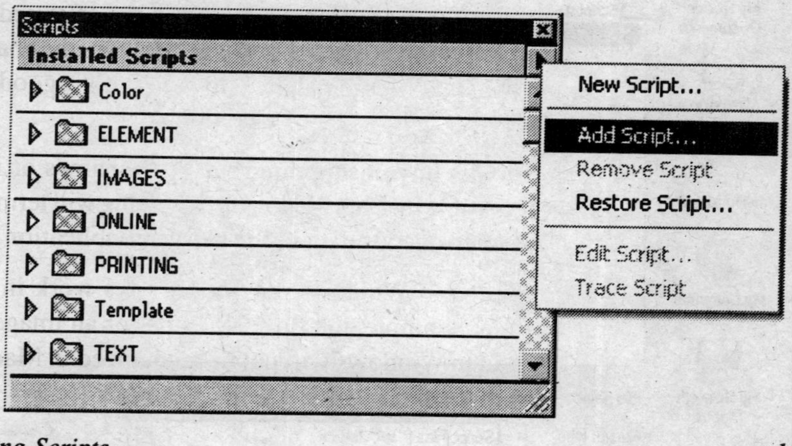

To run a script:

1. Choose Window > Plug-in Palettes > Show Scripts to display the Scripts palette.
2. Double-click a script to run it.

Adding and Removing Scripts

You can add scripts to the Scripts palette either by using the Add Script command on the Scripts palette menu or copying scripts to the Scripts folder. You can also add scripts by dragging and dropping files to the palette.

You can also remove scripts from the Scripts palette. When you remove a script, you merely prevent it from being displayed on the palette; the script file itself is not deleted. Scripts you remove from the palette are moved into the ScriptsD folder. To redisplay a script you've removed from the palette, use the Restore command.

To add a script using the Scripts palette:

1. Choose Add Script from the Scripts palette menu.

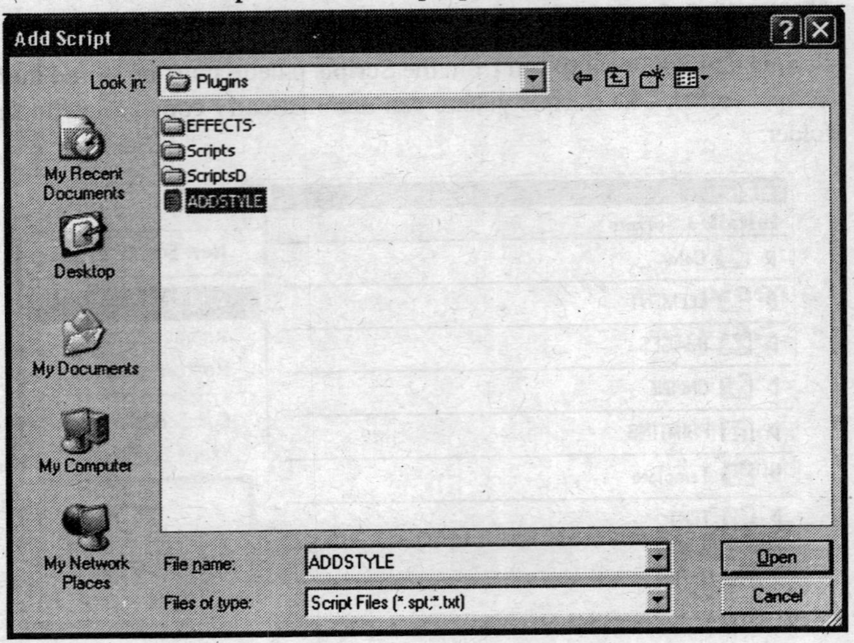

2. In the Add a Script dialog box, select a script, and then click Open.

The script you choose is automatically copied to the Scripts folder and appears in the Scripts palette.

To add a script by dragging and dropping files:

Select a file from the desktop or from Windows Explorer, drag the file over a folder in the Scripts palette, and release the mouse button.

To remove a script from the Scripts palette:

1. Select a script in the Scripts palette. You can remove only one script at a time.

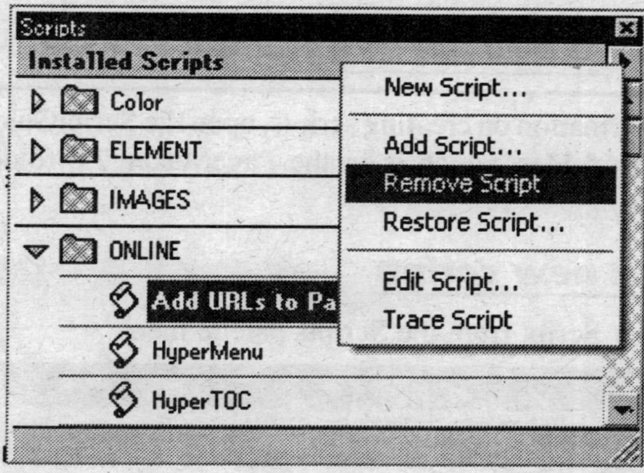

2. Choose Remove Script from the Scripts palette menu.

To restore a script that has been removed from the Scripts palette:

1. C[illegible] Restore Script from the Scripts palette menu.
2. From the list of removed scripts, select a script and click the Restore button.

Creating and editing scripts

You can use the New Script command to create new scripts, and then edit them using the Edit Script command.

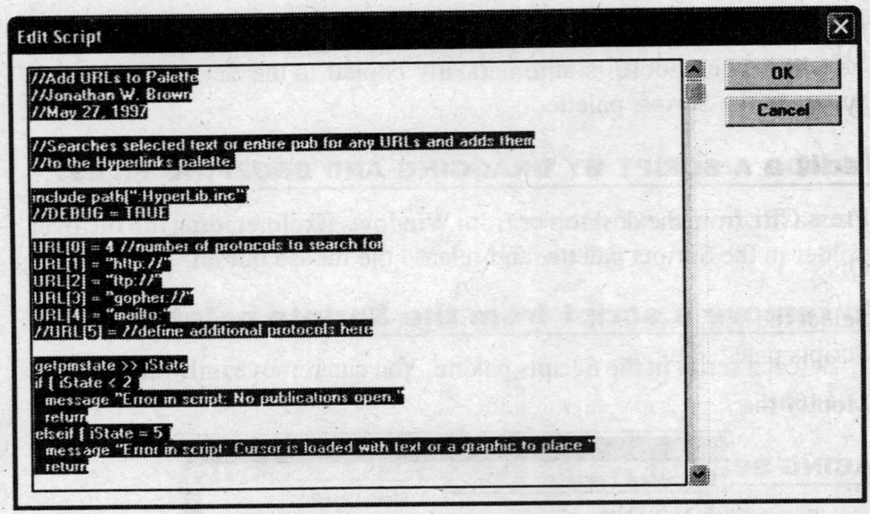

For detailed information on creating scripts, open the ScriptGuide.PDF file in the Tech Info folder, which is in the PageMaker 7.0 folder on your hard drive.

To create a new script:

1. Choose New Script from the Scripts palette menu.

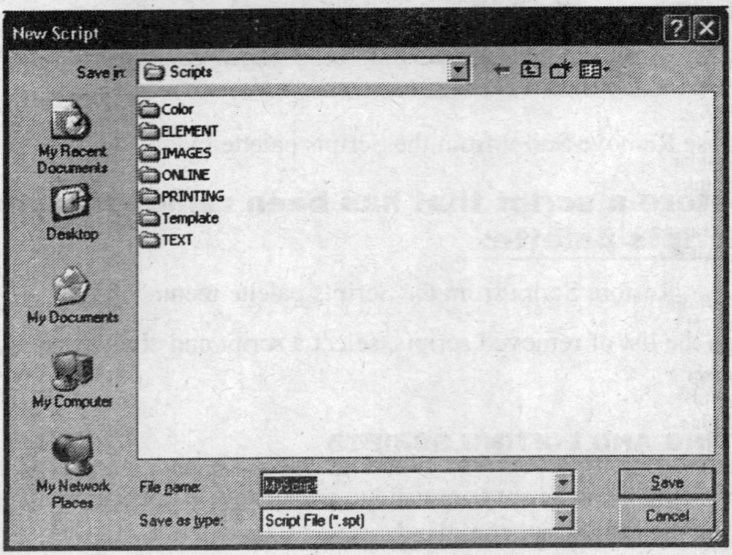

2. Name the script, specify a location in the Scripts folder, and then click OK.
3. Write the new script in the Edit Script dialog box, and then click OK.

To edit a script:

1. Press Ctrl, and click the script.

   Or

   Select the script in the Scripts palette and choose Edit Script from the Scripts palette menu.
2. Modify the script, and then click OK.

TRACING SCRIPTS

Use the Trace Script command to run your script command by command, so that you can see where any problems might be occurring.

To trace a script:

1. Select a script in the Scripts palette.

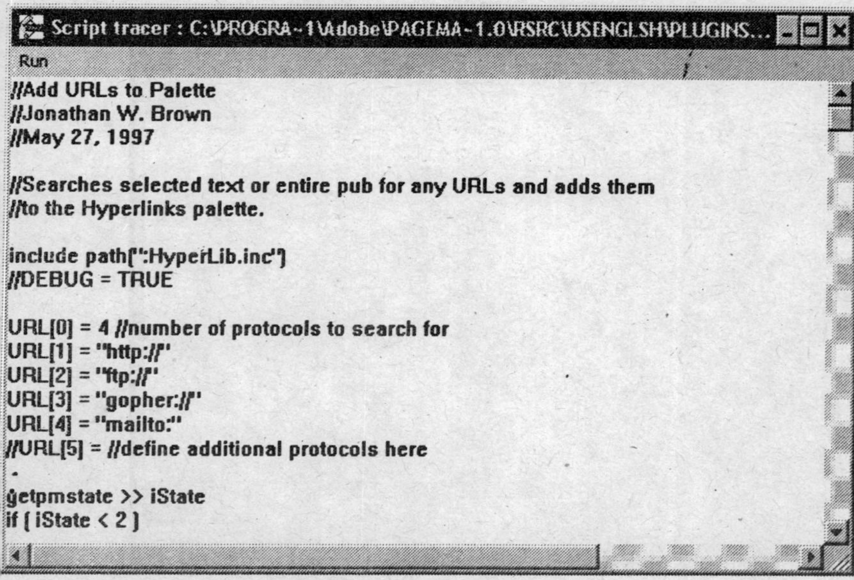

2. Choose Trace Script from the Scripts palette menu.
3. In the Trace Script window, choose one of the following from the Run menu:

- *Run* runs the entire script.
- *Step* runs the script one line at a time.
- *Step Out* runs a series of command subroutines at one time.
- *Reset* stops the script from running without closing the Trace window.
- *Quit* stops the script from running, and closes the Trace window.

10

Working with Colours

Introduction

Each PageMaker publication contains its own collection of colours, available through the Colours palette. In addition to using default colours, you can define colours from scratch, select from a colour-matching system installed with PageMaker, copy from another publication, or import with an EPS graphic.

When you add a colour to a publication, its name appears in alphabetical order on the Colours palette and in any dialog box, such as the Fill and Stroke dialog box, that lists colours.

When you define a colour, you specify whether it is a spot colour, a process colour, or a tint (lightened tones) of a spot or process colour. You can also select predefined spot, process, and high-fidelity colours from colour-matching systems installed with PageMaker, such as the Trumatch® colour library and the PANTONE MATCHING SYSTEM®.

Whether you're specifying a spot or process colour or selecting a colour from a library, do not select a colour based on how it looks on your colour monitor unless you are working with a colour management system supported by PageMaker and you understand its limitations. To specify accurate colours, always use the values printed on process-colour charts or the inks printed in spot and high-fidelity colour swatch books.

Applying colours

You can apply colours and tints to many different objects, including text and graphics created in PageMaker, and monochrome or grayscale bitmap images (such as TIFF images) or EPS graphics that you import into PageMaker.

As with any other text or graphic attribute, you can set the colour for the text and graphics you draw in PageMaker as you create them. For example, you can set text colour in the Character Specifications dialog box for a story you are about to type. Or, you can apply the colour at any time after the text in an object has been created.

To apply colour to most objects (lines, text, and certain imported images), you simply select the text or the object, and then click the colour name in the Colours palette. Applying colour to rectangles, polygons, or ellipses (including frames) drawn in PageMaker involves slightly different steps, because you can apply colours separately to the stroke and the fill of those shapes.

In some instances, you might want to use the Element>Fill and Stroke command rather than the Colours palette. You can use this command to apply fill and stroke colours for rectangles, polygons, or ellipses (including frames); specify whether the stroke or fill of the object should overprint; and set an object-level tint for either the stroke or the fill.

When you apply a colour to an imported EPS graphic, the colour of the graphic does not change on-screen; however, the graphic prints on the separations of the applied spot or process colour. If you remove a colour applied in PageMaker, PageMaker uses the colour information in the imported EPS graphic to determine on which separations it prints.

Use the Colours palette to apply colours or view the name or kind of colour applied to the selected text or graphic.

Icons to the right of color names indicate model—RGB ( ), HLS ( ), CMYK ( ), or multiple ink ( )—and type: Spot ( ) or Process ( ). To hide these, choose the bottommost commands on the palette menu.

To apply a colour with the Colours palette:

1. Select the object or text you want to colour.

   You must select text with the text tool to apply colour to it.

2. Choose Window > Show Colours.
3. If you selected a frame or a rectangle, polygon, or ellipse in Step 1, specify whether you want to change the stroke, fill, or both.
4. Click the name of the colour you want to apply.

5. Optionally, to adjust the percentage of colour applied, select a percentage from the Tint menu in the palette to apply an object-level tint.

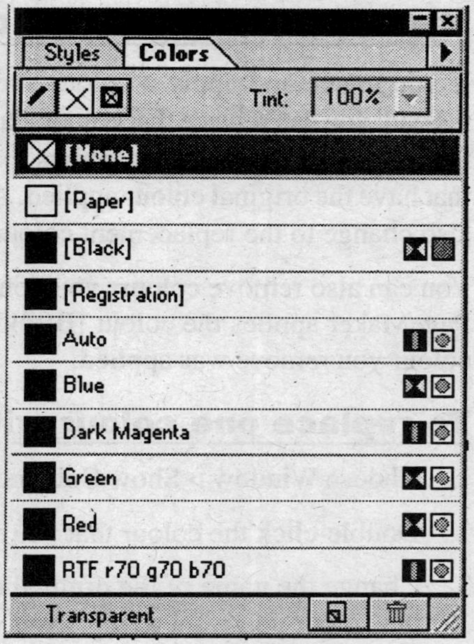

To apply a colour with the Fill and Stroke command:

1. Select the object.
2. Choose Element > Fill and Stroke.
3. Select the type of fill or stroke you want. For more information, see Changing strokes and fills.
4. Select colours for the fill and stroke.
5. Optionally, to adjust the percentage of colour applied, type a percentage or choose one from the Tint menu to apply an object-level tint.
6. Select the Overprint option if you want to make a stroke or fill print over coloured objects placed behind it when imaging colour separations or colour composites, and then click OK.

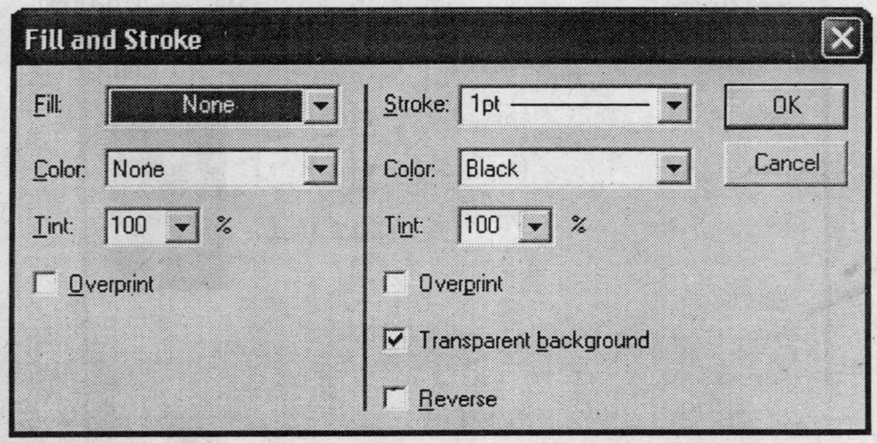

REPLACING AND REMOVING COLOURS

If you create and apply a colour and then decide to use another colour instead, you can replace that colour. PageMaker removes the original colour from your publication and applies the replacement colour to any objects that have the original colour applied. Any tints based on the original colour also change to the replacement colour.

You can also remove colours you don't need. When you remove a colour, PageMaker applies the colour [Black] to any text or graphic to which the colour you remove was applied.

To replace one colour with another:

1. Choose Window > Show Colours.
2. Double-click the colour that you want to replace.
3. Change the name of the original colour to exactly match the name of the colour you want to replace it with, and then click OK.

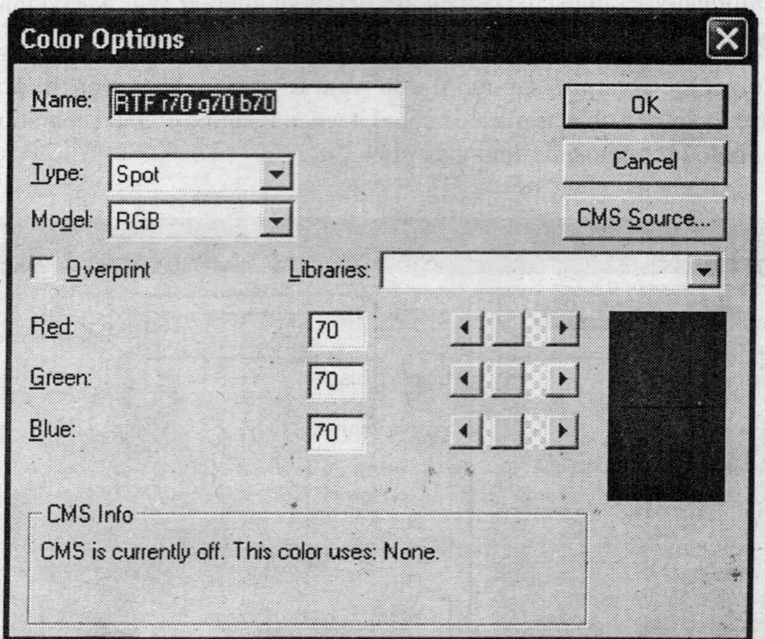

4. When PageMaker displays an alert message asking you to confirm the change of colours, click OK.

To remove a colour from an object:

1. Select the object.
2. For PageMaker-drawn rectangles, polygons, and ellipses (including frames), use the fill and stroke buttons to specify whether it is the fill or stroke colour you want to remove.
3. Click the [None] option in the Colours palette.

To remove colours from a publication:

1. Choose Window > Show Colours.
2. Do one of the following:

   Click a colour that you want to remove, and choose Delete Colour from the Colours palette menu.

   Drag the colour from the palette to the Trash button () at the bottom of the palette.

   Choose Remove Unused Colours from the palette menu to delete all colours not applied in the publication (including unused inks specified as part of a high-fidelity colour). When you select Remove Unused Colours, a dialog box appears in which you can choose to remove all unused colours at once, or one by one. Alternatively, you can remove unused inks when you print. Just click the Remove Unused button in the Print Colour section of the Print dialog box.

EDITING A COLOUR

As with paragraph styles, when you edit a colour, PageMaker automatically updates any objects to which you applied the colour. You can even edit the ink values for a high-fidelity colour, but the colour adjustments appear only on the colour separations—the appearance of the colour on the screen and in a composite proof does not change.

You can edit the definition of a spot colour imported with an EPS graphic, but you cannot change its name or its Overprint setting.

To edit a spot or process colour:

1. Choose Window > Show Colours.
2. Double-click the name of the colour you want to edit.
3. Change the name, colour, or overprint specifications, and then click OK.

When editing a colour, you can switch its type from Spot to Process, or vice versa. However, some spot colours, like metallic gold, cannot be reproduced accurately with process inks. If you choose to convert a spot colour to process, you may need to adjust the resulting colour values (using a printed swatch book as a reference) for the converted spot colour to print as you expect.

To switch a spot colour to a process colour, or vice versa:

1. Deselect all objects, and choose Window > Show Colours.
2. Click the name of the colour that you want to change.
3. Choose the Convert to Process or Convert to Spot command from the Colours palette menu.

Working with imported EPS colours

You can choose what kinds of colours are imported with an EPS graphic, as well as with native Adobe Illustrator files you import directly. Since all spot and process colours defined in the document that generated the EPS are embedded with the EPS graphic, the control PageMaker provides can limit the kinds of colours added to your publication.

PageMaker also lets you edit individual spot colours imported with an EPS graphic. By editing spot colours in an EPS file so that they merge with colours already in your publication, you reduce the number of colour separations PageMaker will produce, and save time and money.

To control the colours imported with an EPS graphic:

1. Choose File > Place.
2. Select the EPS file you want to import.

3. Press Shift as you double-click the filename. (You do not need to press Shift if the Show Filter Preferences option is selected.)
4. In the dialog box, select options to specify the kinds of colours to include.

   The Add Process and High Fidelity Colour Names to Palette option adds the process and high-fidelity colours to the Colours palette.

   In the Preview Options section, select the preference you want. If you are printing to a device other than a PostScript printer, you can experiment with values greater than the 72 dpi default setting (the optimum value depends on your printer's dpi setting), and select Millions of Colours. Another reason to use higher resolution and greater colour depth is if you are exporting to HTML or PDF (where the exported image is derived from the screen preview).

   The Import Nested DCS Images for Separations option includes all of the colour and image data PageMaker requires to colour-separate DCS images embedded in the EPS graphic. If this option is not selected, PageMaker prints a low-resolution version of the DCS image to a single colour plate.

   The Add Spot Colour Names to Palette option ensures that PageMaker has accurate colour data to spot-colour-separate the EPS graphic.

   The Exclude Spot Colour Names option converts the spot colours to their CMYK equivalents during printing. Use this option if you want process-colour separations only, and if it is acceptable that the process equivalents do not exactly match the original spot colours.

If you import an EPS colour that has the same name as a colour in your publication, PageMaker displays an alert. If you press Cancel, PageMaker does not import the colour or list it in the palette. When you print, however, the EPS colour images on the correct separation. If you click OK, PageMaker replaces the colour in your publication with the EPS colour.

To edit a spot colour in an imported EPS file:

1. Choose Window > Show Colours.

2. Double-click the name of the colour you want to edit.

3. Do one of the following:

   To change the spot colour's definition, edit the percentages of its colour components (CMYK, RGB, or HLS).

   - To make the spot colour a process colour, choose Process from the Type pop-up menu.
   - To merge an EPS spot colour with another colour, choose Tint from the Type pop-up menu, and then select another colour as its base colour. Accept the default of 100% for the tint percentage. This makes the spot-coloured areas of the EPS file print on the same separation as the base colour.

4. Click OK to save your changes.

Changes you make to imported EPS spot colours apply when you print on a PostScript printer with the Preserve EPS Colours option deselected in the Print Colour dialog box (File > Print). When Preserve EPS Colours is selected, EPS files print using their original colours. This option is not available when printing to a device other than a PostScript printer.

OVERPRINTING COLOURS

When you print overlapping colour -objects on a printing press, you typically want the top object to print and the bottom object not to print where the top -object overlaps it. In other words, you want the top object to knock out the bottom object.

In some cases, however, you do want a spot or process colour to overprint another colour—to compensate for misregistration, the unintentional gap or hue shift that occurs when colours printed from separate plates are misaligned on the printed piece.

When imaging separations from PageMaker, all graphics, whether you create them in PageMaker or import them from other programs, knock out -objects behind them by default. Black text, however, overprints by default, provided its type size is smaller than 24 point. There are several ways to override the default behavior, if you need to. You can:

Overprint the fill or stroke of a particular object (called object-level overprinting). Use the Element > Fill and Stroke command to set over printing as a fill or stroke attribute. See Applying colours for more information.

Overprint a colour wherever it is applied (colour-level overprinting). Use the Colour Options dialog box to specify that a colour overprints. Then all objects—imported images, lines, ellipses, polygons, rectangles, even text—to which that colour is applied will overprint. See Specifying a spot or process colour or Editing a colour for more information.

Specify that all black strokes, or all black fills, or all black text (below a certain point size) either overprints or knockouts. Use the File > Preferences > Trapping Options command to control how black objects print. See Applying colours and Trapping black for more information.

To overprint a colour to some objects but not to others, you can create a 100% tint of the colour, and set the tint to overprint and the base colour to knock out. (This technique does not work for black objects set to overprint with the Auto-overprint settings in the Trapping Preferences dialog box.)

When PageMaker traps a publication, it does not trap objects set to overprint. Make sure that you understand the requirements for producing your publication before you override overprinting defaults.

Trapping Colours

In commercial printing, it is crucial to anticipate *misregistration*, a situation in which adjacent colours shift slightly to overlap or leave a gap. When imaging separations to PostScript output devices, PageMaker can help compensate for potential gaps between two adjoining colours with a technique called *trapping*. Even if text or an object drawn in PageMaker overlaps several different background colours, PageMaker applies the correct trapping techniques to different parts of the object.

The trapping adjustments are made automatically throughout the publication, although PageMaker gives you control over settings that help define how to trap in particular situations. The effects of trapping appear only on colour separations and composites; you do not see the results on-screen.

CREATING CUSTOM COLOUR LIBRARIES

If the colour libraries included with PageMaker do not suit your needs, you can create your own from scratch. The Adobe Colour File (ACF) format defines a colour library.

To create a custom colour library:

1. Open the sample Crayon.ACF file in a text-editing program.

   The Crayon.ACF file is installed in the Colour folder (within the PageMaker RSRC folder).

2. Add values to the keywords in the file. All of the keywords must appear in the file in the order shown in the following example, even if you do not include values for them.

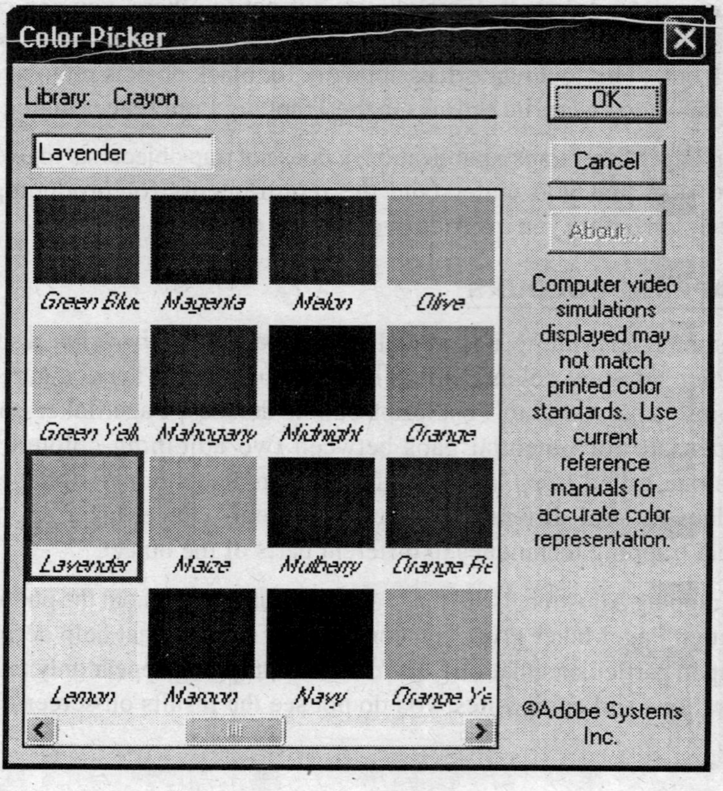

3. Save the file as a text file with a new name in the Colour folder.

Make sure the file is in the Colour folder and that ACF is specified as the filename extension.

WORKING WITH A HIGH-FIDELITY COLOUR PUBLICATION

High-fidelity colour is a variety of print processes designed to achieve a larger gamut range than traditional CMYK colour output processes. PANTONE Hexachrome is a system that uses six inks in combination to accurately simulate over 90% of the current PANTONE solid and spot inks. Those inks are: cyan, magenta, yellow, black, orange, and green (CMYKRG).

Although Hexachrome uses six inks, a maximum of only four inks will be used at one time in combination (cyan and orange use the same screen

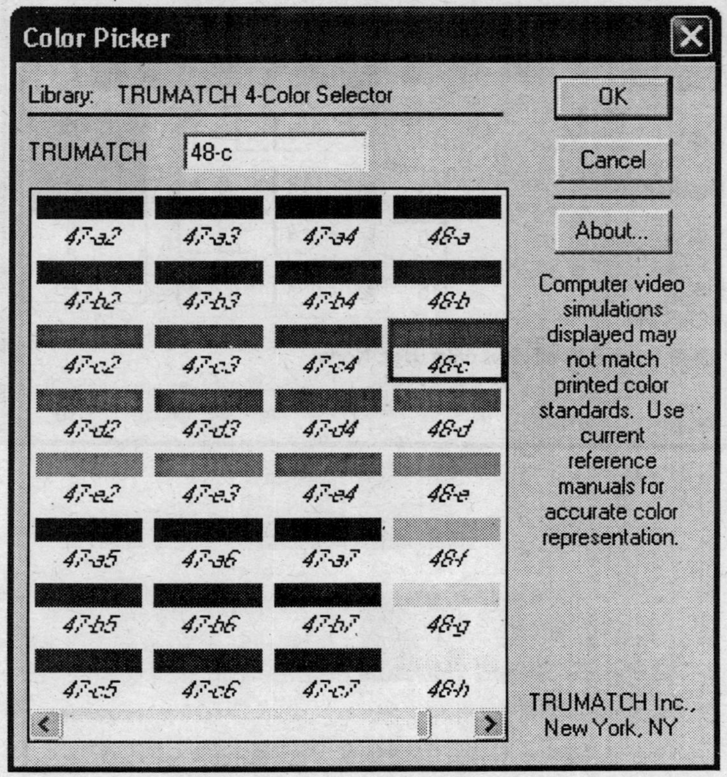

angle; likewise, magenta and green use the same screen angle). Hexachrome CMYK inks are different than traditional CMYK inks.

The High-fidelity Production Guide, a PDF document from Adobe, is available on Adobe's Web site (www.adobe.com) and FTP site (ftp.adobe.com). It describes how to produce high-fidelity output using PageMaker; it also includes a listing of other sources of information. Use Adobe Acrobat Reader or Exchange to view and print the file, which is named "Hificolr.pdf."

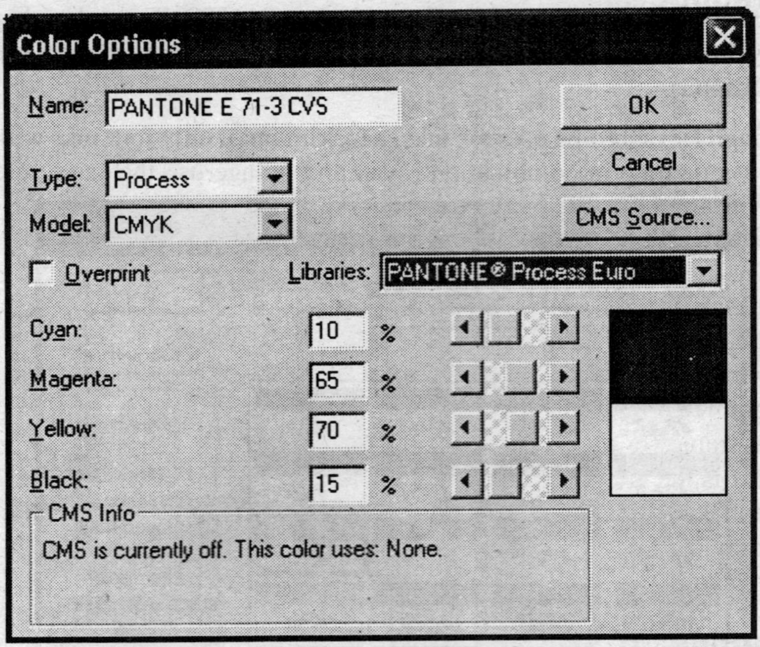

11

DRAWING TOOLS IN PAGEMAKER

INTRODUCTION

Why draw in PageMaker when the results of many great drawing applications on the market can be exported to PageMaker? You could choose to do for several reasons.

First is that it's always easier to remain in one application, rather than moving around in alternate software packages. *Second* it is tool-dependent. If PageMaker's tools offer you capabilities not founding the drawing program you're used to and they fit your needs for a specific project, remaining in PageMaker is the best choice. *Thirdly*, the term "drawing" in a layout application has to be interpreted differently from when you're using vector drawing software. Ninety-nine percent of the time, you "draw" in a layout program to produce larger elements for page design, usually elements that act as frameworks or mortises to hold text. The framing and embellishment of text is the number one priority of a layout program. If the design of a page makes the text clearer to understand (visually and aesthetically), then the drawing that occurs has a purpose. Drawing that is accomplished in a page layout program in meant to accentuate the text.

PageMaker's Drawing Tools

These tools are limited in number and include Line, Restricted Line, Oval, Rectangle and Polygon. This also applies to the frames the address these same general shapes. The Polygon tool is a special case tool because it can be reshaped by control points, making it the most useful shape composition tool of the lot.

PageMaker's Hidden Drawing Tools

Perhaps it is better to call these composition tools rather than drawing tools, although their results contribute to a PageMaker drawing of the same. These tools and processes include layering, masking the application of patterning without strokes and the repurposing of other options not normally considered part of the drawing toolkit.

Drawing Projects to Target within PageMaker

As already mentioned, if your aim is to deyote yourself to digital illustration, than you should get the tools meant for such tasks, including the best drawing and painting applications your budget allows. If, however, your main focus centers upon PageMaker layout composition, you can expand both your creative options and your client base by thoroughly exploring what PageMaker has to offer in these areas. There is limit to the project categories that a knowledge of these tools can open up, but a few general examples might serve as a motivation for further thought:

Message concentrated posters. These are posters whose central headlines dominate the composition. Usually this type of poster consists of nothing more than a short headline and a few lines of text, perhaps just an address and phone number. Examples of these posters are those that call attention to health issues such as AIDS, substance abuse or other dominant social issues. A well-placed graphic or symbol is often required as a backdrop or text mortise for this type of work. A silhouetted face might be used to "say" the main message element inside a voice balloon. The drawing tools within PageMaker, especially the Polygon Reshaping tool, can help you to everything that's needed without leaving the program.

Logo-centered publications. One of the best uses of PageMaker's drawing tools is to trace over an imported logo so that a representation of it can be used as a background element (usually grayed out) for text. Combined with the placement of a photographic or illustrative import of the logo, this can accentuate logo identification and image recognition. The same process can add interesting shadow effects behind an illustration or photographic logo image. The Polygon Reshaping tool, combined with an effective use of screened shading, can serve as a creative choice in this category.

When you trace over lettering to create this publication type, zoom in very close before using the FreeHand Polygon tool. This will minimize jagged curves, because there is no Bezier curve adjustment possible in PageMaker.

- **Certificates and awards.** The correct use of proper text styles, embellishment and framing are all that's needed here. PageMaker's new framing option covers the next handling and an effective use of graphic embellishment option can complete the project.

This is My Sweet
Little Home

- **Customized bulleted lists.** It is often desirable to use a customized graphic shape for a bullet in a data list. Though imported drawings or photo elements are used in this situation, a simpler graphic or image silhouette can suffice. Using the Polygon reshaping process in PageMaker and then coping, pasting and aligning the results makes this tasks almost automatic. This works especially well when creating overhead transparency output.

Shortcut to success

☑ **Hard work**

☑ **Lots of Labour**

☑ **Clear mind**

☑ **Setting up of target**

- **Die-cut work.** Die-cuts are created from exacting keylined shapes and an simple or complex. PageMaker has always been capable of basic die-cut keyline design and with the new polygon reshaping capabilities and layering components of PageMaker, making complex die-cut keylines is a much simpler task. You might want to clone the die-cut shape, resize it and place it on the underlying page so that there's a match between the shapes. There, it can act as the masking outline for a photo, as a frame for a text block or as yet another die-cut to another page. All of this can be accomplished within PageMaker with the Polygon tool, making the importing of die-cut shapes no longer necessary in many cases.

- **Shadowing and shading effects.** Combining the layering, polygon reshaping and screening options offered in PageMaker helps you craft an unlimited number of shadow and shade effects. Three dimensional is always more eye-stopping than 2-D and a simple ways to get a 3-D look is to add a drop shadow to the text block.

Text Shadow Creation In PageMaker

There are dozens of plug-ins on the market that perform one simple task by adding shadows to selected text blocks. You can perform this operation from within PageMaker without the necessity of using a plug-in. Here's how:

1. Select the Text icon in the Toolbox, adjust the type size and style in the Type menus and write your text message.
2. Select the text with the Text tool (pass over it while holding down the mouse button on the Macintosh or the left mouse button for Windows users) and the use the Copy and Paste commands in the Edit menu to clone the next block.
3. Displace the cloned image with the selected color (you can experiment with different colors and tints here). Color selection is accomplished by selecting tints and colors from the Color Palette.
4. Group the two text blocks and move them as a single unit wherever you want them in the composition.

   You also add shadows with the text blocks positioned on different layers. This makes it easier to select elements that are close together for colorizing and image manipulation. You could also sandwich more clones together, colorizing them differently to produce more unique effects

Text in Shadow

Text in Shadow

Text in Shadow

and perhaps even rotate them at different angles. This is definitely a place where layers make work easier.

PageMaker's Drawing Tool and Their Specific Use

Each of the drawing tools in PageMaker has a specific range of uses and each adds creative options for page design. Though PageMaker is not a drawing program as such, its tools offer a wealth of creative possibilities.

The Polygon Tool

The Polygon tool is the single most effective new drawing tool in PageMaker and users will discover a variety of unique uses as they explore its possibilities. We have mentioned some of those possibilities but haven't come anywhere near exhausting the options.

Activating the tool is simple enough. Just click the Hexagon above the Hand icon on the left side of the PageMaker Toolbox. Doing this enables you to generate the specific polygon configuration to which the tool is set. To customize the settings, double-click the icon. This opens the Polygon Specifications dialog box.

The Polygon tool enables you to set both the number of sides of the polygon and the dimension and sides of the possible Star Inset. You can create everything from basic polygons to explosive starbursts by exploring these settings. The real magic begins after you have used the tool to create a polygon on your page. After the polygon is created, double-clicking it while the Selection Arrow is highlighted reveals its control points. The control points can be moved to create new polygon shapes not available in the Polygon Setting dialog box. When the control points are activated, clicking any line that connects the control points adds a new control point. Clicking a control point deletes it. Using all of these options, it's possible to use a basic polygon to create a shape with any number of control points. Moving these points to new positions can be a way to achieve a graphic with any shape.

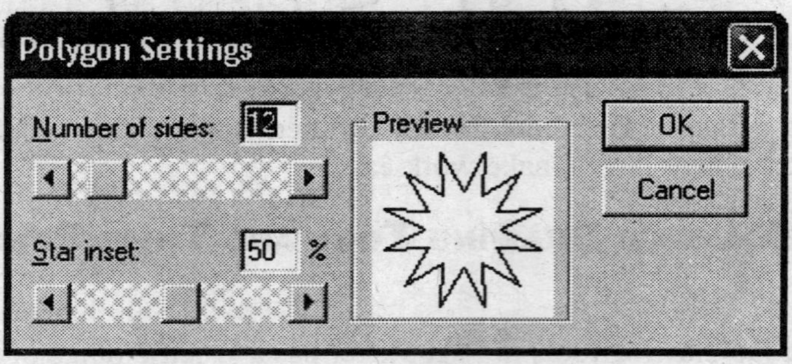

The complex symbol shown on next page was created from a circular polygon with 100 sides and no star points. Points were than moved into place and stroke and fill added. By using the maximum number of points (100), line segments can emulate curves. The graphic could even be exported as an EPS for further manipulation and refinement in a drawing program if needed. After the image is set, you can add apparent 3-D extruded depth by cloning the image and setting it on top of itself with a new fill.

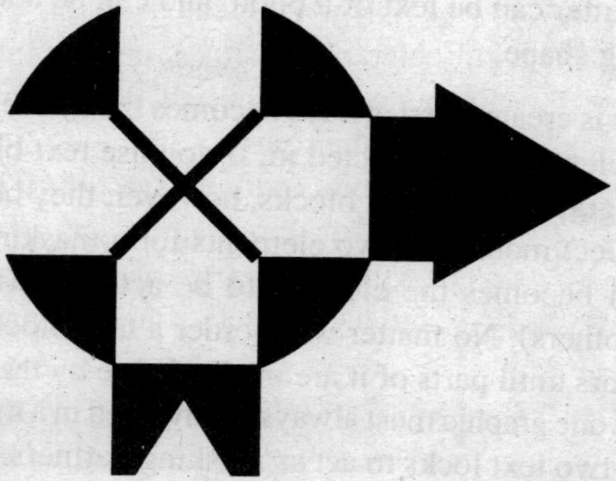

THE POLYGON FRAME TOOL

The Polygon Frame tool works the same way as its non-frame counter part. In fact, whatever settings are used in one automatically transfer to the other. The difference is that a polygon frame is meant to be filled with text. The only way to get text into a standard polygon is to shape text as you create it by using spaces and returns and then manually place it in a polygon (perhaps grouping it with the polygon). If you place text in a polygon frame and then reshape the frame, the text attempts to conform to the new frame. There is no guarantee that the result will meet your expectations or that it will be aesthetically desirable. Stick with non-headline type sizes if you're going to use a customized polygon shape as a frame. It's much easier and more controllable to place headlines in a graphic by masking rather than using the Frame tools. This is because both the graphic and the headline text can be maneuvered freely until you achieve what you want.

POLYGON MASKING

When thinking about drawing tools and operations in PageMaker, a graphic shape's capability to act as an integrated mask for another shape has to stand out in importance. This is because the masking action presents us with limitless ways to achieve visual effects without leaving the PageMaker environment. Masks can be used in two ways to create unique graphics:

- They can be used to erase areas of the receiving graphic, the graphic targeted to receive the mask.

- The mask cutter can be text or a photo and can be added internally to the receiving shape.

The graphic that is created first always becomes the active mask, no matter what order the elements are selected in. If you use text blocks in a mixed composition of graphics and text blocks, however, they became the active mask. If you select more than two elements for a masking operation, the last one chosen becomes the element to be acted on (the element that "receives" the others). No matter what order a text block is chosen in, it always disappears until parts of it are made visible by the one "receiving" graphic. At least one graphic must always be involved in a masking operation. You cannot get two text locks to act as masking partners. The only way to achieve that would be to transform a text block into a graphic (into a path object) in an external application and then to import it into PageMaker as a graphic.

If you want to erase a part of one polygon with another, create the eraser (the cutting form) first. Next, create the object that will be acted upon. No matter in what order the two polygons are selected, the first one created always becomes the active element. The other receives the action. The active element, the first polygon, has to be moved to the top of the stack or in the case of separate layers, to the topmost layer. The receiving and action polygons must be colorized differently or you won't see any results. To make the action polygon an eraser, make sure that its color and fill are set to "Paper" in the action graphic (the "cutter"). Another option is to set both color and fill to 0% black. No Stroke should be set for the receiving graphic or the cut will show the edge. Make sure that the action graphic (the "cutter") is moved to the top of the stack or if layers are in use, that it resides on the topmost layer. Then just move it over the receiving graphic until you have achieved the desired object.

Composite Graphics and Masking

Use the Oval tool in PageMaker to create two circles of approximately equal size. Color the first Paper and no Stroke and the second as 40% Cyan with no Stroke. The first one disappears from view except for its control points. Select both graphics.

1. Go to the Element menu and select Mask. The first graphic is not the

"cutter" for the second. Deselect both graphics and reselect the first one. Go to the Element/Arrange menu and select Bring to Front. The cutter is now positioned correctly in the stack to do its work.

2. Move the cutter over the second graphic and notice that a bite is missing, creating a crescent moon shape. If you want, you can select both graphics and group them and move the shape to another part of a PageMaker document.

3. Very complex shapes can be created by using the mask function to enable one polygon to cut away another.

An Alternate Way to Use the Masking Operation

Now you want to focus on the second way that masks can be used to create unique graphics in PageMaker. This time, instead of cutting away parts of a graphic, you'll add content to the receiving form. The first graphic is always the actor and the second is the shape acted upon. Choose an imported photo as your first graphic and a customized polygon shape as your receiving form.

1. You begin the second mask process the same way you began the first example, only this time you are going to use a CMYK TIFF photo as the first graphic.
2. The Photo and the selected shapes are selected simultaneously and Mask is chosen from the Element menu.
3. After making sure that the photo is brought to the top of the image stack (or placed on the topmost layer), it is moved into place. The polygon shape has now become its graphic frame.
4. Using the command Element/Frame/Attach Content allows for the automatic filling of a frame with either a graphic or a text block. When using a frame instead of mask operation on a non-frame polygonal shape and photo selection, you have much less control over how the image is placed. By using the Mask method, you can reposition the photo in the outlined shape.

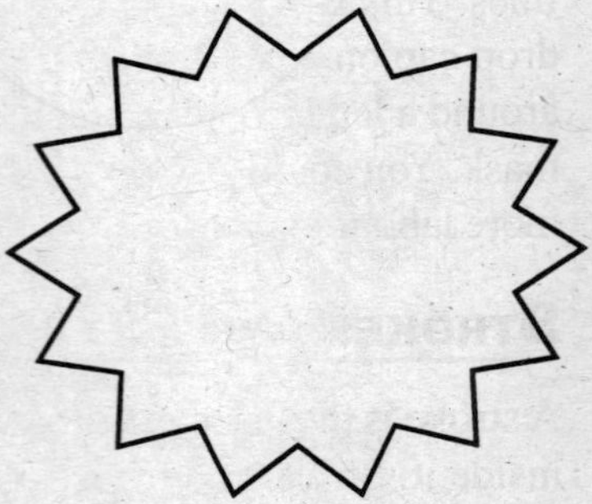

USING OPEN POLYGONS

Open Polygons represent PageMaker's closest approximation to a real drawing tool. The tool is accessed from the same icon as the Closed Polygon is in the Toolbar. Instead of clicking and then dragging to form a closed polygon, however, you just click and release the mouse button to place connected points onscreen. When you're finished with a line, a double-click ends it. Although basically simple to operate, the Open Polygon process can be used to create complex vector drawings. The nicest feature it has is that by drawing short line segments, you are able to approximate gentle curves. True, this is not a Bezier pen or a Freehand pencil or brush, but it does represent a tremendous leap in the right direction for users who want to incorporate more illustration in their layouts without leaving PageMaker.

One of the main shortcomings of PageMaker is its inability to change txt to a path (or to a graphic). Were it able to do so, you could use text as a mask for fills and also reshape text blocks much more intuitively with freer flowing lines. This is especially important to PageMaker users who need to craft a drop cap on a page. With the Open Polygon tool, you can manually trace around a letter to get a graphic that can be filled with patterns or used on a mask. You could also do this to a headline, though the process would be far more labour intensive.

STROKES AND FILLS

A stroke is the perimeter of a selected graphic and a fill is what is contained inside it. Strokes and fills can be considered basic creative ingredients in PageMaker, though limited as far as creative operations go. Strokes are consigned to a limited number of patterns, from solids to multilinear and dashed in various thicknesses. Fills can be patterned or screened solids in a limited palette of colors. Artists are always challenged to work within limited boundaries and to come up with uses and solutions that take advantage of what is available.

With this in mind, you might want to experiment with the multilinear strokes as a design ingredient when using open polygons to craft an illustration. If you transform the strokes in the illustration to multilinear strokes, it abstracts the image, although at the same time maintaining most of its recognizable features.

FILL PATTERNS

Presently no way exists to create your own patterns for the PageMaker library. PageMaker's Fill Pattern library consists of eight basic patterns. You also have to be careful because they are not WYSIWYG as far as printing is concerned. Clicking the Overprint box in the dialog box enables them to overprint when the piece goes to the printer, but you have no way of appreciating what that will look like onscreen. If you are adamant about using patterns for PageMaker art, it's wiser to make other choices than to use the limited Fill Patterns resident in PageMaker. Perhaps importing EPS art from an external illustration program is a strong alternative.

SHADETREE PATTERNZ FOR PAGEMAKER

Patternz, from ShadeTree Software is a collection of 100 PageMaker patterns. Patternz is a PageMaker plug-in that must be installed separately form the PageMaker application. Of the 100 patterns, 20 are editable so that you can create customized patterns to fit your current PageMaker projects. Unlike PageMaker's native patterns, you can place Patternz top of each other to create a pattern sandwich and the results can be viewed onscreen. Patternz shapes can be masked with other PageMaker elements and can be rotated to create angular results, which is not possible with PageMaker patterns.

Making Your Own Patterns with Patternz

The last 20 boxes in the ShadeTree Patternz dialog box contain patterns you can customize and save in the library. By selecting one and clicking the Edit button, a separate Patternz Edit dialog box appears. From there, it's an easy and fun process to craft your own patterns. By using a pencil tool, you can select to fill the pixels boxes or erase them. Finished customized patterns can then be written to the document and manipulated as desired.

ShadeTree Arrowz

A PageMaker document requires the addition of arrows at times, whether as pointers or as stand-alone graphic elements. You can use the Open Polygon tool to craft arrows when this need arises, or you can create them in a simple point-and-click fashion with the Arrowz plug-in, also from

ShadeTree Software. With Arrowz, draw a straight line on the page and leaving it selected, open the Arrowz plug-in dialog box. Here, the tail and head of the arrow can be chosen from a list of possibilities and the thickness adjusted. Tails and heads can be placed on either one or both ends of the arrow. Remembering that the original shape the arrow is being written to is a line, there are no possibilities for internal fills. There is, however, the capacity for colorizing the arrow from within the dialog box.

ShadeTree Starz

If you like the way the PageMaker's Polygon tool enables you to configure polygons and star shapes, you will love the PageMaker Starz plug-in from ShadeTree Software. The ShadeTree Startz dialog box enables you to craft star graphics with two shapes at time, with color for each as well. The thickness and distance parameters of each separate pattern can be altered independently. The result is a near limitless variety of star shapes, medallions, flowers and other symbolic graphics useful to the PageMaker user.

ShadeTree Fraemz

With ShadeTree Softwar's Fraemz plung-in, the PageMaker user can add certificates or fancy borders to any selection. Fraemz come in a collection of separate libraries and install easily into PageMaker as a plug-in. The process for using one of the Fraemz designs is as follows:

1. Select the graphic
2. Open the Fraemz plug-in PageMaker's Utility/Plug-ins list.
3. Choose a Fraemz style.
4. Apply (place) the Fraemz border.

Fraemz attach themselves to PageMaker frame graphics permanently, but may not be resized. Faemz can be moved away from non-frame graphics selections and then can be rezised.

Creating Special Effects with Frames

PageMaker's new Framing tool gives you many opportunities for graphics and layout creativity. When it comes to placing text in a frame, it is strongly suggested that you keep the frame shape somewhat rectangular, especially for headlines. This is because large type gets randomly displaced it placed in a curvy frame. If the text size is small (relative to the frame graphic), you can explore more curve-oriented frames. Nothing is "poured" into a frame as some other layout applications allow, but text must be placed thee with the command Element/Frame/Attach Content. After text is placed in a frame, it can be resized and restyled according to your needs. This is often necessary when working with larger type sizes. You cannot attach frames inside other frames as content, but you can manually drag them into, or over, the targeted central frame graphic. Once inside, set the inserted graphics Stroke to None in the Stroke dialog box. You could, of course, add borders and fills to an internal framed element if you want to set it off from the larger frame's background.

The Frame Options dialog box must be mastered if you want to make the most out of framed graphic and text. It enables you to justify and resize frame content to best fit graphics; all that a frame can address when the content is a PageMaker or an imported text block is justification. Frames can be resized to the graphic content's configurations and graphic content can be resized to a frames dimensions and shape. This becomes all the more necessary if you plan to use curved or reconfigured Polygon Frames for graphic content, to avoid unpleasant surprise.

You can place imported graphics or photos inside a frame, but frames do not address other frames as components, nor are they able to digest PageMaker rectangles, ovals or polygons. You cannot incorporate grouped elements or multiple elements in a frame. You can, however, place any or all of these elements in a framed area manually, taking care to adjust their Strokes and Fills as needed.

12

USING TABLE EDITOR

INTRODUCTION

Adobe Table is installed in the PageMaker 7.0 folder on your hard disk. Start the application as you would any other application—for example, by double-clicking the application icon. You can also start the application from within PageMaker, in which case you can import a table as an OLE-embedded object.

SETTING UP A NEW TABLE

Each time you start Adobe Table or choose File > New within Adobe Table, the New Table dialog box appears, where you specify the number of rows and columns you want (up to 100 each), and the height and width of the table (up to 40 inches by 40 inches). You can also specify the kinds of borders you want around the table and inside it, as well as the size of the gutter, or space, you want between text in neighboring rows and columns. You can change any of the settings at any time while working in Adobe Table.

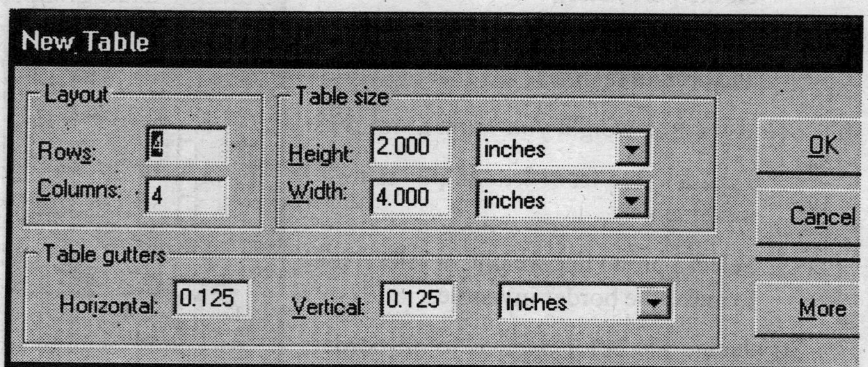

To create a new table:

1. Start Adobe Table and choose File > New.
2. Type the number of rows and columns you want, and the height and width of the table.

   The dimensions of the table determine the height of the rows and the width of the columns.
3. In the Table Gutters section, specify the horizontal space between blocks of text in columns and the vertical space between blocks of text in rows.
4. Click OK, or click More to further define border and fill attributes.
5. To change the border weights, select the borders you want to specify, as follows:
   - Click a line in the borders proxy. Dashes appear at the ends of the selected line.
   - Click the Outside icon to select all borders on the perimeter of the table.
   - Click the internal icon to select all borders within the table (excluding the borders on the perimeter).
   - Click the All icon to select all vertical and horizontal lines.

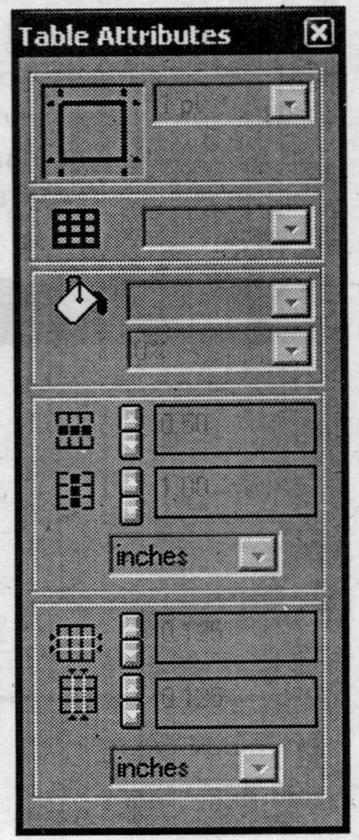

6. Select the line weight you want, as follows:
   - Type a value from 0 to 36 points in 0.1 increments.
   - Select a preset line weight, or select None to make the border invisible.
7. To change the color applied to all borders with widths, select a defined color from the Colors pop-up menu. Selecting the color None resets all border weights to 0 pts.

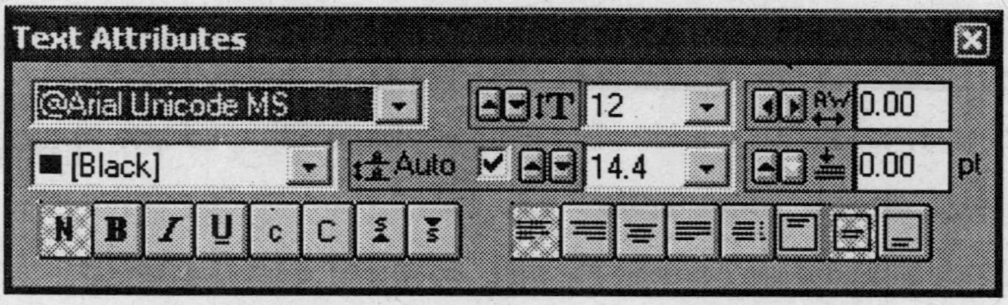

8. To apply a fill (a color background) to all cells in the new table, select a defined color from the Colors pop-up menu in the Fills section of the dialog box. Then, use the Tint option to type or select a percentage of the fill color to apply. You can type a percentage value between 0 and 100% in 1% increments.
9. Click OK.

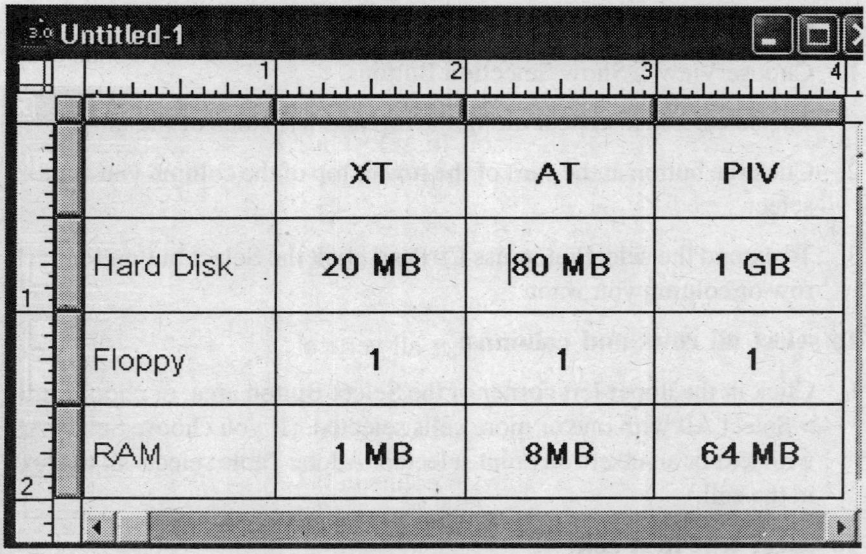

Closing tables and quitting Adobe Table

Use the File > Close command to close the active table. Use the File > Exit command to close all tables and end the Adobe Table work session. If you have made changes to a table without saving or updating at the time you close the table or end the work session, Adobe Table prompts you to save the changes.

Selecting text, cells, rows, and columns

Select text, cells, rows, and columns in a table using a variety of methods.

To select one or more cells:

1. Click an insertion point in the cell.
2. To select additional cells, use one of the following techniques:

   To select contiguous cells, either drag in any direction, or press Shift and click another cell to select all cells between it and the first cell you selected.

   To select a discontiguous range of cells, press Ctrl and click the cells you want.

To select entire rows or columns:

1. Choose View > Show Selection Buttons.

   The select zones appear along the top and left sides of the table.

2. Click the button at the start of the row or top of the column you want to select.
3. To extend the selection, press Ctrl and click the Select button for each row or column you want.

To select all rows and columns:

1. Click in the upper left corner of the Select Button area, or choose Edit > Select All with one or more cells selected. (If you choose Select All with text or an insertion point selected, Adobe Table selects all the text in the cell.)

To select text in a cell:

1. Drag-select a range of text, or, to select all of the text in a cell, click an insertion point in that cell, and then choose Edit > Select All.

Typing, editing, and formatting text

Click in a cell to type, edit, and format text within it. Formatting changes can also affect all text in a selected range of cells.

Formatting text in tables

You should be familiar with formatting text in PageMaker before using Adobe Table to format text. The character- and paragraph-level text attributes you can set are a subset of those that PageMaker offers, with only two exceptions: the Vertical and Decimal alignment options (described below).

To format text in the active table:

1. Select the range of text you want to format, or select one or more cells containing text you want to format.
2. Choose Window > Show Text Palette or Format > Format Text.
3. Specify the settings you want.

To set text defaults for all new tables you create:

1. Close all open tables.

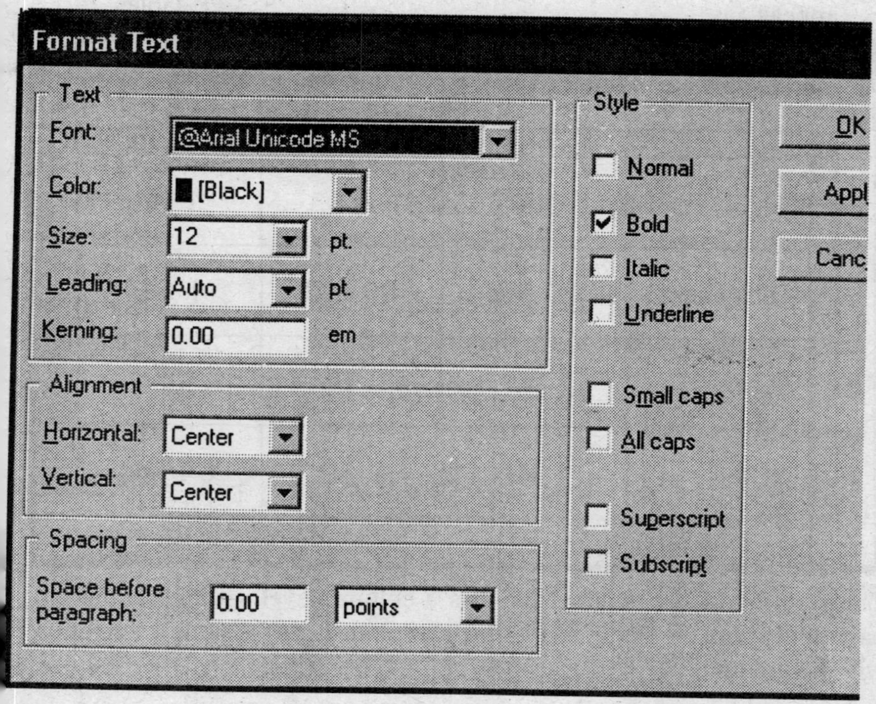

2. Choose Format > Set Default Text Format.
3. Specify the settings you want, and click OK.

To align numbers in a column:

1. Select the paragraphs that contain the numbers you want to align, choose Window > Show Text Palette, and select decimal-horizontal alignment.
2. Insert a single tab—Ctrl+. (period)—immediately before each number you want to align by decimal point.

   If you want to override the default position of the tab stop (the place where the decimal point is positioned within the column), complete steps 3 and 4.
3. Choose View > Show Tab Markers, and choose View > Show Selection Buttons.
4. In the Select Button of the column containing the numbers you are formatting, drag the tab marker to where you want the decimals to appear.

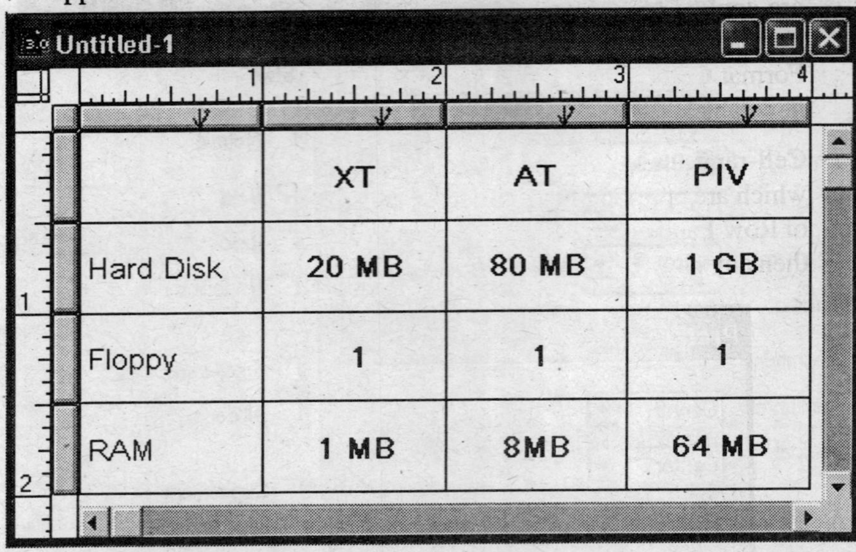

The position of the decimal point is a column-level setting, so that all paragraphs with the Decimal alignment attribute have the same tab position within a column.

Cutting, copying, and pasting information

The Adobe Table Edit menu includes the standard editing commands—Cut, Copy, Paste, and Clear—for moving information back and forth from a table to the Clipboard (or with Clear, for removing information entirely). Note that these commands apply only to text and fills (not to borders), with one exception: if the entire table is selected when you choose Cut or Copy, the table is placed on the Clipboard as an Enhanced Metafile.

The Paste command changes to read Paste Text, Paste Cells, or Paste Table, depending on the contents of the Clipboard. When you paste text into one or more cells, the text attributes of the Clipboard contents are preserved. (The vertical alignment of the cell into which you paste text is preserved, since vertical alignment is a cell attribute, not a text attribute.)

Setting defaults and preferences

Like PageMaker, Adobe Table has two kinds of defaults:

Application defaults, which you set when no table is open and which are applied to all new tables you create. For example, if you choose Format > Set Default Cell Format before you open a table and, in the Format Cells dialog box, change the number of rows to six, then all new tables you create will have six rows.

Cell-range defaults, which you set with one or more cells selected and which are applied only to selected cells. For example, if you select all of Row 1 and choose Center paragraph alignment from the Text palette, then any new text you type in Row 1 is aligned to the center of the cell.

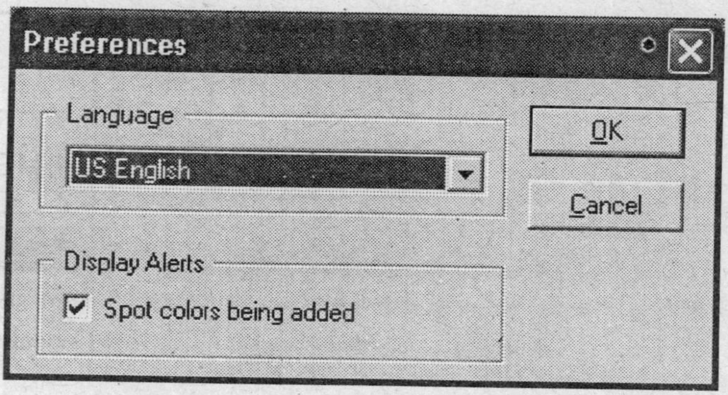

Adobe Table also has a Preferences command that controls various attributes of tables.

To set preferences:

1. Choose File > Preferences.
2. For the Language option, select the version of English you want to appear in Adobe Table dialog boxes, messages, and palettes, and then click OK.

The settings stay in effect until you change them.

IMPORTING AND EXPORTING

Although you'll typically want to import a native Adobe Table file directly into your publication by embedding or linking the table as an OLE object, you can also choose to export a table as a text-only file or as a graphic. You can also import text-only files into Adobe Table (you cannot import graphics).

13

TIPS AND TRICKS

INTRODUCTION

In this chapter I give you various options which you would not otherwise find in any book, specially of this size. These tricks have been collected over the years working with the software.

USING OVERSIZED STROKE CLONES WITH LINE TOOL

Oversized Stroke Clones sounds like the title of a grade-B horror film, but the results of mastering this process can be beautiful as far as PageMaker layouts are concerned.

Here's what to do to get them:

1. Double-click the Line or Constrained Line tool inPage Maker (constrained lines are written either vertically, at 45 degree angles, or horizontally). The Custom Stroke dialog box appears.

   In it you will see a pop-out lit for Stroke style, a Stroke weight box (in Points), a Transport background and Reverse stroke checkboxes. Leaving the Transparent background box checked as a default for all cases is OK, as your interest centers upon the other three items.

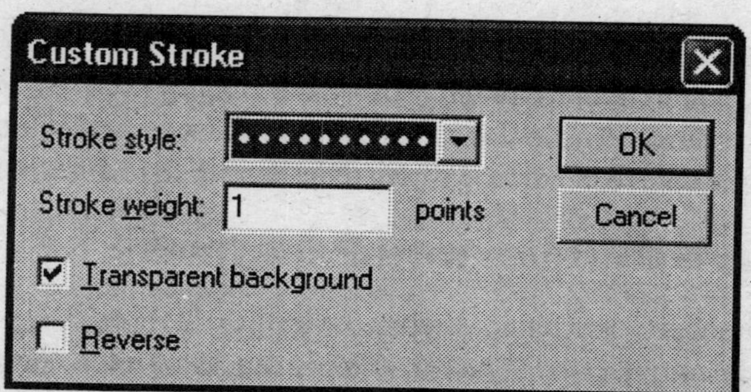

2. Select a stroke style from the list.
3. Enter a large point size in the Stroke weight input box, from 72 to 120.
4. Goto the page and draw a line. Notice that it is very large, rather like drawing with a rectangular block.
5. Draw a pattern of oversized lines on the page to get used to the tool and the process. You can open the Stroke and Fill dialog box in the Element menu (Command-U) to change the color of the line to another hue or a screened tint.
6. Select another stroke style and repeat the process. Notice that the lines now contain even repetitions of the pattern, a designer's layout dream. Each of the patterns can become an element in a page design and more you get used to the process, the more your design ideas will flow. Any of the stroke styles can be used as interesting frames for placing text or graphics. At large sizes, the dotted line Style generates large circles.

Why is this method of oversized stroke clones valuable for page design? The shapes are always in sync, both in styles and measurement. When you use one of the broken styles to draw with, the elements are automatically adjusted internally to the length of the line. Reversing the styles allows them to overprint in interesting symmetries. Reversed shapes also can be used as cutters for shapes they're placed over-masks without masking! Finally, very exacting compositions can be generated and the shapes can act as mortises for text blocks (text can be reversed out of the solid colored lines).

Custom strokes can be solid, multiple line (four options) or broken (rectangles, squares and circles). All of the patterns can be colorized or percentage screened by opening the Elements/Stroke and Fill dialog box. All patterns are perfect clones without ever having to resize them to match.

Creating Primitives with Primitives

In the computer arts, basic shapes (whether 2-D or 3-D) are called primitives. Primitives are the literal building blocks of more complex scenes and compositions. In 2-D applications, primitives are commonly consigned to circles/ovals and squares/rectangles. In 3-D applications, these same primitives are given volume and appear as spheres and cubes. Primitives can include more shapes than these, but these remain the basics. It also can lead to graphics that are unique in their simplicity and strength. You are going to add a triangle as another primitive in this PageMaker exercise.

The most common way to use primitive to form a 2-D shape is to focus on the human form. Stick figures are the first human forms that children learn to draw and using primitive basic shapes to construct graphics grows out of that same stick figure basis. Circles are always the primary building block of the human form, so we will definitely use circles in our constructs. Squares are used less often, usually for the torso areas. Triangles, apex down, can be used effectively for heads. All of the basic shapes we start with should have a 2 point Stroke and a 50% fill. It's best to group the primitives into larger elements as you go. Heads can be completed with all of their elements grouped and so can other larger body parts. The reason is that by utilizing a handful of grouped elements, you can alter the forms quickly by using rotation on grouped objects. This enables you to develop characters that you can copy and choreograph. Some of you may want to copy the grouped elements to the Clipboard and Special Paste them back in as PICT graphics. Here's an exercise that should allow you to develop needed experience with this process:

1. Create a triangular shape in the Polygon Specifications dialog box by double-clicking the Polygon tool and setting Number of slides to 3 and Star Inset to 12 (you are free to change these settings to your own liking, especially the Star setting). Draw the shape in PageMaker and rotate the shape 180 degrees.

2. Use other basic shape tools to add facial elements as needed. Group all the facial elements together and either save the graphic to a file or to the PageMaker Library.

3. Build figures from the saved and grouped elements. You can even build groups of figures as an illustration or use them as ornaments to point to certain text blocks. Besides being useful, building primitives with primitives is a lot of fun.

Here the figure illustrates an example of what your grouped figure elements might look like. Except for a few straight lines the elements used to make

these groups relied strictly on PageMaker ovals, rectangles and polygons. All of the elements are now ready to act as building blocks in a larger page composition. When you find composite figures you like, save them to a file. These can then be imported and recombined into a larger work. Finished figures that utilize this method take on a cubist look and can act as powerful graphic elements in your PageMaker projects.

PageMaker Gradient Depth Stacks Revealed

Gradients are commonly created in PageMaker by cloning a shape several times and with Strokes set to None, placing he cloned shapes either in a straight line or concentrically with each one smaller tan the next. Then, each clone adjacent to the next is selected and a progressively lighter (or progressively darker) screen tint is applied as fill. The result is what appears to be a smooth gradient in the overall shape, as long as care is taken to make each adjacent screen tint no more than 5% different from its neighbor. That's all well and good, but it doesn't explore any variations on this theme. For that reason, here's a project that enables you to appreciate PageMaker's gradient capabilities:

1. First, click the Oval tool and go to the Fill and Stroke dialog box. Set the Fill to None and the Stroke to Custom, which opens the Customizing dialog box. Select the dotted line as the Stroke Style an select a size of 40, with a color of 100% Black.

2. Test on oval our on the page. Notice that what you get is a round string of large Black Ovals. All are evenly spaced from each other. Now select Copy from the Edit menu.

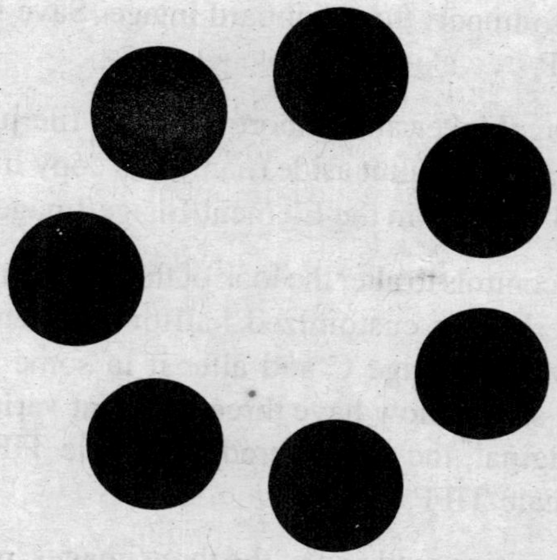

3. Select Paste Multiple from the Edit menu and set both the horizontal and vertical numbers to zero. This pastes a clone of the oval shape exactly over itself.

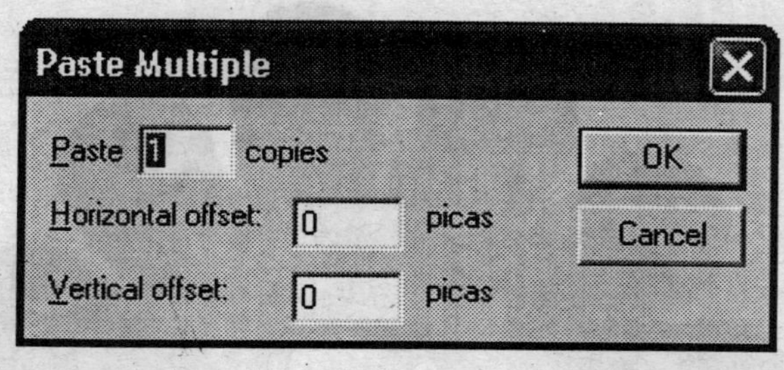

4. After selecting the center Control in the Controls palette, change he size of the selected clone of ovals to about 5% less than the original it came from (this can be done in the Control palette by number or percentage). Activate the settings. Notice that the clones ovals are now smaller and that they rest within the center of the original ovals. Go to the Fill and Stroke menu and make the cloned ovals Strokes 5% lighter than they are.

5. Repeat these steps until you have a series of oval rings more or less centered upon each other, whose tints get progressively lighter as they reach the center. Select all of the rings and group them as one.

6. Copy the new graphic to the Clipboard. Use an image application such

as Photoshop to import the Clipboard image. Save it to disk as a 256 grayscale TIFF.

7. Go back go PageMaker and import the TIFF file just saved. Make a copy of the image and put it aside (name this copy Image C). Open the Image Control window in the Element/Image/Image Control menu.

8. Use the image controls to alter the look of the image, making it a negative of itself or perhaps a customized halftone screen. Then apply the changes. Now take Image C and alter it in some way under Image Controls. You should now have three different variations of the same image: the original, the first altered Grayscale TIFF and the second altered Grayscale TIFF .

9. Create a composition made up of the three images, placing the original graphic above the rest. Notice that when you place an image above a negative clone of itself, it seems to fly off the page. This is what is called a Gradient Depth Stack.

You can also use a variant of this effect for developing speed lines for a graphic. Speed lines is a cartoonist's term for what you perceive as an object that moves past you quickly. You see transparent frames of the object fading into the distance away from the direction it's heading. To appreciate speed lines on your own, move your forearm while holding it in front of you from a vertical position to a position parallel to the ground. If you move it at just the right speed, you should see transparent clones of your arm following along behind it. (If you can't see them, not to worry; this PageMaker speed-line example will work anyway).

Creating 3-D Text Cubes

If you want a text block to be noticed more than the text that surrounds it, here's guaranteed method that will do the trick.

1. Place a rectangular frame on the page, using the Frame tool in the PageMaker toolbox. Create a line of text, appropriate in size to the Rectangular Frame. Select both the frame and the text. Go to the Element/Frame/Attach Content (command-F) command and watch as the text is placed inside of the frame.

This text is typed to show the 3-D effect created in Page Maker.

This text is typed to show the 3-D effect created in Page Maker.

2. Go to the Fill and Stroke dialog box in the Element menu and make the Strokes around the frame equal to a 100% Black border. Leave the Fill set to None.

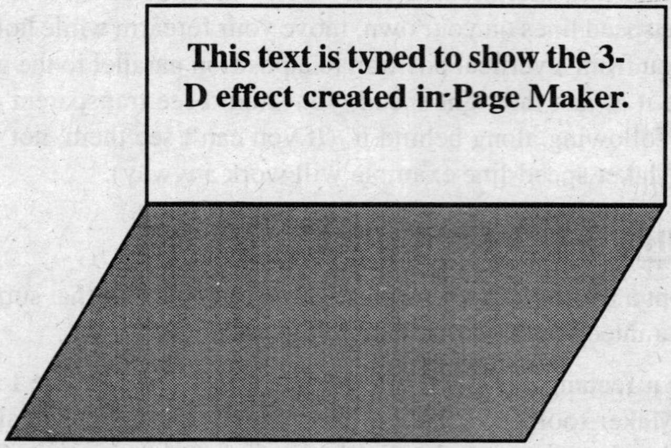

3. With the Rectangular tool, create a rectangular about the same size as the frame and butt it up against the bottom of the frame.

4. Using the Control palette, with the rectangle selected, set the Skew function to 40% by inputting that number into the box provided (on the right of the Control palette).

5. Place a 1-point stroke on the rectangle and tint it a 40% Black, using the Fill and Stroke dialog box.

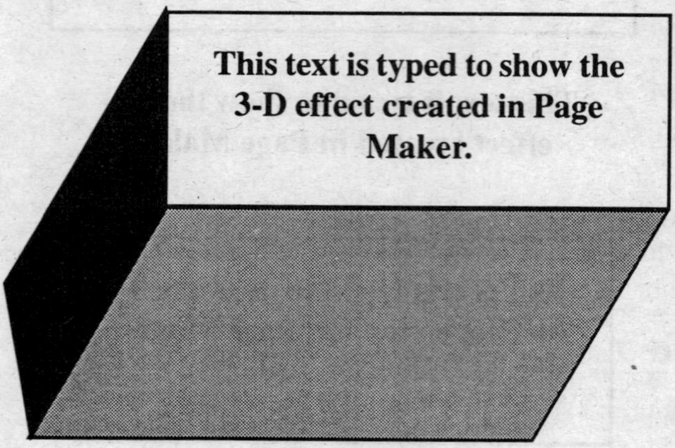

6. Using the Polygon tool, create the third side of your box. Click the points necessary to make this third side look as if it's connected to both the frame and the rectangle on the left. Remember, you can always tweak it if the sides need adjusting. There you have it! Group all of the elements so you can move it if needed and save the results to disk so that you have a reminder of how it was accomplished.

Creating Unique PageMaker Drop Shadows

Drop shadows are an extension of the 3-D topic covered in the last tutorial – making flat, 2-D objects appear to be 3-D. With PageMaker, you can use several options to generate drop-shadowed art. Let's investigate three cases: Text Drop Shadows, special Photo Drop Shadows and Rotated Zoom Shadows.

Text Drop Shadows

Text Drop Shadows are the highest in demand and the basic process couldn't be simpler. Users commonly just clone (copy and paste) the text and place the duplicate lighter version underneath the darker original one. That works, but it's also boring (been there, done that!). Shadows in the real world are not the same size as the objects that cast them and they're often more or less condensed than the object. To get a better drop shadow, create your text and clone a copy of it. Make the clones' filled area light by using 40% or lighter tint in the Color Palette.

Copy the text and get rid of the text object you just copied again. Use the Paste Special command to write another copy back to the screen as a PICT image. Now you should have the original text block and a PICT copy of it. The PICT version is light, so make the original a dark color. The nice thing about PageMaker PICT text blocks is they can be resized, so make the lighter "shadow" text larger and more condensed. Now place the original dark colored text over it. The shadow seems to be enlarged compared to the text, which makes it look more realistic, like a large shadow cast on a wall in the background.

Rotated Zoom Shadows

This effect utilizes the basic shadow techniques at the start, making clones of selected text. Select some text and copy then paste about six clones of it on a PageMaker screen. Select each clone and vary its ting by about 10% by using the Color palette to edit the Fill color. The lightest clone should be rotated 70% with the next lightest rotated at less of an angle. Continue this process until all of the clones, except the original text, are rotated. You could rotate the original as well, but we'll leave this to your explorations. Place the lightest clone at the bottom of a stack and place the rest on top of it in a linear increase of the tints, with the darkest text block on tcp. You should end up with an interesting stack of text blocks.

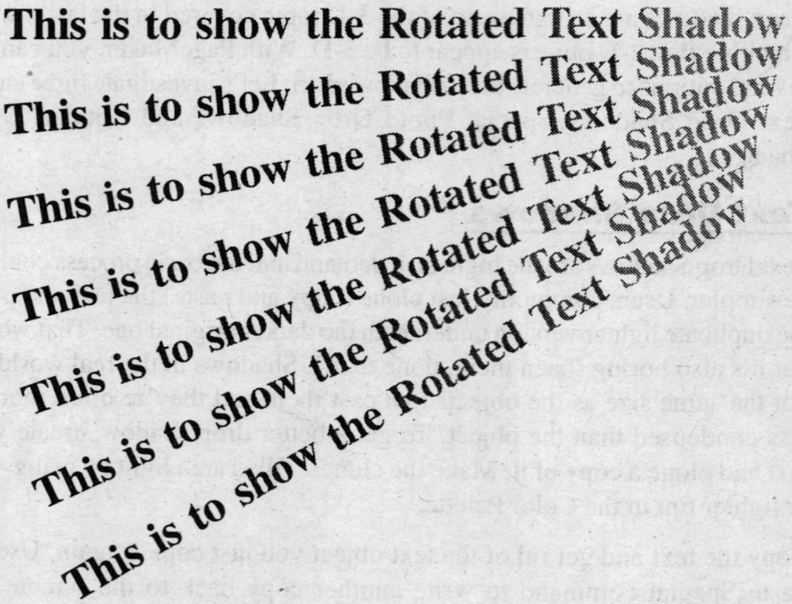

SPIRALS

The Spiral is one of the oldest world-class symbols in existence and is still attracts attention when used in a publication. The eye is always drawn to the center of a spiral, so spirals make great frames for important text. You can, however, create a selection of spiral shapes and effects without too much trouble.

1. Start by drawing four circles, each about 2/3 the size of its largest neighbor and call them A, B, C and D. A is the largest and d is the

smallest. Place them on the page so that B touches A at the top of A, C touches B at the bottom of B and D touches C at the top of D.

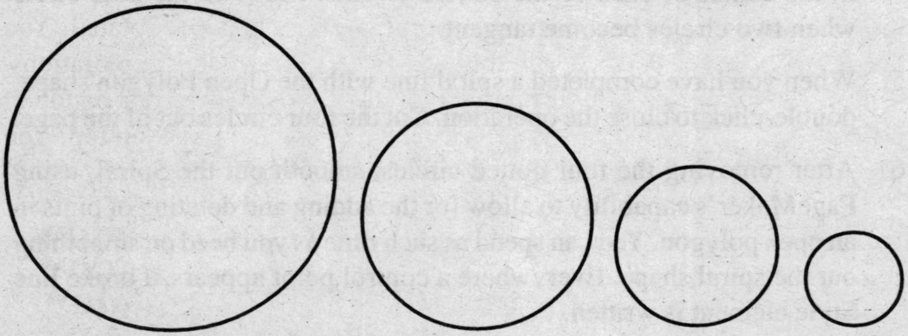

2. Select all the circles and open the Stroke and Fill dialog. Select None for Fill and Custom for Stroke. When the Custom dialog box appears, choose the dotted line as the Stroke Style, with a Size of 22. Now apply the settings.

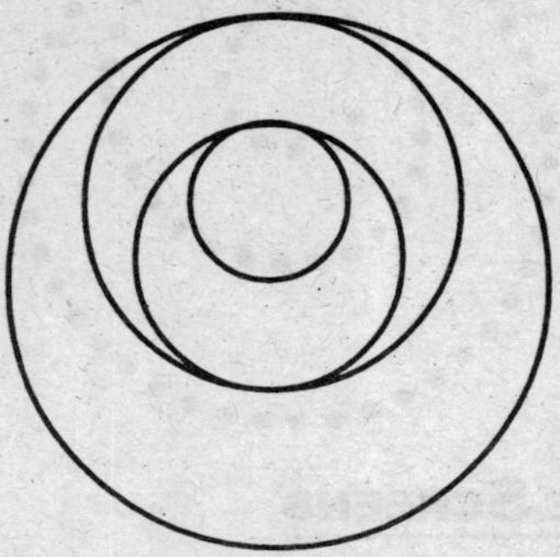

3. The four circle snow transform into a series of dots. This will be your form for constructing the Spiral graphic.

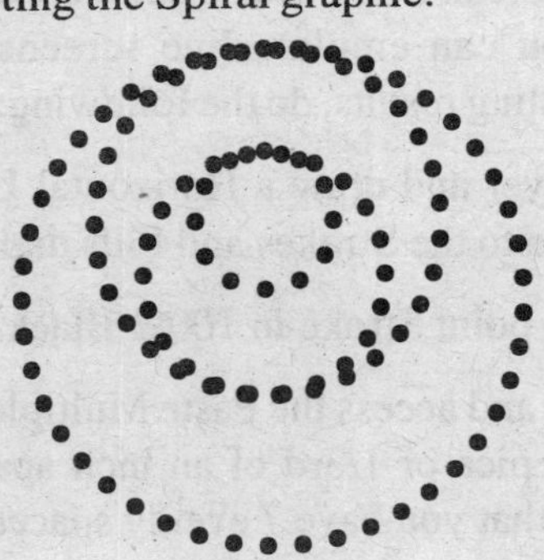

4. Select the Polygon tool. You want to use an Open Polygon to construct the Spiral. Starting at the smallest circle of dots, click the moue button in the center of each of the circles of dots. Move to the next circle when two circles become tangent.

5. When you have completed a spiral line with the Open Polygon shape, double-click to close the operation. Cut the four circles out of the page.

6 After removing the four dotted circles, smooth out the Spiral, using PageMaker's capability to allow for the adding and deleting of pints in an open polygon. You can spend as such time as you need on smoothing out the spiral shape. Everywhere a control point appears, a broke line Style element is written.

7. You can now use the Spiral as an element in your page design.

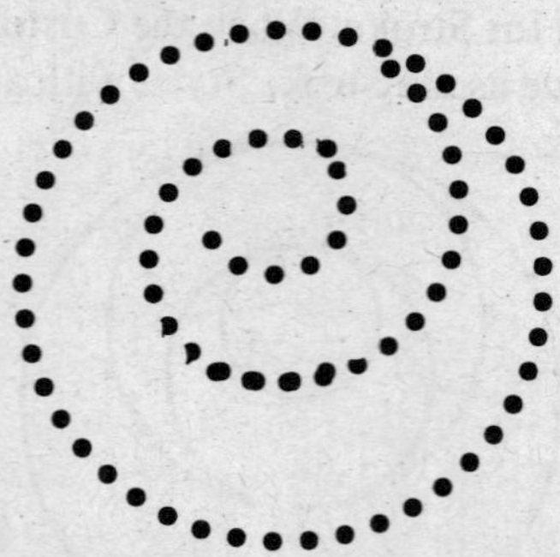

SMOKIN' STROKE SCREENS

Most PageMaker users are aware of the effect that linear screens have on an image. They not only break it up but also add a certain illustrative quality. Did you know that you can emulate line screens in PageMaker? To accomplish some interesting results, do the following:

1. Create a second Layer and draw a Horizontal Line at the top of the page, select it and go to the Strokes and Fills dialog box.

2. Set the line as a one point Stroke in 100% Black.

3. Select the line again and access the Paste Multiple dialog box. Clone 6 copies of the line 2 pica or 1/3rd of an inch apart, with zero for the Horizontal shift, so that you have 7 evenly spaced lines.

4. Select the 7 evenly spaced lines one at a time from the bottom up. Use the Stroke command to make the bottom one 12 points, the next up 8 points, the next 6 and so on. Then reverse the process, so that the very top line will be 12 points thick. Then group the lines.

5. Bring in a photo on Layer 1 and place it under the newly created Stroke group.

6. Go to the second layer and set the Stroke color to the paper, making the lines knock out the color in the photo beneath. We are creating a line screen for the photo. To explore the possibilities further, use dots and dashes for the solid lines or vary their thickness, number and spacing. If you're brave enough to devote some time to explore this process, you can create concentric circles and other screens to apply to an image in the same fashion.

Radial and Other Gradient Fills

Creating gradients, subtle changes in tone in an image, is a simple process in PageMaker. Combined with other possibilities, however, some of which you already investigated, a range of interesting results can be achieved. PageMaker's internal gradients are limited to jumps of 5% increments in screen percentages, but this is usually enough for page layout purposes. For graphics however, it forces you to work in less subtle gradient washes.

To construct a concentric gradient, follow these steps:

1. Draw a series of circles, starting with the outermost first and processing to the smaller one at the center.
2. Select them all and choose Align from the Element menu (Shift-Command-E) to center all of the selections.
3. Select the outermost circle only and using the Stroke and Fill dialog box, set it to Stroke None and Fill 100% Black. Move toward the next one inward and decrease the Fill by 20%. Repeat this action until you have reached the central circle. Select all of the object that seems to have a central glow. If you reverse the order of percentage Fills, you will end up with a dark central circle that seems to be glowing.

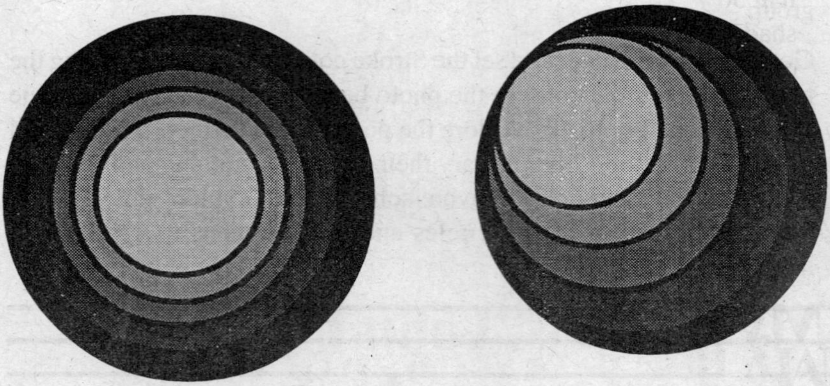

Another option is of aligning the circles to one corner, as shown above.

Reflected Text Options

Although most PageMaker uses realize how easy it is to create text with a drop shadow, few explore the topic any deeper. All sorts of text shadows and reflections can be created without leaving the PageMaker environment.

This section investigates how to create text with a reflective shadow and also how to manipulate the shadow for more dynamic effects.

1. Create a block of text in any font at a size of 24 points. Zoom in so the text block can be seen clearly. Copy the text and paste it in again.
2. Select the text and use the Flip Vertical button in the Control palette. Butt the cloned and flipped version up against the original text line. Color the original whatever hue you desire and color the new reflection a 60% Black. This serves as a straight reflection, as if the text were sitting on a sheet of ice, but it has little character.
3. To give it more pizzazz, clone the reflective text block and resize it to 130% taller than the original by first making the typeface larger and then using the Horizontal Scale command in the Type menu to shrink its width. You'll have to play around with this to get it exact. Place this new block in the back layer (Element/Arrange/Send to Back) and get rid of the original reflection.
4. Now take the reflection and turn it into a cast 3-D shadow by Skewing it at 50% (use the Skew input in the Command palette). Color the new shadow dark and the original text lighter (or vice versa). This same operation can be used to make the text cast a shadow in front or in back of itself, just by moving it and altering its position in the stack..

CREATING GRAPH IN PAGEMAKER

You can generate complex charts and graphs, PageMaker is not the place to do it. But, for those who want to create a graph in a hurry, using PageMaker anyway, this is how you can do it.

1. Open the Layout/Column Guides dialog box. Enter 6 for the number of columns and 2 pica (1/3rd of an inch).
2. Select the rectangle tool and use the ruled measurements on the side of the PageMaker Pasteboard to determine the relative height of your bars to each other. Make sure Snap to Guides is turned on in the View menu.
3. Draw the bars with different colours or screen tints.
4. Create a Bar Key, a box that shows what data each of the bars represent, and save the Bar Chart.

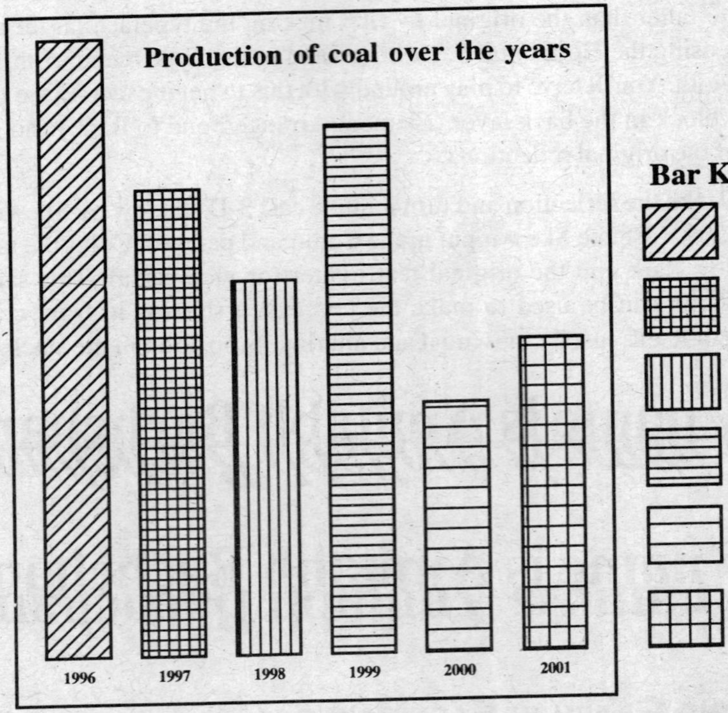

14

TEMPLATES

INTRODUCTION

In this chapter I give you various templates, ready to use pages, which can be used for creating your own similar pages.

These templates come under various categories and are numbered. The categories are:

Ads	Brochures
Business Cards	Business Sets
Cards	Certificates
Direct Mail	Flyers
Label Sets	Menus
Miscellaneous	Newsletters
Post Cards	Posters
Presentation Folders	Presentations
Programs	Reports
Signs	TriPack

On the next few pages, I show you an example of each of the above categories.

ADS

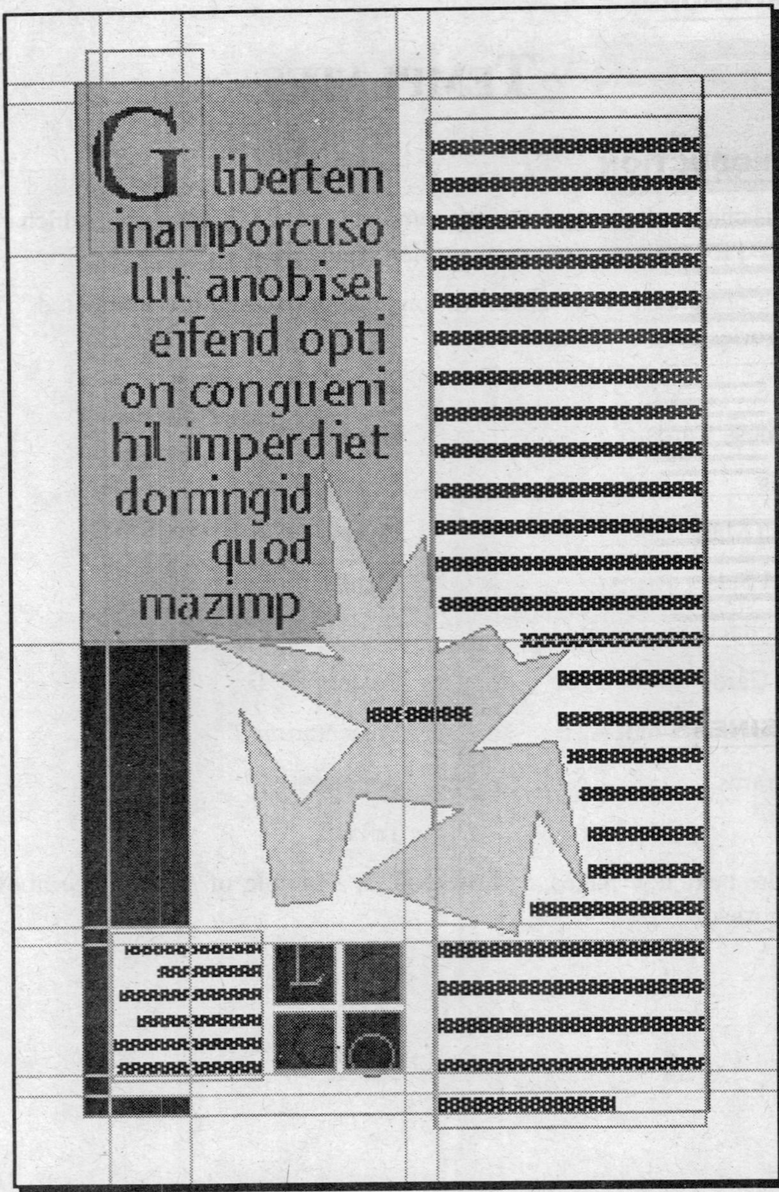
G libertem
inamporcuso
lut anobisel
eifend opti
on congueni
hil imperdiet
domingid
quod
mazimp

Brochures

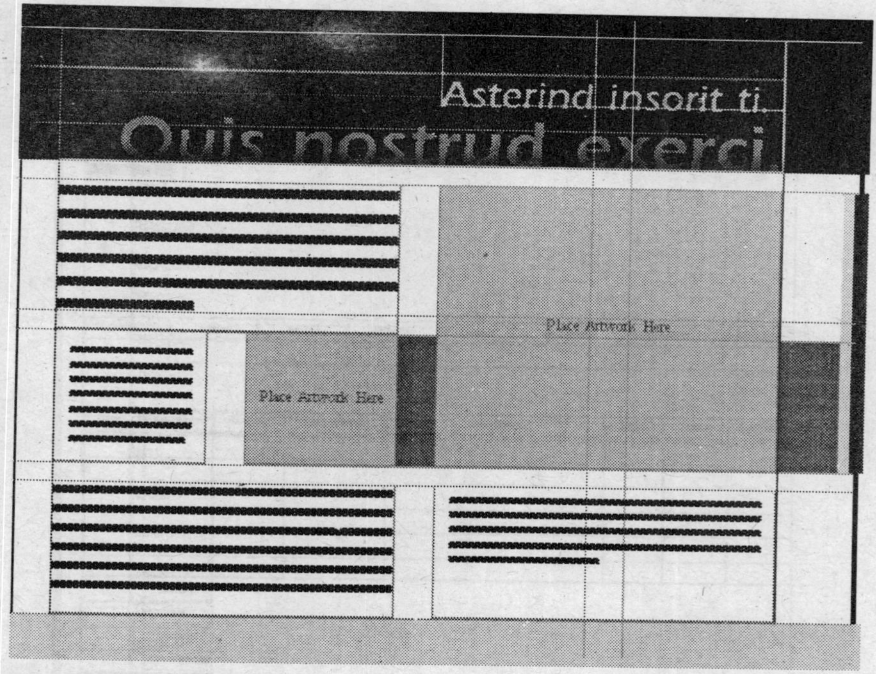

Business Cards

Business Sets

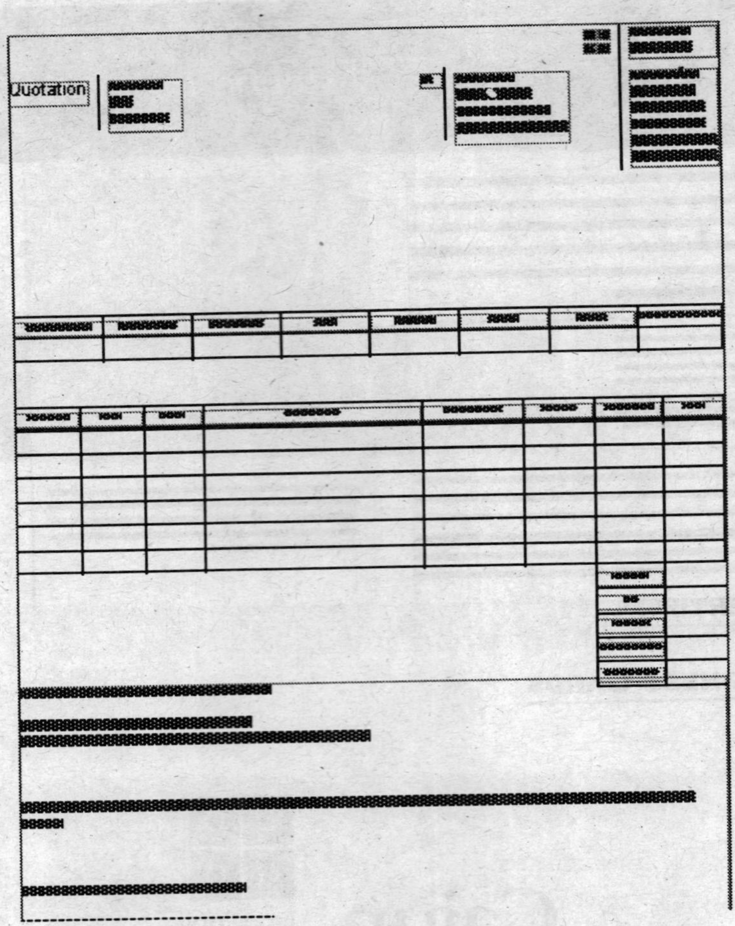

CARDS

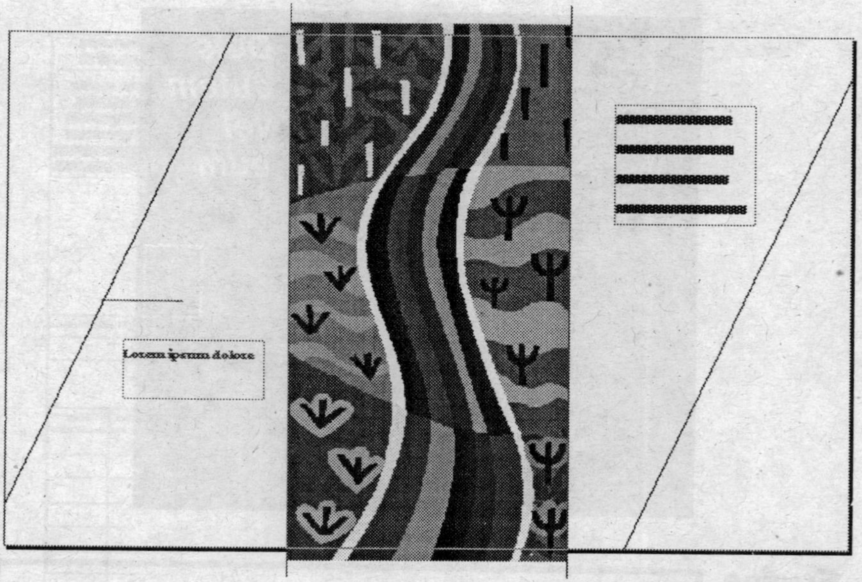

CERTIFICATES

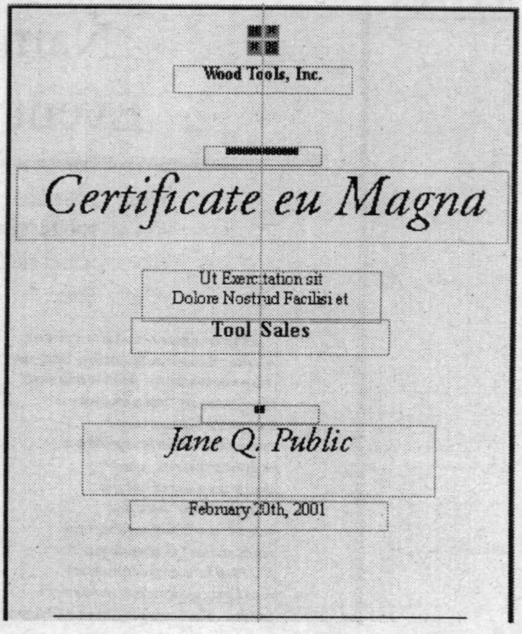

Direct Mail

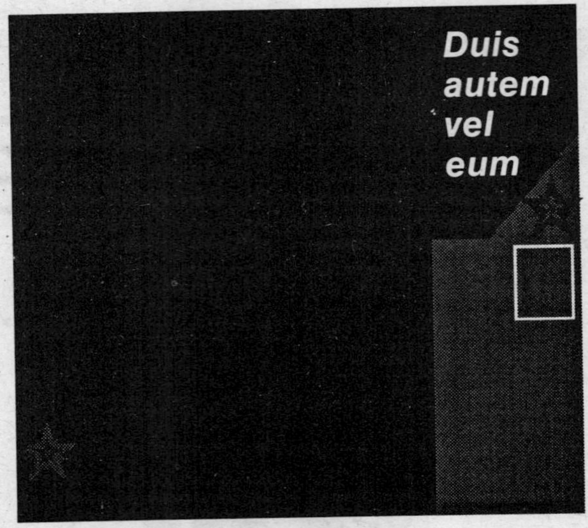

Flyers

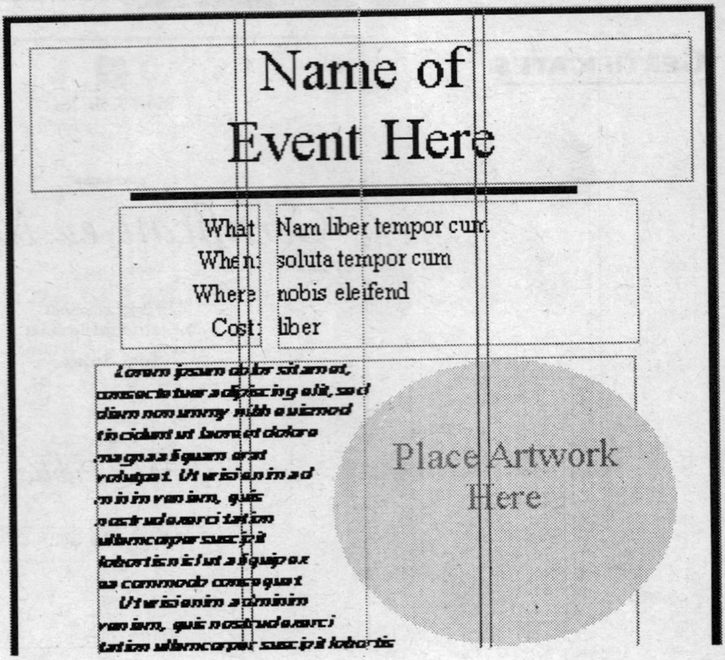

Label Sets

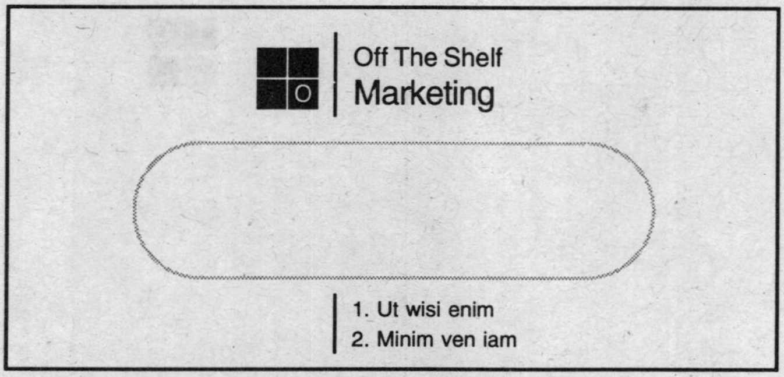

Menus

Miscellaneous

Newsletters

Post Cards

Posters

PRESENTATION FOLDERS

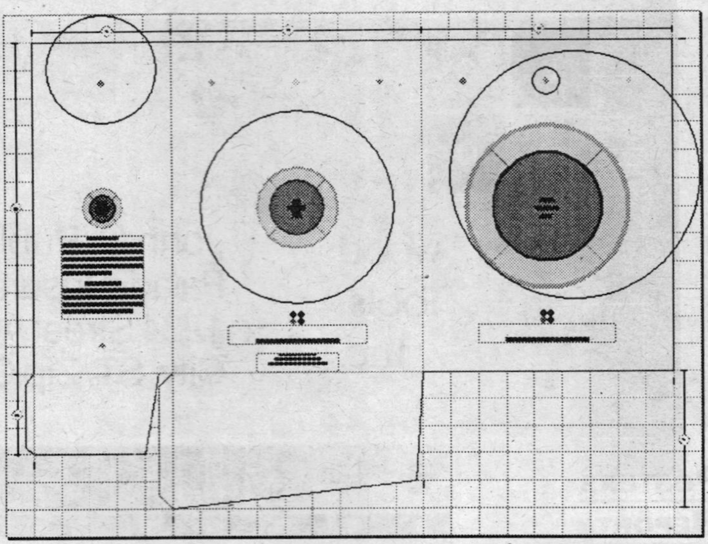

PROGRAMS

Presentations

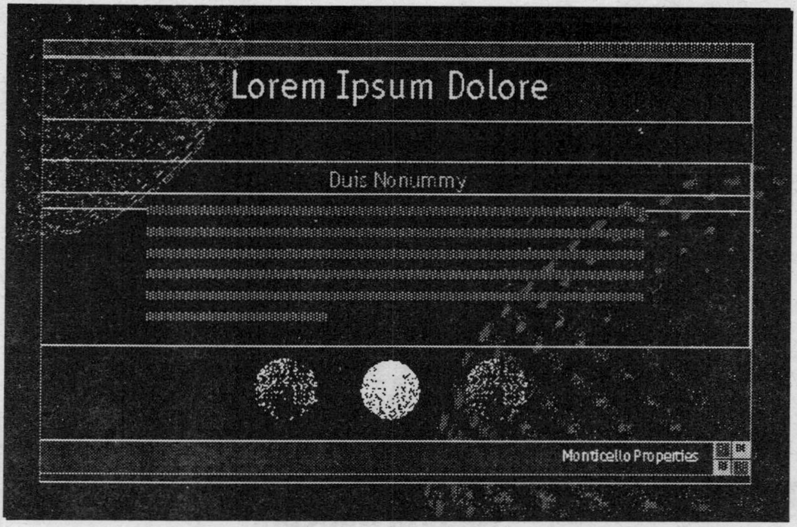

Reports

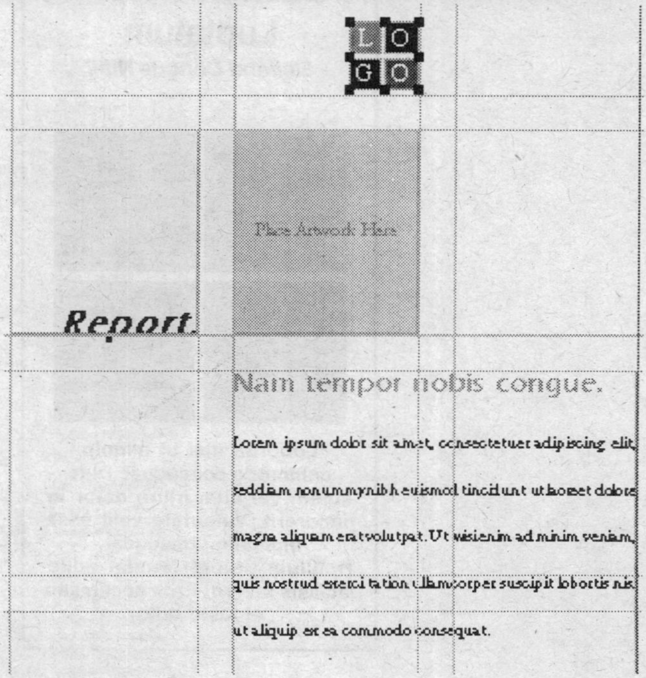

SIGNS

TRIPACK

Blandit Paesent Luptatum

Eleifend Congue Nihil

Lobortis nisl ut aliquip commodo consequat. Duis autem vel eum iriure dolor in hendrerit. Vulputate velit esse molestie consequat. Helillum dolore feugiat nulla facilisis atvero. Eros accumsan et iusto odio

15

KEYBOARD SHORTCUTS

100%/FIT IN WINDOW

Ctrl + Alt + Click

200% SIZE

Ctrl + 2

200%/100% TOGGLE

Ctrl + Alt + Shift + Click

400% SIZE

Ctrl + 4

50% SIZE

Ctrl + 5

75% SIZE

Ctrl + 7

ACQUIRE

Alt + F + Q

ACTIVATE CONTROL PALETTE

Ctrl + ‘

ACTUAL SIZE

Alt + V + A or Ctrl + 1

ADD PAGES

Ctrl + Alt + Shift + G

Align center

Ctrl + Shift + C

Align left

Ctrl + Shift + L

Align Objects

Alt + E + A or Ctrl + Shift + E

Align right

Ctrl + Shift + R

Alignment

Alt + T + A

All caps

Ctrl + Shift + K

Apply change and return to layout in control palette

Shift + Enter

Apply change and stay at same option in control palette

Enter

Arrange Icons

Alt + W + A

Attach/detach content and frame

Ctrl + F

Auto leading

Ctrl + Alt + Shift + A

Autoflow

Alt + L + F

Bold

Ctrl + Shift + B or F6

Book

Alt + U + B

Bring Forward

Ctrl + Shift +]

Bring to Front

Ctrl +]

Bullet

Alt + 8

Carat

Shift + 6

Cascade all open stories

Shift + [Cascade]

Cascade

Alt + W + D

Change character

Ctrl + H

Change page to fit in window

Shift + click page icon

Change to frame

Ctrl + Shift + Alt + F

Change in Story Editor

Alt + U + H

Character specifications dialog box

Ctrl + T or Alt + T + T

Clear Ruler Guides

Alt + V + C

CLEAR

Alt + E + L

CLICK SELECT PARAGRAPH

Triple click with text tool

CLICK SELECT WORD

Double click with text tool

CLOSE ALL OPEN DOCUMENTS

Shift + Close on the File menu

CLOSE ALL STORIES

Shift + [close story]

CLOSE CURRENT STORY WINDOW

Ctrl + W or Alt + F + C

COLOUR PALETTE

Ctrl + J

COLUMN GUIDES

Alt + L + C

CONSTRAIN MOVE VERTICAL/HORIZONTAL

Shift + drag item (first move sets constrained direction)

CONSTRAINED LINE TOOL

Alt + Shift + F3

CONTROL PALETTE

Ctrl + '

COPY BOOK LIST TO ALL BOOK PUBLICATIONS

Ctrl + [book]

COPY EXISTING TOPICS FOR NEW ENTRY

Ctrl + Ok in topic dialog box

Copy Master Guides

Alt + L + M

Copy

Alt + E + C or Ctrl + C or Ctrl + Insert key

Copyright symbol

Alt + G

Create fast index entry in story editor

Ctrl + Shift + Y

Create index entry

Ctrl + Y

Create Index

Alt + U + I

Create proper name entry

Ctrl + Alt + Y

Create TOC

Alt + U + T

Cropping tool

Alt + Shift + F2

Cut

Alt + E + T or Ctrl + X or Ctrl + Delete key

Decrease one point size

Ctrl + Shift + <

Decrease to next standard size

Ctrl + Alt + <

Define Colors

Alt + U + C

Define new Color in Colors Palette

Double or Ctrl + click

Define new master page in Master Pages Palette

Ctrl + click

Define new style in styles palette

Ctrl + click

Define Styles

Alt + T + D or Ctrl + 3

Deselect All

Alt + E + D

Discretionary hyphen

Ctrl + Shift + hyphen

Display all except tools

Shift + Tab

Display list valid value for option in control palette

Esc

Display Master Items

Alt + V + D

Display Non-printing items

Alt + V + N

Display/hide all palettes

Tab

Display/hide Color palette in Colors Palette

Ctrl + J

Display/hide control palette

Ctrl + (lower case tilde)

Display/hide Hyperlinks in Hyperlinks Palette

F10

Display/hide Hyperlinks palette in Hyperlinks Palette

Ctrl + 9

Display/hide Master Pages palette in Master Pages Palette

Ctrl + Shift + 8

Display/hide nonprinting

Ctrl + Alt + N

Display/hide Styles palette in styles palette

Ctrl + B

Document Setup

Alt + F + M or Ctrl + Shift + P

Down one line

Down arrow or keypad 2

Down one paragraph

Ctrl + down arrow or Ctrl + keypad 2

Down one screen

Page Down or Keypad 3

Drag left indent marker only

Shift + drag indent

Edit Color in Colors Palette

Double click or Ctrl + click

Edit Hyperlinks in Hyperlinks Palette

Double click item

Edit item in Palette list

Double click or Ctrl + Click

Edit Master Page in Master Pages Palette

Double click or Ctrl + click

Edit original (OLE)

Double click object

Edit original

Alt + Double Click Object or Alt + E + O

Edit Story

Alt + E + E

Edit story in Layout View

Triple click text block with pointer tool

Edit style in styles palette

Double click or Ctrl + click

Ellipis

Alt + 0133

Ellipse (Oval) tool

Shift + F5

Em dash

Alt + Shift + hyphen

Em space

Ctrl + Shift + M

En dash

Alt + hyphen

En space

Ctrl + Shift + N

End of paragraph

Enter

Entire Pasteboard

Alt + V + P or Ctrl + Shift + 0

Exit

Alt + F + X

Expert Kerning

Alt + T + K

Expert Tracking

Alt + T + R

Export

Alt + F + E

Fill and Stroke

Alt + E + A or Ctrl + U

Fill

Alt + E + L

Find character in story editor

Ctrl + F or Alt + U + F

Find next character

Ctrl + G or Alt + U + X

Fit in Window

Alt + V + W or Ctrl + 0

Font

Alt + T + F

Force Justify

Ctrl + Shift + F

Forced line break

- Shift + Enter

Frame dialog box

Alt + E + F

General Preferences dialog box

Ctrl + K

Go Back

Alt + L + B

Go Forward

Alt + L + W

Go to next frame

Ctrl + Alt +]

Go to next option in control palette

Tab or arrow key

Go to Page

Alt + L + G or Ctrl + Alt + G

Go to previous frame

Ctrl + Alt + [

Go to previous option in control palette

Shift + Tab or arrow keys

Grabber constrained

Alt + Shift + drag or Shift + F7

Grabber hand

Alt + Drag or Shift + F7

Grabber hand, constrained

Option + Shift + drag pan

GRABBER HAND, PAN THE VIEW

Option + drag

GROUP

Alt + E + G or Ctrl + G

GUIDES (TOGGLE)

Ctrl + ;

HIDE GUIDES

Alt + V + G

HIDE RULERS

Alt + V + R

HIDE SCROLL BARS

Alt + V + B

HIDE TOOLS

Alt + W + T

HORIZONTAL SCALE

Alt + T + S

HYPHENATION

Alt + T + H

IMAGE

Alt + E + I

INCREASE ONE POINT SIZE

Ctrl + Shift + >

INCREASE TO NEXT STANDARD SIZE

Ctrl + Alt + >

INDENTS/TABS

Alt + T + I or Ctrl + I

Index Entry

Alt + U + E

Insert Object

Alt + E + I

Insert Pages

Alt + L + I

Installed filter list

Ctrl + About PageMaker on toolbar

Italic

Ctrl + Shift + I or F7

Justify

Ctrl + Shift + J

Kern apart .01 em

Alt + Right arrow

Kern apart .04 em

Ctrl + Alt + Right arrow

Kern together .01 em

Alt + Left arrow

Kern together .04 em

Ctrl + Alt + Left arrow

Layers palette

Ctrl + 8

Layout/Story Editor (toggle) in LayoutView

Ctrl + E

Leading

Alt + T + L

LEFT ONE CHARACTER

Left arrow or keypad 4

LEFT ONE WORD

Ctrl + Left arrow or Ctrl + keypad 6

LINE TOOL

Shift + F3

LINK INFO

Alt + E + N

LINK OPTIONS

Alt + E + O

LINKS MANAGER

Alt + F + K or Ctrl + Shift + D

LOCK GUIDES

Alt + V + L

LOCK POSITION

Alt + E + L or Ctrl + L

MAGIC STRETCH PROPORTIONAL

Ctrl + Shift + drag handle of bitmap

MAGIC STRETCH REGULAR

Ctrl + drag handle of bitmap

MAGNIFYING TOOL

Alt + Shift + F7

MAGNIFYING TOOL—BIGGER IN LAYOUT VIEW

Ctrl + spacebar + click or drag

MAGNIFYING TOOL—SMALLER IN LAYOUT VIEW

Ctrl + spacebar + Alt + click

Mask and Group

Ctrl + 6

Mask

Alt + E + M

Master page palette

Shift + Ctrl + 8

Measurement system in control palette

Ctrl + Alt + M

Minimize Palette size

Double click palette tab

New document

Ctrl + N or Alt + F + N

No track

Ctrl + Shift + Q

Non breaking hyphen

Ctrl + Alt + hyphen

Non breaking slash

Ctrl + Alt + /

Non breaking space

Ctrl + Alt + spacebar

Non-Printing

Alt + E + R

Normal

Ctrl + Shift + spacebar or F5

Nudge object

Use arrow keys or Ctrl + palette nudge buttons

Nudge regular in control palette

nudge buttons

Nudge, power move in control palette

Ctrl + [nudge]

Ok/Cancel all open dialog boxes

Shift + Ok/Cancel

On/Off selected button in control palette

Spacebar

Open document

Ctrl + O or Alt + F + O

Oval Frame tool

Alt + Shift + F5

Page number marker

Ctrl + Alt + P

Page turn (next)

Page Up

Page turn (previous)

Page Down

Paragraph symbol

Alt + 7

Paragraph dialog box

Alt + T + P or Ctrl + M

Paragraph/character view

Ctrl + Shift + (lower case tilde)

Paste Multiple

Alt + E + M

PASTE SPECIAL

Alt + E + S

PASTE

Alt + E + P or Ctrl + V

PLACE

Alt + F + L or Ctrl + D

PLUG-IN PALETTES

Alt + W + L

PLUG-INS

Alt + U + P

POINTER TOOL

F9 or Ctrl + spacebar

POLYGON FRAME TOOL

Alt + Shift + F6

POLYGON SETTINGS

Alt + E + P

POWER NUDGE

Shift + arrow or Shift + nudge buttons

POWER PASTE

Ctrl + Alt + V

PREFERENCES

Alt + F + F

PRINT

Alt + F + P or Ctrl + P

PRINTER STYLES

Alt + F + Y

Proportional stretch

Shift + drag corner handle

Proportions, restore

Shift + drag corner handle

Proxy control point in control palette

Arrow keys

Question mark

Shift + /

Quit/Exit

Ctrl + Q

Quotation mark single close

Alt +]

Quotation mark single open

Alt + [

Quotation marks close

Alt + Shift +]

Quotation marks open

Alt + Shift + [

Recent Publications

Alt + F + R

Rectangle Frame tool

Alt + Shift + F4

Rectangle tool

Shift + F4

Redraw, high resolution

Ctrl + Shift + view

REGISTRATION TRADEMARK

Alt + R

REMOVE ALL CROSS-REFERENCES

Ctrl + Shift + [remove]

REMOVE ALL ENTRIES

Ctrl + Alt + Shift + [remove]

REMOVE ALL MASTER OBJECTS IN MASTER PAGES PALETTE

Ctrl + none

REMOVE ALL PAGE REFERENCES

Ctrl + Alt + [remove]

REMOVE OBJECTS AND ALL GUIDES IN MASTER PAGES PALETTE

Shift + click

REMOVE OBJECTS AND COLUMN GUIDES IN MASTER PAGES PALETTE

Alt + Shift + click + [none]

REMOVE OBJECTS ONLY IN MASTER PAGES PALETTE

Alt + Click

REMOVE PAGES

Alt + L + R

REMOVE TRANSFORMATION

Alt + E + T

RETURN TO PREVIOUS PAGE

Ctrl + Page Up or Ctrl + Page Down

REVERSE

Ctrl + Shift + V

Revert to last mini-save

Shift + Revert on the File menu or Alt + F + V

Right one character

Ctrl + right arrow or Ctrl + keypad 6 or Right arrow or keypad 6

Rotate 45 degree increments

Shift + Rotate tool

Rotate around center of object

Ctrl + Rotate tool

Rotating tool

Shift + F2

Rounded Corners

Alt + E + C

Rules (toggle)

Ctrl + R

Save all documents

Shift + Save from File menu

Save As

Alt + F + A or Ctrl + Shift + S

Save

Alt + F + S or Ctrl + S

Scaling/cropping in control palettf

Arrow key toggle

Section symbol

Alt + 6

Select All

Alt + E + A or Ctrl + A

Select multiple elements

Shift + Click

Select multiple subordinates

Ctrl + Shift + Click

Select subordinate item

Ctrl + click

Selection mode

Hold down Shift key while using a navigation shortcut

Send Backward

Ctrl + Shift + [

Send Guides to Back

Alt + V + U

Send mail

Alt + F + D

Send to Back

Ctrl + [

Set all page to same view

Alt + desired view

Show Colours

Alt + W + C

Show Control Palette

Alt + W + P

Show Hyperlinks

Alt + W + H

Show index

Ctrl + [show index] or Alt + U + W

Show Layers

Alt + W + L

Show Master Pages

Alt + W + M

Show Styles

Alt + W + S

Size

Alt + T + Z

Snap to Guides

Alt + V + S or Ctrl + Shift + ;

Snap to Rulers

Alt + V + T or Ctrl + Alt + R

Sort Pages

Alt + L + S

Spelling

Alt + U + S

Spelling in story editor

Ctrl + L

Story Editor/Layout

Ctrl + E

Strikethru

Ctrl + Shift + /

Style

Alt + T + E

Styles palette

Ctrl + B

Subscript

Ctrl + \

Superscript

Ctrl + Shift + \

Tab

Tab

Text flow, Auto/Manual

Ctrl + flow text (toggle)

Text flow, Semi-automatic

Shift + flow text

Text link tool

Ctrl + Shift + Alt + Click

Text tool

Alt + Shift + F1

Text wrap redraw, interrupt

Hold down spacebar during adjustment

Text Wrap

Alt + E + W

Thin space (¼ em)

Ctrl + Shift + T

Tile all open stories

Shift + [Tile]

Tile

Alt + W + I

To beginning of line

Home key or keypad 7

To beginning of sentence

Ctrl + keypad 7

To beginning of story

Ctrl + keypad 9

To end of line

End or keypad 2

To end of sentence

Ctrl + keypad 1

To end of story

Ctrl + keypad 3

Trademark symbol

Alt + 0153

Trigger screen redraw

Ctrl + Shift + F12

Type Style

Alt + T + Y

Underline

Ctrl + Shift + U or F8

Undo

Alt + E + U

Ungroup

Alt + E + U or Ctrl + Shift + G

Unlock

Alt + E + N or Ctrl + Alt + L

Unmask and Ungroup

Ctrl + Alt + 6

Unmask

Alt + E + U

Up one line

Up arrow or keypad 8

Up one paragraph

Ctrl + Up arrow or Ctrl + keypad 8

Up one screen

Page Up or Keypad 9

Zero Lock

Alt + V + K

Zoom In

Alt + V + I

Zoom Out

Alt + V + O

Zoom To

Alt + V + Z

16

QUESTIONS

MARK THE FOLLOWING STATEMENTS TRUE(T) OR FALSE(F)

CHAPTER 1 — PAGEMAKER BASICS

1. PageMaker is introduced by Aldus Corporation.
2. New version allows you to import Illustrator files as it is.
3. Polygons were introduced for the first time in PageMaker.
4. A lot of new templates are introduced in this new version.
5. You cannot do most of the word processing options in this new version of PageMaker.
6. PageMaker is very useful for typing of the text.
7. You need not leave any margin on all sides of the paper.
8. There are two ways of looking at the paper.
9. 7 inches by 9 inches is a popular size for the books.
10. A4 is the popular page size.

CHAPTER 2 — UNDERSTANDING PAGEMAKER

1. PageMaker can be started using the Start button.
2. Pointer tool is used to rotate the text.
3. Hand in the toolbar is used to move the text.
4. Formatting tool has the various tools for formatting.
5. You cannot hide toolbar from the screen.
6. Page boundary and the paper boundary is the same.

7. Acquire command is used to acquire text.
8. You cannot send e-mail using PageMaker.
9. Paste command allows to paste the matter from clipboard.
10. Insert Pages command inserts new pages into the publication.
11. With Character command you can set the various character options.
12. Using Alignment command you can set the alignment of the text.
13. With the help of Image command you can set the brightness of the object in the publication.
14. Plug-in commands are available under the Utilities menu.
15. You can view the publication in various sizes.

Chapter 3 — Creating a Publication

1. PageMaker can be started from the floppy too.
2. Page size should be set according to the paper size.
3. Zero pointer is over the left hand side ruler.
4. You cannot manually place the text in PageMaker.
5. You cannot change the width of the character in PageMaker.
6. You cannot set rulers under the text in a paragraph.
7. You cannot change the spacing between the words and letters.
8. You can set various special characters as leaders in Indents/Tabs.
9. You cannot copy styles from one publication to another.
10. Hyphenation allows to select how a word should be hyphenated.
11. Headers are placed at the bottom of the page.
12. Close option is under the File menu.

Chapter 4 — Editing Publication

1. Word Processor in PageMaker is called Story Editor.
2. Find command is available under the Utilities Menu.
3. You cannot change words in Story Editor in PageMaker.
4. You cannot change all Bold text to Italics text in PageMaker.

5. Spell checking in PageMaker is done through a dictionary loaded into the software.
6. You can do the simple Cut and Paste commands in PageMaker.
7. You cannot paste multiple copies of the copied matter in PageMaker.
8. PageMaker allows you to work with more than one column.
9. Control Palette is an easy way of working under PageMaker.
10. Book command creates a list of publications belonging to the same document.
11. PageMaker allows you to generate a Table of Contents.
12. Index in PageMaker is generated by more than 1 step.
13. You can print more than 1 copy of pages of the publication.
14. You can print pages of various colours using Print command of PageMaker.

Chapter 5 — Working with Graphics

1. An object can be inserted in the PageMaker publication using Insert Object command.
2. Paste Special command allows you to paste the object in the best suited method.
3. An object can be linked into a PageMaker publication.
4. Link Info gives you the information about the linked object.
5. Using Text Wrap command you can wrap the text around an object.
6. Bring to the Front command can be used only with the text.
7. There are 4 Frame options on the toolbar.
8. PageMaker does not allow you to work with colours.

Chapter 6 — Working with Layers

1. Layers has been introduced to the PageMaker version 7.0 for the first time.
2. A new layer can be created for any publication page.
3. You cannot hide a layer in the publication of PageMaker.

4. A layer cannot be locked in PageMaker.

Chapter 7 — Using Frames

1. There are 4 type of frame tools on the toolbar.
2. You cannot merge text with figure using frames.

Chapter 8 — Working with DataMerge

1. DataMerge is used to merge data from other software.
2. A PageMaker file is not used in DataMerge.

Chapter 9 — Using Scripts

1. Using Scripts you can automate PageMaker.
2. Scripts use the script language.

Chapter 10 — Working with Colours

1. PageMaker uses many colour libraries.
2. You cannot mix 2 colours in PageMaker.

Chapter 11 — Drawing Tools

1. Polygon tool can be used to make different figures.

Chapter 12 — Adobe Table

1. A table created in Adobe Table cannot be transferred to PageMaker.
2. You cannot highlight the text in rows.

Chapter 13 — Tips and Tricks

1. You can create different figures using simple tools.
2. Shading can be done using the lines.

Chapter 14 — Keyboard Shortcuts

1. You can see the screen in Actual size by pressing Ctrl + 1.
2. You can make a character bold by pressing F6.

3. Story Editor can be called by pressing Ctrl + E.
4. A copyright symbol can be called by pressing Alt + G.
5. Cut command can be called using the keys Ctrl + X.
6. You can call Ellipse tool by pressing keys Shirt + F5.
7. You can see the whole pasteboard by using the keys Shift + Ctrl +0.
8. Indents/Tabs can be called by using the keys Ctrl + I.
9. Line tool can be called by keys Shift + F3.
10. For creating a new publication, you press the keys Alt + N.
11. Print command can be given using the command Alt + P.
12. You can quit PageMaker using the keys Alt + Q.
13. You can select all the text by using keys Ctrl + A.
14. You can underline the text by using the key F8.

Answer the Following Questions

Chapter 1 — PageMaker Basics

1. Describe the various new features of PageMaker.
2. Describe, briefly the activities of PageMaker.
3. Which are the various popular paper and page sizes?
4. Describe how two pages are made on one page.

Chapter 2 — Understanding PageMaker

1. Describe the various tools on the toolbar.
2. Describe the various commands on the File menu.
3. Which are the various commands on the Edit menu?
4. Describe the various commands on the Layout menu.
5. Which are the various commands on the Type menu.
6. Describe the various commands on the Element menu.
7. Describe the various options on the Utilities menu.

8. Describe the various commands on the View menu.
9. Describe the various options on the Window menu.
10. Describe the various commnads on the Help menu.
11. Their are various commands on the toolbar, describe them.
12. Describe the various otpions available under Preference.
13. Which are the extra preference commands in PageMaker?

CHAPTER 3 — CREATING A PUBLICATION

1. Describe the various methods of starting PageMaker.
2. Describe how would you setup the dimensions of a new page.
3. How would you check the size of a page? Explain.
4. Explain the steps taken in placing the text in the publication.
5. What all you can change from the character dialog box? Explain.
6. Describe the various options of the Paragraph dialog box.
7. How would you set up paragraph rules? Explain.
8. Describe the process of setting Indents/Tab.
9. Describe the usefulness of setting Styles.
10. How dows the hyphenation command works? Explain.
11. What are master pages?
12. How would you set the page numbers in a publication?

CHAPTER 4 — EDITING PUBLICATION

1. How would you open a PageMaker publication? Describe.
2. Describe how would you Find a word in Story Editor and Change it to other?
3. Describe briefly the process of Spell Checking in PageMaker.
4. Explain the difference between Cut and Copy commands.
5. Describe the use of Multiple Paste.
6. Describe the process of setting up of 2 pages on a single sheet of paper using the columns command.

7. How would you use the command Control Palette? Explain.
8. What are the uses of Book command? Explain.
9. Explain the process of creating Table of Contents.
10. Describe the completer process of creating Index in PageMaker.
11. What are the various options under the Print command? Explain.

Chapter 5 — Working with Graphics

1. What types of objects can be inserted in a publication? Explain.
2. Describe the various type of links..
3. Describe the various option of wrapping the text around an object.
4. Describe the steps taken to make the text Reverse.
5. Describe the various Frames and their working.
6. How are colours used in PageMaker?

Chapter 6 — Working with Layers

1. What are layer? Explain their working..
2. How would you create a new layer in a publication?
3. Describe the process of deleting a layer.
4. How would you lock a layer? Explain.

Chapter 7 — Using Frames

1. Describe the various type of frames.
2. How do you use frame and text together?

Chapter 8 — Working with DataMerge

1. How does DataMerge work?
2. What sort of files can you use in DataMerge?

Chapter 9 — Using Scripts

1. How do you use Scripts in PageMaker?
2. How is script run?

Chapter 10 — Working with Colours

1. What sort of colours can you use in PageMaker?

Chapter 11 — Drawing Tools

1. Which are the drawing tools used in PageMaker?

Chapter 12 — Adobe Table

1. How is a table create in Adobe Table?

Chapter 13 — Tips and Tricks

1. Describe the process of creating Spirals.
2. How would you give 3-D effect to the text?

NOTES

NOTES